Free DVD   Free DVD

Essential Test Tips Video from Trivium Test Prep

Dear Customer,

Thank you for purchasing from Trivium Test Prep! Whether you're looking to join the military, get into college, or advance your career, we're honored to be a part of your journey.

To show our appreciation (and to help you relieve a little of that test-prep stress), we're offering a **FREE TExES English Language Arts and Reading** *Essential Test Tips* **Video** by Trivium Test Prep. Our video includes 35 test preparation strategies that will help keep you calm and collected before and during your big exam. All we ask is that you email us your feedback and describe your experience with our product. Amazing, awful, or just so-so: we want to hear what you have to say!

To receive your **FREE TExES English Language Arts and Reading** *Essential Test Tips* **Video**, please email us at 5star@ triviumtestprep.com. Include "Free 5 Star" in the subject line and the following information in your email:

1. The title of the product you purchased.

2. Your rating from 1 – 5 (with 5 being the best).

3. Your feedback about the product, including how our materials helped you meet your goals and ways in which we can improve our products.

4. Your full name and shipping address so we can send your **FREE TExES English Language Arts and Reading** *Essential Test Tips* **Video**.

If you have any questions or concerns please feel free to contact us directly at 5star@triviumtestprep.com.

Thank you, and good luck with your studies!

TExES English Language Arts and Reading 7-12 (331) Study Guide

2 Practice Tests and TExES ELAR Exam Prep [5th Edition]

Eric Canizales

Copyright ©2024 Trivium Test Prep

ISBN-13: 9781637987827

ALL RIGHTS RESERVED. By purchase of this book, you have been licensed on copy for personal use only. No part of this work may be reproduced, redistributed, or used in any form or by any means without prior written permission of the publisher and copyright owner. Trivium Test Prep; Accepted, Inc.; Cirrus Test Prep; and Ascencia Test Prep are all imprints of Trivium Test Prep, LLC.

Image(s) used under license from Shutterstock.com

TABLE OF CONTENTS

Introduction i

Foundations of Reading Instruction and Assessment 1
    Instruction Planning 1
    Characteristics of Reading Difficulties and Disabilities 6
    English Language Learners 8
    Answer Key 13

Vocabulary Development 14
    Vocabulary 14
    Vocabulary Development 18
    Resources 20
    Answer Key 23

Reading Comprehension 24
    Literary Elements 24
    Poetic Devices and Structures 31
    Themes 35
    Literary Theory 36
    Building Comprehension of Fiction 39
    Strategies for Developing Reading Comprehension 42
    Answer Key 45

Reading Literary Texts 46
    Constructivism 46
    Literary Traditions 48
    American Literature 48
    British Literature 53
    World Literature 59
    Young Adult Literature 64
    Literary Context 66
    Literary Genres and Instructional Strategies 68
    Answer Key 76

Reading Informational and Argumentative Texts 77
Author's Purpose 77
Text Structure 79
Identifying Central Ideas 80
Textual Evidence 81
Argumentation 83
Rhetorical Strategies 85
Audience Appeal 87
Nonfiction Instructional Strategies 88
Selecting Texts 90
Answer Key 93

Composition 94
The Recursive Writing Process 94
Organizing Writing 96
Writing Well 98
Strategies for Writing Instruction 101
Rules and Guidelines of English Language Usage 104
Syntax 112
Punctuation 115
Capitalization 119
Answer Key 120

Inquiry, Research, and Media 122
Research Resources 122
Citing Sources 124
Media Literacy 127
Answer Key 133

Listening and Speaking 134
Listening and Speaking 134
Nonverbal Communication Skills 141
Listening Skills 142
Answer Key 144

Differentiation Strategies and Communication 145

Instructing Students with Reading Difficulties and Disabilities 145

    Culturally Responsive Practices and Considerations 151

    Code of Ethics and Standard Practices for Texas Educators 152

    Communication with Stakeholders 153

    Answer Key 156

Data-Driven Practices and Assessments 158

    Assessment 158

    Types of Assessments 159

    Assessing Reading and Writing Skills 161

    Answer Key 165

Developing Data-Driven Instruction 166

    Overview of the Constructed-Response Portion of the Exam 166

    Sample Prompt 167

    Sample Constructed Response 168

    Sample Response Analysis 168

Practice Test 170

Answer Key 190

Constructed-Response Prompt 196

Sample Response and Analysis 198

ONLINE RESOURCES

Trivium includes online resources with the purchase of this study guide to help you fully prepare for the exam.

Review Questions

Need more practice? Our review questions use a variety of formats to help you memorize key terms and concepts.

Flash Cards

Trivium's flash cards allow you to review important terms easily on your computer or smartphone.

Cheat Sheets

Review the core skills you need to master the exam with easy-to-read Cheat Sheets.

From Stress to Success

Watch "From Stress to Success," a brief but insightful YouTube video that offers the tips, tricks, and secrets experts use to score higher on the exam.

Feedback

Let us know what you think!

Access these materials at: cirrustestprep.com/texes-ela-online-resources

Introduction

Congratulations on choosing to take the Texas Examination of Educator Standards (TExES) English Language Arts and Reading (ELAR) 7 – 12 (331) exam! By purchasing this book, you've taken a vital step toward becoming an English language arts teacher.

This guide will provide you with a detailed overview of the TExES ELAR exam, so you will know exactly what to expect on test day. We'll take you through all of the concepts covered on the test and give you the opportunity to evaluate your knowledge with practice questions. Even if it's been a while since you last took a major test, don't worry; we'll make sure you're more than ready!

What is the TExES ELAR Exam?

TExES tests are a required part of earning your certification to be a teacher in Texas. Along with the successful completion of an educator preparation program, TExES exam scores are used to fulfill the requirements for the state application for teacher certification in Texas. The ELAR exam ensures that the teacher candidate has the skills and knowledge necessary to become an educator of English language arts in Texas public schools.

What's on the TExES ELAR Exam?

The TExES ELAR exam consists of 90 multiple-choice questions and one constructed-response question. Test taking slots are five hours each:

- 15 minutes for a computer tutorial and to sign compliance documents
- 4 hours and 45 minutes to complete the exam.

The breakdown of questions and content domains is described in the table below.

Domain	Domain Title	Approximate Number of Questions	Percentage of Exam
I	Reading Instruction and Assessment	28	25%
II	Text Comprehension and Analysis	19	17%
III	Oral and Written Communication	28	25%
IV	Educating All Learners and Professional Practice	15	13%
V	Constructed Response	1	20%

The constructed-response portion of the exam requires you to submit a written answer to a prompt that asks you to achieve a stated learning goal. The prompt will be accompanied by additional information, known as "exhibits," that you must consider when forming your response. You must provide a thorough description of the strategies and instructional principles you would use to meet the stated learning goal. The instructional plan you describe must be based on educational standards and driven by proven data.

How is the TExES ELAR Exam Scored?

Multiple-choice (i.e., selected response) questions that are answered correctly are worth one raw score point each. The total raw score is the equivalent of the total number of multiple-choice questions that are answered correctly. A scale of 100 – 300 is used to report scores; a scaled score of at least 240 is required to pass the exam. There is no penalty for guessing on TExES exams, so be sure to eliminate answer options and respond to every question. If you still do not know the answer, guess; you may get it right!

Education experts will score the constructed-response portion of the exam. Those tasked with scoring this portion of the exam have undergone extensive training to ensure that standardized scoring metrics are utilized. Exams that have a high number of test takers are scored using an independent double-scoring model, in which two scorers each provide an initial rating. If the two ratings differ more than one point, additional ratings are used to determine the final score.

A consensus-scoring model is used on exams that do not have a high number of test takers. With this scoring model, a scoring leader works with a team to review the written responses; together, they reach a consensus score for each test taker.

When Will I Get My Score?

Your score report will be available online through your Pearson account approximately four weeks after you take the exam. Scores are automatically made available to the Texas Education Agency (TEA) and your educator preparation program (EPP), so you do not have to manually report your scores. You score report will be emailed to you within 28 days of your exam if you requested this option.

How is the TExES ELAR Exam Administered?

TExES exams are administered at Pearson VUE testing centers throughout Texas and the United States. You can register for the exam at www.tx.nesinc.com and take tutorials on the website to acclimate yourself to the computerized format.

About Cirrus Test Prep

Cirrus Test Prep study guides are designed by current and former educators and are tailored to meet your needs as an incoming educator. Our guides offer all of the resources necessary to help you pass teacher certification tests across the nation.

Cirrus clouds are graceful, wispy, and characterized by their high altitude. Just like cirrus clouds, Cirrus Test Prep's goal is to help educators "aim high" when it comes to obtaining their teacher certifications and entering the classroom. We're pleased you've chosen Cirrus to be a part of your professional journey!

Foundations of Reading Instruction and Assessment

Instruction Planning

Standards and Objectives

To ensure their students are getting the most they can from language and content lessons, effective teachers organize their instruction around the content and objectives. To do this successfully, teachers must have clearly defined content and language objectives that fall under the umbrella of the academic standards.

Content area standards identify what students are supposed to learn throughout a given time period in a specific subject area. Each content area has its own set of standards, which can be yearly or unit standards. Both yearly and unit standards are intended to guide instruction and clearly define learning goals. Content area learning is intended to be aligned to these standards to ensure that all students are learning the same material:

- Yearly standards identify goals and expectations for students' annual learning; the Common Core State Standards are one example.
- Unit standards are created by the teacher and clearly lay out expectations for student achievement in a single unit.

Content objectives identify what students should be able to do at the end of a content area lesson and are related to the key concepts being taught; they are usually the same for all students in the classroom. Content objectives should be clearly stated so that students can understand them without explanation. They should have measurable goals that are achievable in the given time for the lesson.

One example of a well-written content objective is, "Students will explain three contributions made by George Washington that improved the lives of people living in the United States." This objective clearly states what students should be able to do at the end of the lesson and can be measured in a number of ways.

Language objectives describe how students will learn and/or demonstrate their mastery of materials by reading, writing, speaking, or listening. A strongly written language objective provides a precise look at the expectations for students' learning.

For example, the objective "Students will make predictions about the events in the short story using future tense and conditional verbs," states what students will be expected to do, what materials they will use, and what kind of language they will use. Each element of the objective is clear and measurable. Effective language objectives meet several criteria:

- They are formed using the tasks of the content area lesson.

- They emphasize the communicative skills of speaking and writing without neglecting the importance of listening and reading.
- They use active verbs to name targeted functions.
- They specify the target language that students will need to complete the task.
- They focus on language that is suitable for students' use in other contexts.

Practice Question

1) Which of the following statements is a clearly written language objective?
   A. Students will learn about the life of Mark Twain.
   B. Students will write a summary of their science lab.
   C. Students will identify and define the adjectives used in character description.
   D. Students will listen to two pianists' interpretations of Beethoven's Fifth Symphony.

Promoting Mental Development of Students

While students can develop many mental skills on their own, teachers can promote this development through lessons and activities that are aimed at increasing understanding and awareness of cognitive and metacognitive strategies. Mental skills differ from the skills students use inherently since they require some thought to determine which strategy should be used.

Cognitive strategies help students remember and organize both content and language learning information. Deliberate instruction in cognitive strategies can help all students become more successful in their learning. For example, it is common to skim the title, headings, and pictures for information when reading. These strategies are taught to children as they are learning to read. Cognitive strategies develop into skills and often become habitual with good readers. **Skimming** is a cognitive strategy that assists students in anticipating what they are about to read and aids them in making predictions.

Another common practice is **grouping** information. When presented with large amounts of material, it is helpful to separate the information into chunks that relate to one another. Some teachers show students how to do this with graphic organizers, diagrams, or outlines.

Regardless of the strategy used, direct instruction in cognitive practices aids students in understanding the content and linguistics they are learning. The five types of cognitive strategies used to aid students in their learning are discussed in Table 1.1.

Table 1.1. The Five Types of Cognitive Strategies		
Strategy	**Purpose**	**Steps**
Comprehension strategies	- help students understand and remember content	- broken into subcategories: monitoring, using text structure, summarizing, elaborating, and explaining - When explicitly taught to use these strategies, students can more easily

Table 1.1. The Five Types of Cognitive Strategies

Strategy	Purpose	Steps
		retain and comprehend information.
Writing strategies	<ul><li>help students complete unstructured tasks</li><li>teach students the importance of planning in order to conceive and organize ideas</li></ul>	<ul><li>After they plan their work, students begin generating their pieces.</li><li>After the initial draft, revisions and edits are made before presenting the final product.</li><li>Students who complete all of the steps in writing strategies are more likely to create comprehensive, well-composed pieces.</li></ul>
Problem-solving strategies	<ul><li>help students see ways in which they can achieve specific goals</li></ul>	<ul><li>Students are presented with a problem and must identify steps to solve it.</li><li>The most popular steps involve teaching students to understand the problem and then develop a plan for solving it.</li><li>Students then carry out the plan and look back to see what can be learned from their process and solution.</li></ul>
Reasoning strategies	<ul><li>help students determine what they believe to be true or false, correct or incorrect</li></ul>	<ul><li>Successful reasoning involves the creation of arguments and counterarguments, fair evaluation of evidence, and consideration of sources.</li></ul>
Self-regulation strategies	<ul><li>help students monitor their behaviors</li></ul>	<ul><li>Students who master self-regulation are capable of successful self-monitoring and evaluations, time management, and goal setting.</li><li>These skills aid them in their learning endeavors</li></ul>

Table 1.1. The Five Types of Cognitive Strategies		
Strategy	Purpose	Steps
		by contributing to their metacognitive processes and focus.

Metacognitive strategies are those that focus on thinking about thinking. They involve knowledge of one's own thinking processes, one's own knowledge, and the limitations of that knowledge. Metacognition is not an inherent process; students must be taught how to analyze their knowledge in order to successfully plan, monitor, evaluate, and revise their thinking in order to engage in various learning environments and subjects.

Metacognitive strategies teach students how to identify their prior knowledge of a topic, recognize what they do not know about something, and what it is that they still need to learn. Such strategies help students plan their learning, self-regulate, and choose appropriate cognitive strategies to aid them as they study new material. Direct instruction in metacognitive strategies can lead to increases in learning; implementing these strategies results in success and self-sufficiency.

Table 1.2. Metacognitive Strategies	
Strategy	Description
Identifying what is known and what is not	- Students need to recognize their prior learning and then move forward in determining what they do not know, what they need clarification on, and what knowledge has stuck with them.
Planning	- Estimating the time a task will take, organizing materials, scheduling group or individual work time, and determining procedures for completing a task all require planning. - Students should assume responsibility for these components of planning in order to become self-directed. - Criteria for evaluating their planning processes should be established and taught as students proceed through an activity.
Keeping a thought journal	- Logging their own thoughts and ideas can help students reflect upon their thinking and understanding of a topic and understand any difficulties they are struggling with as they work through a problem or process.
Talking about thinking	- This process must be modeled for students.

Table 1.2. Metacognitive Strategies

Strategy	Description
	- Teachers should think aloud during problem-solving and planning activities to show students what this process looks like. - This will enable students to understand what it means to talk about their thinking and demonstrate the benefits of doing it.
Self-evaluating	- This process should be modeled for students. - Providing students with checklists or one-on-one conferences can help them develop the skills necessary for determining their own understanding. - As students come to recognize how to implement strategies and where they are most useful, they will develop the ability to evaluate their use of them for success as well as their understanding.
Debriefing	- Activities that focus on closure help students develop awareness of the strategies they implemented as well as where their successes and areas of improvement are. - Debriefing helps students recognize the cross-curricular uses of many of the strategies they employ.

Activating students' prior knowledge can help them make connections between what they already know and what they are going to learn. In order to activate students' prior knowledge, there are several strategies that teachers can use to encourage students to think about what they already know:

- **Introduce vocabulary before content:** Presenting students with words and learning about them prior to being expected to apply them will allow students to gain comfort and familiarity with new words and demonstrate their understanding and practice of words they already know. This strategy can also help students recall familiar topics within given content.

- **Use graphic organizers, outlines, and diagrams:** Helping students visualize content can aid them in recall. By creating a visual aid to organize information, students are able to see the material in the topic and potentially recall prior learning.

- **Brainstorm ideas about the topic or content:** Students are able to toss out ideas they have and make connections with what they already know when completing brainstorming activities. It may help students generate connections that they did not know existed.

- **Ask questions about the content or topic and things related to it:** This kind of exercise can help students use vocabulary they already know and prepare them to use what they are going to learn in communicative ways.

Practice Question

2) Which of the following strategies is NOT intended to aid students in activating prior knowledge?
   A. asking questions about the content
   B. introducing vocabulary before content
   C. using graphic organizers, diagrams, and outlines
   D. listening to an expert speaker discuss the content

Characteristics of Reading Difficulties and Disabilities

Reading Difficulties

Students progress toward full literacy at different rates. Those who do not meet (or are at risk of not meeting) grade-level expectations have reading difficulties, which are different from reading disabilities. When students have **reading difficulties**, they fall behind grade-level expectations in reading but do not qualify for special education services under the category of a **specific learning disability (SLD)**. Reading difficulties fall into three categories:

- **Specific word-reading difficulties (SWD)** describe when students have trouble reading or decoding individual words. Students may also have below-average fluency and comprehension levels because they struggle to decode on the word level; however, when presented with texts they are able to decode, these students may have strong reading comprehension skills.

- **Specific reading comprehension difficulties (SRCD)** are experienced by students who can decode on a basic level but lack the vocabulary knowledge or inferencing skills necessary to fully comprehend texts.

- **Mixed reading difficulties (MRD)** describe when students have deficits in both decoding and comprehension.

Practice Question

3) A ninth-grade student struggles to understand the main idea of a new text that has been introduced to the class that uses vocabulary and expressions which he has trouble decoding; however, the student easily understands higher level texts he has not yet read but which mostly contain words with which he is familiar and can easily decode. Which reading difficulty does this student MOST likely have?
   A) a specific reading comprehension difficulty
   B) dysgraphia
   C) a mixed reading difficulty
   D) a specific word-reading difficulty

Reading Disabilities

Reading disabilities are formally diagnosed learning disabilities. Students with reading disabilities will typically qualify for special education services and are served through an **Individualized Education**

Program (IEP), which is a legal document that is designed to promote adequate educational progress in students with formally diagnosed learning disabilities. Reading disabilities also fall into three categories:

- **Phonological deficits** occur when students struggle with word recognition due to weak phonological processing. Students with phonological deficits face a range of challenges, including trouble with letter-sound correspondence, sounding out words, and spelling. Seventy to 80 percent of students with reading-related learning disabilities have phonological deficits, which are usually described by the term *dyslexia*, sometimes called a **language-based learning disability (LBLD)**. Dyslexia is a very common SLD thought to affect at least 15 percent of the global population.

- **Processing speed/orthographic processing deficits** occur when students do not read quickly or accurately. Orthographic coding differs from phonological coding in that it does not rely solely on letter-sound correspondence and knowledge to decode but rather on memory (of letters, groups of letters, or entire words). This type of deficit is typically milder than a phonological deficit and may be co-occurring or distinct from a phonological deficit. There is some debate as to whether this type of deficit is a subtype of dyslexia or a distinct disability.

- **Specific comprehension deficits** describe challenges with vocabulary, language learning, and abstract reasoning. Comprehension deficits might co-occur with phonological or processing deficits as well as with other conditions, particularly autism spectrum disorder (ASD). This type of deficit is also referred to as **hyperlexia** because word recognition skills are average or even advanced.

It is important to recognize signs of dyslexia and dysgraphia within students. Generally speaking, **dyslexia** affects reading, while **dysgraphia** affects writing. Signs may include difficulty spelling, writing, or using a pencil. If reading or writing struggles continue and a diagnosis is confirmed, it is then up to instructors to accommodate students. Evidence-based instruction for dyslexia and dysgraphia should be implemented to help students improve their reading and writing proficiencies. This may include paired reading for students with dyslexia or speech-to-text writing for students with dysgraphia. Extra time on assignments may be beneficial in both cases.

> **Did You Know?**
>
> **Dysgraphia** is an SLD that describes writing skills that fall below expectations for a student's age.

Students who qualify for special education services under another category (e.g., intellectual disability, speech and language impairment, or developmental disability) may have other disabilities that cause reading difficulties. Their IEPs may therefore list reading-related modifications and accommodations even though these students have not been diagnosed with specific learning disabilities. A more complete discussion of IEPs and legal considerations concerning reading and other specific learning disabilities is provided in Chapter 9.

> **Helpful Hint:**
>
> **Least restrictive environment** emphasizes placement in the general education classroom with as many supplemental aides and services as possible.

Practice Question

4) Specific comprehension deficits often co-occur in students diagnosed with which one of the following?
    A. dyspraxia
    B. dysgraphia
    C. autism spectrum disorder (ASD)
    D. emotional or behavioral disorders (EBD)

English Language Learners

Second Language Acquisition

Researchers agree that second language acquisition occurs through a series of stages, much like first language acquisition. Learners must pass through each of the five stages (described in Table 1.3.) on their way to proficiency, though the time spent in each stage varies from person to person.

Table 1.3. Stages of Second Language Acquisition

Stage	Description
Preproduction (silent period)	<ul><li>Learners may have upward of 500 words in their receptive vocabulary, but they refrain from speaking.</li><li>Learners will listen and may copy words down.</li><li>Learners can respond to visual cues, such as pictures and gestures.</li></ul>
Early production	<ul><li>Learners achieve a 1,000-word receptive and active vocabulary.</li><li>Learners can produce single-word and two- to three-word phrases and respond to questions and statements.</li></ul>
Speech emergence	<ul><li>Learners have a vocabulary of about 3,000 words.</li><li>Learners are able to chunk simple words and phrases into sentences that may or may not be grammatically correct.</li></ul>
Intermediate fluency	<ul><li>Learners have a vocabulary of about 6,000 words.</li><li>They can speak in more complex sentences and catch and correct many of their errors.</li><li>Learners may communicate well but have large gaps in their vocabulary, grammar, and syntax skills.</li></ul>

Table 1.3. Stages of Second Language Acquisition	
Stage	**Description**
Advanced fluency	<ul><li>Learners achieve cognitive language proficiency in their learned language.</li><li>Learners demonstrate near-native ability and use complex, multi-phrase and multi-clause sentences to convey their ideas.</li></ul>

As language learners progress through levels of study, they usually develop an interlanguage to aid them in their progression. **Interlanguage** is a learner's current understanding of the language being learned. It is a rule-based system that develops over time and tends to blend aspects of the learner's first language with those of the second language.

When language learners stop progressing and the development of their interlanguage stops, their understanding can become fossilized. **Fossilization** is the point in second-language acquisition when a learner's growth freezes, and further linguistic development becomes highly unlikely.

Practice Question

5) Lucia enjoys listening to songs in English. She memorizes the choruses and sings them to herself. She notes words she does not recognize and integrates phrases from the songs into her everyday language practice. When asked about the songs, Lucia responds in single words and short phrases but struggles to compose complete sentences. In which stage of second-language acquisition might Lucia be?
   A. preproduction
   B. early production
   C. speech emergence
   D. intermediate fluency

First-Language Influence on Second Language Learning

Students' native languages will always impact their learning of English. The influences of their native languages will occur in all parts of language learning, from grammatical understanding to vocabulary acquisition to syntactical awareness. English language learners (ELLs) are bound to transfer their understanding of their first language to their studies of English to make sense of what they are learning.

Transfer occurs when a student applies knowledge of a first language to another language; it can be both positive and negative:

> **Helpful Hint**:
>
> Sometimes students will repeat what they hear in a process called **parroting**. This can help them build their receptive vocabulary, but it should not be mistaken for producing language.

- **Positive transfer** occurs when students find similarities between their native languages and English and use those similarities to help them learn. For example, a Spanish-speaking student may recognize the English verb *to comprehend* because it looks like the Spanish verb *comprender* ("to understand").
- **Negative transfer**, also called **interference**, occurs when students incorrectly apply rules from their native languages to their learning of English. For example, a Spanish-

speaking student may place an adjective after a noun ("the house red") because of the noun-adjective structure in Spanish. In English, however, the adjective comes before the noun ("the red house").

Words that are visually similar are known as **cognates**. Words that look similar but have different meanings are **false cognates**. For example, the Spanish verb *comprar* means "to buy," not "to compare." Students who are learning a new language should understand that both cognates and false cognates exist.

Code-switching is also frequent among language learners. When **code-switching**, students mix in words from their first language with the language they are learning. This often happens when students have forgotten a term or do not know how to express themselves in the second language. For example, a Spanish-speaking student who is looking for the bathroom and cannot recall a vocabulary word might ask, "Where is the baño?" This type of linguistic back-and-forth is very common with bilingual and multilingual individuals.

> **Helpful Hint**:
>
> **Cognate awareness** describes a student's ability to recognize cognates and use them as tools for understanding a second language.

Finally, students' accents will impact their learning and pronunciation of English. Speakers will often substitute the sounds of their first language for ones they think are the same in English. For example, some Spanish speakers may pronounce the /v/ sound like the English *b*. Additionally, stresses and intonations of words can be carried over from first languages, and both of these speech patterns can change the meanings of English words. For example, the meanings of the words *read* and *read* can lead to an unclear message.

Practice Question

6) Jamie has just moved from Mexico to Texas, where his mother enrolled him in an ESOL class. A few weeks in, Jamie is still reluctant to speak because he mixes in words from his first language with the English he is learning. Which linguistic behavior is Jamie demonstrating?
   A. code-switching
   B. cognate awareness
   C. difficulty with accent
   D. language interference

Instruction of English Language Learners

Like all students, ELLs need developmentally appropriate systematic instruction to build content knowledge and English proficiency. While students are working to master content-specific standards, they will also be working to master **English Language Proficiency (ELP) standards**. Such standards may be created by the state or by the WIDA Consortium (a group of state and government agencies that uses a shared set of ELPs). These standards aim to help students develop language proficiencies related to language arts, mathematics, science, social studies, and the social and instructional language of the school environment.

Within a broader framework of overarching ELPs, educators should create language objectives for ELLs that correspond with each lesson's focus. In schools with a large population of English language learners, some classes may be sheltered. **Sheltered classes** focus on the content area and English language learning, with an emphasis on developing language objectives in conjunction with content-area proficiency.

If, on the other hand, ELL students are taught in the general education setting, content-area teachers will need to embed English learning objectives in their lessons. They will also need to modify lessons and assessments to meet the needs of all learners. Lesson modification and assessment strategies are discussed in Table 1.4.

Table 1.4. Lesson Modification and Assessment Strategies for English Language Learners

Lesson Modification Strategies	Assessment Strategies
using picture dictionaries or electronic translators	- giving students a word bank or other explicit prompting
eliminating portions of assignments or assessments of which students may not have background knowledge	- allowing a test to be read aloud or completed orally in its entirety using peer tutors or collaborative learning strategies that build on each student's strengths - giving students assessments with simplified language
using multimedia or visual elements to aid in understanding	- administering assessments in smaller portions
preteaching core vocabulary or vocabulary scaffolding, such as digital texts with click-through definitions	- allowing students to use a dictionary or translating device on tests and/or allowing for extra or unlimited time
limiting teacher talk and, when used, speaking slowly and avoiding colloquialisms	- not penalizing students for spelling or grammar errors (as appropriate)
verifying that instructions are understood before students begin a task	- using informal assessment measures, such as observational records or oral assessments whenever possible
providing both print and oral versions of instructions	
using manipulatives or authentic learning situations whenever possible	
providing copies of lecture notes or allowing audio recordings	

> **Helpful Hint:**
>
> Some schools use bilingual education to transition to solely English instruction. Other schools use full English immersion with ESOL services through co-teaching, pull-out services, or sheltered or specialized classes.

Reading and English/language arts teachers are in a slightly different position from content area teachers: they must teach basic literacy skills along with the foundations of English as a language students might not be familiar with. Their focus will be on best practices in reading instruction with an emphasis on the needs of English language learners.

Phonemic awareness is important when teaching English language learners. English phonemes are distinct and should be taught explicitly, particularly for sounds that do not exist in the student's native language; however, sounds that are present and already known in the student's native language can be transferred rapidly. In such cases, instruction in phonemes should focus on those that differ from the student's first language.

Systematic phonics instruction is also an important component of teaching English to ELLs. Systematic phonics instruction is effective with students whose first language is not English as well as students whose native language is English. **Decoding** through phonics is a two-step process:

- Teachers must give ELLs the tools to sound out words.
- These students must be able to make meaning of the words based on their oral language vocabulary, which should be developed in tandem.

Automatic word recognition (sight reading) can also be very helpful for ELLs, since it can speed up reading rate and sometimes prevent difficulties that are encountered when words deviate from standard phonetic structures.

Fluency in reading follows oral language fluency; however, ELLs may have trouble with strategies like reading aloud in front of others. Students may lack confidence and focus on mistakes instead of the growth they have achieved over time. Oral reading practice with English language learners should be carefully orchestrated, making use of a trusted peer whenever possible.

Vocabulary instruction for ELLs will vary considerably from that of their native-speaking classmates. English language learners will need instruction in idioms and basic "connector words" like *because* and *and*. They will also need explicit and direct instruction in the vocabulary of the classroom. This includes words frequently used in giving instructions, words associated with subject area, high-frequency words used in speech and texts, and all vocabulary necessary to understand a text. Whenever possible, vocabulary should be taught explicitly and backed up with images or objects.

Comprehension must be carefully scaffolded in a variety of ways. Teachers should provide as much background knowledge as possible to students who are unfamiliar with aspects of American culture. Like developing readers, ELLs are better able to comprehend text with low complexity; such texts should be used to build comprehension skills. Graphic organizers, visual aids, and films or multimedia elements to promote comprehension may also be helpful.

Cultural sensitivity describes an awareness of cultural differences. While cultural sensitivity is important for all students, it is especially relevant for English language learners, who may be unfamiliar with elements of American culture that many people take for granted. Assumptions about religious beliefs, dietary preferences, clothing choices, family structures, and so on should be avoided. Teachers should select a variety of texts and curricular resources to promote an understanding of diverse cultural perspectives. While many publishers now promote multicultural awareness, teachers should consider curricular resources that also include diverse authorial voices.

Practice Question

7) A reading specialist is helping a high school teacher make her unit on *Romeo and Juliet* more accessible to English language learners. What is the BEST suggestion for the reading specialist to make?
   A. provide an alternate dramatic text on a different topic for ELL students to read
   B. encourage ELL students to use context clues to identify new vocabulary as they read the play
   C. preteach important roots and affixes to ELL students to aid in their decoding of new words in the play
   D. give ELL students a list of words used frequently in the play, along with their definitions

Answer Key

1) C: This objective is clear, measurable, transferable to other contexts, and indicates the target language for students' use.

2) D: Listening to an expert speaker discuss a topic may be beneficial to students' understanding of the material, but it will not activate their prior knowledge.

3) D: With a specific word-reading difficulty, students struggle to decode on the word level and may therefore have below-average comprehension and reading fluency. When students encounter words they are able to decode, however, they may exhibit strong comprehension skills.

4) C: Specific comprehension deficits commonly co-occur in students with ASD.

5) B: Lucia is using language chunking and song lyrics to build vocabulary; these are features of early production.

6) A: In code-switching, students mix in words from their first language when they speak their second language.

7) D: Common Shakespearean words like *thine* and *thou* may be new to English language learners and should be concretely defined before the students read the play.

Vocabulary Development

Vocabulary

Vocabulary plays an important role in language development. Students—both native English speakers and English language learners (ELLs)—benefit from continuous word acquisition, especially when they are seeing, learning, and studying new words in context. Teachers must therefore be able to support students by instructing them in the use of word clues and reference materials to acquire new vocabulary.

Phonics Instruction

Explicit phonics instruction is part of the early childhood and elementary education curricula; however, secondary ELA teachers should understand the basic principles of phonics instruction and apply these principles as they continue to develop students' reading, writing, and vocabulary skills.

Phonics is an age-old strategy for helping students read by connecting written language to spoken language or by correlating certain sounds with certain letters or groups of letters. Essential to phonics instruction is the concept of **letter-sound correspondence**—the knowledge that specific sounds are associated with specific letters.

Phonemes are distinct units of sound and the basic units of language. There are twenty-six letters in the alphabet, and most researchers agree that there are at least forty-four phonemes in English. (Some letters represent different phonemes, and some phonemes are made up of more than one letter.)

> **Helpful Hint:**
>
> **Sight words** require no decoding because they are instantly recognized and read automatically. Young students will work on memorizing sight words with basic sound structures that cannot be sounded out.

Phonics instruction draws on the strategy of **decoding**, or the ability to pronounce the sounds of written words orally and understand their meanings. Some of the most common strategies for phonics instruction include the following:

- **Synthetic phonics** is one of the most common and effective types of phonics instruction. Students are explicitly taught to break down words into their component phonemes and sound them out.

- **Analytic phonics**, or **implicit phonics**, does not involve sounding out each phoneme in a word; instead, students begin to recognize word families by identifying the initial sound (onset) and the rime (the letters which follow the onset).

- **Embedded phonics**, or **phonics through context**, is an approach to phonics instruction that relies on incidental learning; whole texts are the primary curricular resources. Explicit phonics instruction is only used when students have trouble reading a particular word.

- **Phonics through spelling** is a combined approach whereby reading and spelling are taught in tandem. Students are taught to spell words phonetically by sounding them out or breaking them into their individual phonemes.

> **Helpful Hint**:
> Fluency refers to the rate, accuracy, and expression of a text when read. It is an important measure of a student's reading development because it affects comprehension and reading enjoyment.

According to research, the synthetic phonics approach is the most universal method of phonics instruction that can meet the needs of the most learners. Research also indicates that systematic phonics instruction occurring in a particularly designed sequence is the most effective.

Phonics instruction is also highly effective when it includes connected texts, or words, in sentences and paragraphs instead of only in isolation or lists.

Practice Question

1) A kindergarten teacher is working with a student to read a short sentence: *He ran to the woods.*

The student becomes stuck on the word *woods*. Which question should the teacher ask in order to stay aligned with synthetic phonics instruction?
   A. What do the pictures tell you this word might be?
   B. What sound do the letters in the word make?
   C. Where would someone run?
   D. What other words do you know that rhyme with *wood*?

Word Analysis

The human brain uses three cueing systems to determine the meanings of words: semantic, syntactic, and graphophonic. Together, these systems form **word analysis strategies**, or **word-attack strategies**—methods of decoding unfamiliar words.

Semantic cues offer prompts to a word's meaning and are drawn from background knowledge or context clues. Since words are immediately retrieved from memory and processed, semantic cues are the brain's most efficient cueing system. Semantic cues rely on students to activate knowledge and make reasonable predictions and inferences regarding a word's meaning.

Semantic cues based on the text itself are called **context clues**. Context clues can be other words in the text or graphics. Students should be explicitly taught to identify other words in a sentence, paragraph, or passage that provide possible clues to the meaning of an unknown word. Students of all ages can also look to illustrations or charts to understand new words. This is particularly helpful with subject-specific vocabulary, such as terminology associated with organelles within plant cells.

Syntactic cues are based on the structure of language and are regarded as the brain's second-most efficient cueing system while reading. They include sentence structure and word order, structural clues within words, and structural analysis of the word. A word's meaning can sometimes be clued or determined by its placement in a sentence. For example, figuring out whether a word is used as an adjective, noun, or verb can help with determining its meaning.

Structural analysis of a word can also be a useful strategy. Students can decode a compound word, for example, by breaking the word into its two component parts.

Structural clues within words, such as **affixes** (prefixes and suffixes) and **roots** (base words with no affixes), can also offer clues to a word's meaning. The use of structural clues is sometimes referred to as

morphemic analysis, or the analysis of morphemes (the smallest units of meaning within words). (Affixes and roots are discussed in more detail in the next section.)

The **graphophonic cueing system** is based on applying sound (phoneme)-symbol (grapheme or letter) knowledge while reading. It is the most basic level of decoding and tends to be the least efficient since its focus is on individual units (letters and letter patterns, for example) instead of larger chunks of text, like words and ideas.

Homophones are words that have the same pronunciation but differ in meaning and, in some cases, spelling:

- gate/gait
- role/roll
- cue/queue

Homographs are words that are *spelled* the same but have different meanings; in some instances, the words are pronounced differently:

- tear
- fair
- bow

The word *homonyms* refers to words that are either homophones or homographs.

Students should be taught to use context clues to identify the meanings of homonyms they encounter while reading.

For graphophonic cueing to be most effective, readers must have some knowledge of the word they are sounding out to make meaning. For example, a ninth-grade student might be able to apply graphophonic cueing to successfully sound out the word *meticulous*; however, this word is not truly decoded unless the student can use other clues to determine the word's meaning. For this reason, many educators use whole-language instruction, which does not use any cueing system smaller than the word level. In a whole-language approach, students must use semantic and syntactic cues as the only methods for decoding new words.

Practice Questions

2) Which activity would MOST likely help students develop the knowledge to use semantic cues effectively?
   A. reading books that provide information on a variety of places and cultures
   B. underlining confusing sentences and diagramming them
   C. reading a text aloud twice, once to oneself and once to a partner
   D. encouraging students to increase their reading rates to retain more information

Practice question 3 is based on the following passage:

The Bastille, Paris's famous historic prison, was originally built in 1370 as a fortification, called a bastide in Old French, to protect the city from English invasion during the Hundred Years' War. It rose 100 feet into the air, had eight towers, and was surrounded by a moat more than eighty feet wide. In the seventeenth century, the government converted the fortress into a prison for upper-class felons, political disruptors, and spies. Residents of the Bastille arrived by direct order of the king and usually were left there to languish without a trial.

3) Which of the following phrases from the passage could be used as a context clue to help students determine the meaning of the word *fortification*?
   A. "surrounded by a moat more than eighty feet wide"
   B. "arrived by direct order of the king"
   C. "converted the fortress into a prison"
   D. "to protect the city from English invasion"

Root Words and Affixes

Roots are the building blocks of all words: every word is either a root itself or has a root. The root is what is left when you strip away the prefixes and suffixes from a word. For example, if you take away the prefix *un–* from the word *unclear*, you have the root *clear*.

Roots are not always recognizable because they often come from Latin or Greek words, such as *nat*, a Latin root meaning "born." The word *native*, which refers to a person born in a referenced place, comes from this root. So does the word *prenatal*, meaning "before birth." It is important to keep in mind, however, that roots can have several spellings and do not always match the original definitions of words.

Prefixes are elements added to the beginning of words, and **suffixes** are elements added to the end of words; together they are known as **affixes**. Affixes carry assigned meanings and can be attached to words to completely change their meanings or enhance their original meanings. For example, in the word *prefix*:

- The word *fix* means "to place something securely."
- *Pre–* means "before."
- Therefore, the word *prefix* means "to place something before or in front of."

An example of a suffix can be found in the word *feminism*:

- *Femin* is a root that means "female."
- The suffix *–ism* means "act," "practice," or "process."

Therefore, *feminism* is the process of establishing equal rights for women.

Practice Questions

Which option offers the BEST definition of the underlined word in the following sentences?

4) The <u>bellicose</u> dog will be sent to training school next week.
   A. misbehaved
   B. friendly
   C. scared
   D. aggressive

Vocabulary Development

5) The new menu <u>rejuvenated</u> the restaurant and made it one of the most popular spots in town.
    A. established
    B. invigorated
    C. improved
    D. motivated

Vocabulary Development

Vocabulary can—and should—be broadened through a variety of strategies. Vocabulary knowledge makes reading more expedient and fluent since readers can simply decode a word semantically without having to resort to other cueing systems. Vocabulary development should focus on retention—not memorization. The goal is for students to be able to not just recognize words but also understand and use them appropriately. Vocabulary is developed through one of two ways:

- **Incidental vocabulary learning** occurs while reading, either independently or through teacher-guided oral reading activities.

- **Intentional vocabulary teaching** requires educators to more explicitly direct vocabulary acquisition.

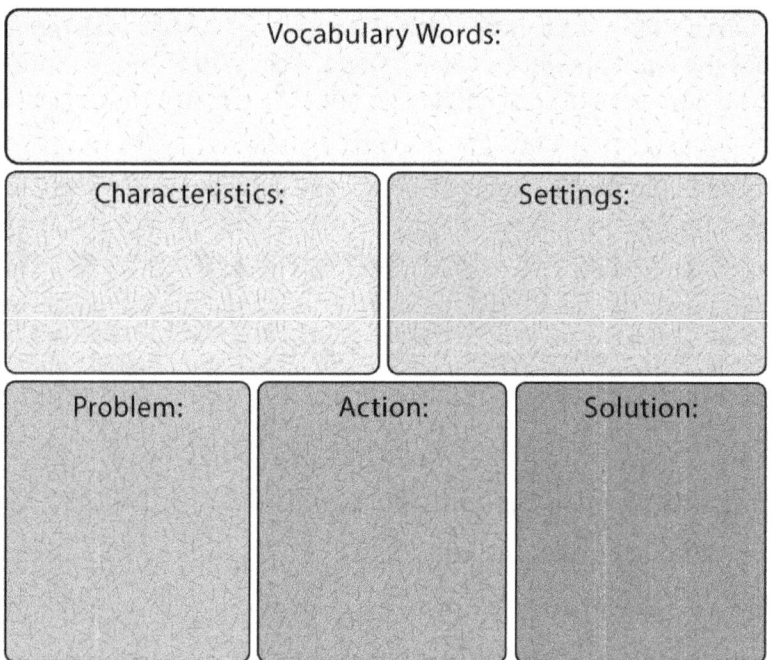

The following strategies can be used for intentional vocabulary teaching:

- **Predict-O-Gram:** Students are given a list of words and predict how they will be used in a text. This strategy can be used effectively for both fiction and nonfiction texts, though it is most often used with fiction since it can be easily integrated into existing knowledge about plot structure.

- **Semantic impressions:** Students are given a list of words in the order in which they appear in the text. The definition of each word is then briefly discussed by the teacher. Students write their own stories using the words in the same order, using each word only once. Students then read the text and compare their finished stories to the original.

- **Semantic feature analysis:** Also called a **semantic grid**, this strategy functions as a graphic organizer that helps students think deeply about the features or properties of each vocabulary word.
- **Frayer model:** This is a specific type of semantic analysis with four grids on which students write the definition of a word, along with its characteristics, examples, and nonexamples.
- **List-group-label:** In this semantic mapping strategy, students brainstorm all the words they can think of that relate to a particular topic. They then divide the list of words into subcategories based on common features. For example, words like *dorsal fin*, *gills*, and *teeth* might be placed in the category of "parts of a fish's body."
- **Possible sentences:** Students are given a list of vocabulary words from the text they will read. They then write a "possible" sentence for each word, illustrating the word's possible meaning. After reading the text, students return to their possible sentences to see if they are accurate or if the sentences need to be changed based on the word's actual meaning as revealed in the text.
- **OPIN:** Short for the word *opinion*, this strategy is similar to a **cloze exercise** in which students fill in the blank with a word they think belongs in a sentence. Students then break into groups to "defend" their word choices to other members of the group. This strategy helps reinforce other skills since students use context clues and background knowledge to justify their answers.

Assessments should be used to guide vocabulary development. How students perform on such assessments will guide the instruction and pacing of new content. Information on how to assess vocabulary skills appears in Chapter 11 ("Data-Driven Practices and Assessments").

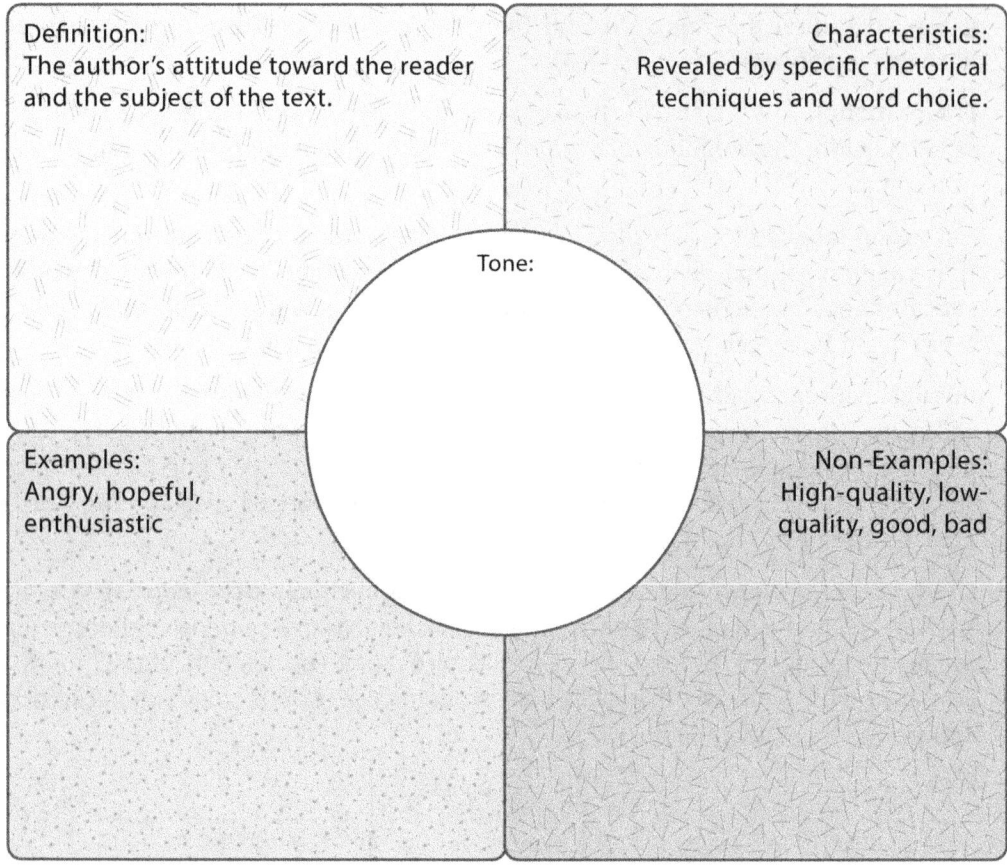

Figure 2.3. Frayer Model

Practice Question

6) Which exercise could BEST be used to incorporate vocabulary acquisition into a creative writing unit?
    A. list-group-label
    B. OPIN
    C. semantic impressions
    D. semantic grids

Resources

Despite their best efforts, students will inevitably encounter a word that they cannot decipher based on usage alone; therefore, in order to assist students in the acquisition of new words, teachers must be knowledgeable about the tools and resources that are at their students' disposal in the modern age. Teachers must understand the purpose and usage of each kind of resource, the limits of the various tools, and the advantages and disadvantages of dependence on reference materials.

Spellcheckers come as a default on many word processing systems and can be helpful as a first line of defense against spelling (and even grammar) errors; however, spellcheckers should not be used in isolation since they are limited in their abilities to catch certain kinds of errors. For example, a spellchecker might recognize the word *therre* as an incorrect spelling of *there*, but it would not recognize *their* as incorrect in context. Though improvements are always being made to automatic spelling and grammar-checking technology, students would be prudent to continue doing their own editing as well.

Style manuals are guidebooks for general language usage and the documentation of sources within a written document, anthology, or field of study. While some style manuals, such as *The Chicago Manual of Style*, exist to serve a general readership, many serve specific audiences or professional groups. One such example is the *Publication Manual of the American Psychological Association*, which is used in most social science publications. Students should be familiarized with some of the more common style manuals and be able to apply them to their own work.

Dictionaries provide the definitions of words along with a few other important details, such as a word's part of speech and other forms. Dictionaries are therefore especially useful tools for vocabulary acquisition. With a good dictionary, students can

- look up the meaning of a word;
- check the spelling of a word;
- check the plural of a noun or past tense of a verb;
- find out other grammatical information about a word;
- find the synonym or antonym of a word;
- check the part of speech of a word;
- find out how to pronounce a word;
- find out about the register of a word (formal or informal, for example);
- find examples of a word's usage.

Bilingual dictionaries can be used to translate words and/or phrases between two languages. While some bilingual dictionaries allow the user to translate only from one language to the other, many actually allow the reader to translate in both directions—to and from the secondary language.

A thesaurus is useful when considering alternate word choices. A **thesaurus** provides synonyms and antonyms and helps writers vary their language or find just the right word to communicate a particular idea. Students should be taught, however, that a thesaurus should be used cautiously: replacing words for the sake of choosing ones that are interesting or more advanced can sometimes complicate the true meaning of a text. Enhancing word choice without overwriting is challenging but generally makes for the most effective writing. Indeed, as long as the voice of the writer is maintained, a thesaurus can become a tool to add creativity to the text. For example:

Starting Sentence:

The man walked toward his house in the wind and snow.

Ineffective Use of Synonyms:

The fellow ambulated in the orientation of his household, against the strident gale and frigid precipitation.

Effective Use of Synonyms:

The man trudged toward his distant house, against the harsh wind and unrelenting snow.

A **glossary** is a list of terms and definitions found in a specific text; it is usually located at the end of the book. Glossaries are common in textbooks and other technical publications.

Teachers should emphasize to students that the resources mentioned are designed to be *tools* for students—not substitutes for their own knowledge. For instance, after looking up a new word in the dictionary, students should make an effort to learn the word.

Students may refer to these resources throughout their academic careers, but they should also be encouraged to do their best to enhance their own knowledge.

Practice Question

7) A student in Mr. Moreno's class is writing an essay and needs to find a suitable replacement for the word *justify*. Where should the student look FIRST?
   A. the dictionary
   B. a glossary
   C. a bilingual dictionary
   D. a thesaurus

Answer Key

1. B: Asking about the sounds the letters make will help the student decode the word *woods* by sounding it out.

2. A: Reading a broad array of books builds background knowledge, which can then be applied and retrieved.

3. D: A fortification is a defensive structure meant to protect.

4. D: Both *misbehaved* and *aggressive* look like possible answers given the context of the sentence; however, the prefix *belli–*, which means "warlike," can be used to confirm that the word *aggressive* is the correct answer.

5. B: All of the answer options could make sense in the context of the sentence, so it is necessary to use word structure to find the definition. The root *juven* means "young," and the prefix *re–* means "again," so *rejuvenate* means "to be made young again." The answer option with the most similar meaning is the word *invigorated*, which means "to give something energy."

6. C: The semantic impressions strategy involves having students write a story with the words from the text.

7. D: A thesaurus provides a list of synonyms and antonyms for each word.

Reading Comprehension

Literary Elements

Just as visual artists have the tools of color and shape to communicate ideas, so have writers their literary tools. These tools include point of view, plot, setting, character, tone, and figurative language. Each of these elements contributes to the overall idea that is developed in the text and, as such, can provide valuable insight into the theme of the work.

Setting and Character Development

Setting is the time and place of events in a story. When considering setting, students should look at the following elements of a story:

- how the characters interact with their surroundings
- how the characters are influenced by the societal expectations of the time and place in which the story takes place
- how the location and time period impact the development of the story

Since students could have difficulty understanding the differences between setting and plot, teachers can ask, "How would this story change if it were set in a different time or place?" to help students understand setting.

An author uses **character development** to create characters that are complex and, to some degree, believable. Authors might develop their characters directly by telling the reader explicitly what the character is like by describing traits and values.

Sometimes, authors include the thoughts and feelings of the characters themselves, offering readers even more insight. Authors also develop their characters indirectly by revealing their actions and interactions with others. They might do this by including what one character says or thinks about another and allowing readers to draw their own conclusions. Most authors combine direct and indirect characterization, which ensures that readers know what they need to know and provides opportunities for reflection and interpretation.

Practice Question

1) A reading specialist suggests that the eighth-grade English teacher should invite a guest speaker to present a lecture on the historical background and setting of *Johnny Tremain* before the class reads a portion of the text. What is the MOST appropriate strategy to use with the guest speaker?
    A. listen-read-discuss
    B. Predict-O-Gram
    C. peer tutoring
    D. reader's theater

Tone and Mood

The **tone** of a literary work is created by the author's attitude toward both the reader and the subject of the text. In a sense, it is the tone of voice the author uses to speak to the reader.

Depending on word choice, an author's tone can range from playful, familiar, or sincere to detached, sarcastic, or indifferent. It can be alarmed and forceful or philosophical and serious. It might be concerned or careless, saddened or overjoyed, triumphant or defeated.

Whatever the case, students should be encouraged to consider how the author uses language to convey tone by thinking about what the author is suggesting through language choice. This process will reveal the author's attitude and, ultimately, the theme of the work.

Students should also be able to distinguish the author's tone from the **mood**, which is the emotional atmosphere of a literary work that shapes the reader's experience with the text.

Mood is created through an interplay of the literary elements of plot, character, setting, point of view, tone, and figurative language. By examining the emotional effect of the author's choices, readers can further develop their understanding of the text's larger meaning.

Practice Question

2) Which of the following strategies would BEST help a student identify the tone of a literary work?
   A. implementing pre-reading strategies like previewing, scanning, and predicting
   B. using a list-group-label process to dig deeper into key concepts from the work
   C. focusing on the morphology and orthography of words found in the text
   D. identifying specific words in the text that evoke feelings or emotions

Point of View

Point of view is the perspective from which the action in a story is told. By carefully selecting a particular point of view, writers are able to control what their readers know. Most literature is written in first-person or third-person point of view:

- In the **first-person** or **"I" point of view**, the action is narrated by a character within the story, which can make the story feel more believable and authentic to the reader. The reader's knowledge and understanding, however, are limited to what the narrator notices and influenced by what the narrator thinks and values.

- A **third-person point of view** is a voice outside the action of the story—what an observer knows, sees, hears, and shares with the reader. A third-person narrator might be
    - **omniscient** (able to see into the minds of the characters and share what they are thinking and feeling);
    - **partially omniscient** (able to see into the minds of just one or a few characters); or
    - **limited** (unable to see into the minds of any of the characters and only able to share what can be seen and heard).

- The **second-person point of view** uses "you" and can be read as the narrator speaking directly to the reader. It is used mainly in nonfiction texts, particularly in introductory and concluding paragraphs in which the writer might make a direct appeal to the reader to reflect on the points about to be made or already made.

Practice Question

3) Which passage below from "A Mystery of Heroism" by Stephen Crane BEST exemplifies the third-person omniscient point of view?
- A. "In the midst of it all, Smith and Ferguson, two privates of A Company, were engaged in a heated discussion, which involved the greatest questions of the national existence."
- B. "An officer screamed out an order so violently that his voice broke and ended the sentence in a falsetto shriek."
- C. "The officer's face was grimy and perspiring, and his uniform was tousled as if he had been in direct grapple with an enemy. He smiled grimly when the men stared at him."
- D. "No, it could not be true. He was not a hero. Heroes had no shames in their lives, and, as for him, he remembered borrowing fifteen dollars from a friend and promising to pay it back the next day, and then avoiding that friend for ten months."

Plot

Plot structure is the way the author arranges the events of a narrative. In a conventional plot line, the story is structured around a central conflict—a struggle between two opposing forces. Conflicts in literature can be categorized in general terms as either internal or external, though most stories have a combination of both.

Internal conflicts take place inside the mind of the main character, who might be making a difficult decision, struggling with change, or sorting out priorities. **External conflicts**, on the other hand, occur when a character is in conflict with something or someone in the external world—the elements of nature, another character, supernatural forces, destiny, or society. A traditional plot structure is usually organized as follows:

- The author begins by introducing the **exposition**—important background information about the setting, the characters, and the current state of the world.
- An **inciting incident** then introduces the antagonist and establishes the conflict.
- As the story progresses, the conflict becomes more complicated and tension increases, moving the story toward a **climax**, or turning point, in which the conflict reaches a crisis point.
- Finally, there is a resolution to the conflict, followed by **falling actions**—events that move the characters away from the conflict and into new lives.

To facilitate deep comprehension of literary texts, teachers can help students understand key elements through a **plot diagram**. In studying plot, students should be encouraged to focus on cause-and-effect relationships between events in the story, the conflict, and its resolution. By analyzing how the author chooses to resolve the conflict, the reader can gain a better understanding of the story's theme.

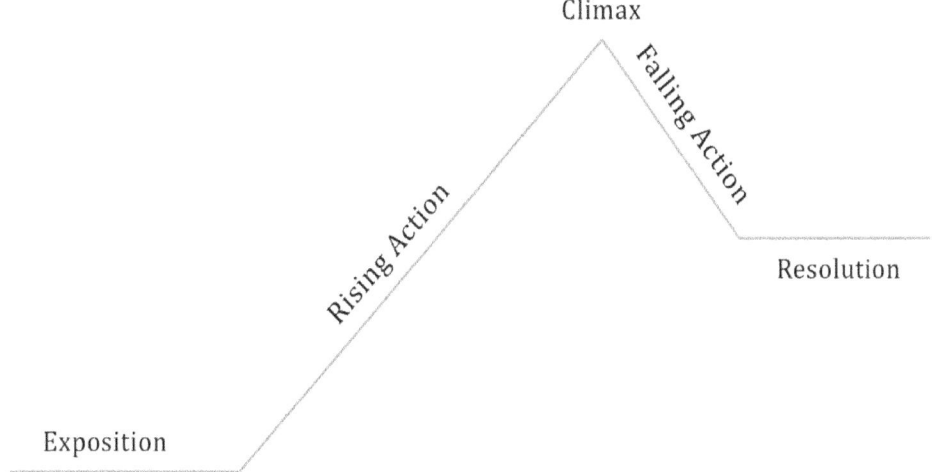

Figure 3.1. Plot Diagram

Practice Question

4) Which of the following BEST describes an internal conflict?
   A. In Jack London's "To Build a Fire," the protagonist tries to survive the freezing weather of the Yukon.
   B. In Virginia Woolf's *Mrs. Dalloway*, Clarissa Dalloway questions her choice of husband as she prepares for a party.
   C. In Margaret Atwood's *The Handmaid's Tale*, a group of women try to escape a dystopian society in which they have been enslaved.
   D. In Shakespeare's *Romeo and Juliet*, two lovers try to marry despite the objections of their families.

Figurative Language

Figures of speech are expressions that are understood to have nonliteral meanings. Rather than stating their ideas directly, authors use figurative language to suggest meaning by speaking of a subject as if it were something else. For example, when Shakespeare says, "All the world's a stage, / And all men and women merely players," he is speaking of the world as if it is a stage. Since the world is not *literally* a stage, the reader has to ask how the two are similar and what Shakespeare might be implying about the world through this comparison. Figures of speech extend the meaning of words by engaging the reader's imagination and adding emphasis to different aspects of their subject.

A **metaphor** is a type of figurative language that describes something that may be unfamiliar to the reader (the topic) by referring to it as though it were something else that is more familiar to the reader (the vehicle). A metaphor stands in as a synonym, interchangeable with its corresponding topic. As readers reflect on the similarities between the topic and the vehicle, they form a clearer understanding of the topic. For example:

- In Shakespeare's *Romeo and Juliet*, Romeo says that "Juliet is the sun."
- By making this comparison, Romeo is comparing Juliet's energy to the brightness of the sun, which is familiar to readers.

Important Works

Romeo and Juliet

Author: William Shakespeare

Publication Date: 1597

Summary: Juliet, a member of the Capulet family, is engaged to Count Paris per her father's wish; however, she falls in love with Romeo, a member of the Montague family, with whom her family has a longstanding and sometimes violent feud. The two marry in secret, knowing their love will not be permitted by their families.

Juliet's cousin Tybalt confronts Romeo about his affections for Juliet; a fight breaks out, and Tybalt kills Romeo's best friend, Mercutio. After killing Tybalt in retribution, Romeo is banished from the city of Verona. Now scheduled to marry Count Paris, Juliet obtains a potion to make her seem dead and devises a plan for Romeo to rescue her; however, a letter explaining the plan never reaches Romeo, and he believes that Juliet actually died. In Juliet's burial crypt, Romeo poisons himself, thinking he has lost his only love. Juliet awakens, finds Romeo dead, and commits suicide.

Themes, Motifs, and Symbols: star-crossed love, fate, role of family, youth and foolishness

A **simile** is a type of figurative language that directly points to similarities between two things. As with a metaphor, the author uses a familiar vehicle to express an idea about a less familiar topic. Unlike a metaphor, however, a simile does not replace the object with a figurative description; it compares the vehicle and topic using *like*, *as*, or similar words. For example:

- In his poem *The Rime of the Ancient Mariner*, Coleridge describes his ship as "idle as a painted ship / Upon a painted ocean."
- He speaks about the boat as if it were painted (unlike Romeo above, who says explicitly that Juliet is the sun itself). The reader understands that paintings do not move, so Coleridge uses this comparison to show the reader that the ship in the poem is completely motionless.

Imagery is vivid description that appeals to the reader's senses of sight, sound, smell, taste, or touch. This type of figurative language allows readers to experience through their senses what is being described. As readers use their imaginations to visualize or recall sensory experiences, they are drawn into the scene of the story or poem.

Hyperbole is an overstatement, or an exaggeration, intended to achieve a particular effect. Hyperbole can create humor or add emphasis to a text by drawing the reader's attention to a particular idea. For example:

- A character might say, "I am so hungry, I could eat a horse." Though the character probably will not literally eat a horse, the reader understands that the character is extremely hungry.

Personification is a type of figurative language in which human characteristics are attributed to objects, abstract ideas, natural forces, or animals. For example, writers referring to "murmuring pine trees," are attributing to the pine trees the human ability of murmuring. The writer is using the familiar vehicle of the sound of murmuring to help readers understand the sound pine trees make in the wind.

Symbolism is a literary device in which the author uses a concrete object, action, or character to represent an abstract idea. The significance of the symbol reaches beyond the object's ordinary meaning. As readers notice an author's use of symbolism, they begin to make connections and formulate ideas about what the author is suggesting. Familiar symbols include the following:

- roses representing beauty
- light representing truth
- darkness representing evil

An **allusion**—not to be confused with an *illusion*—is a reference to a character or event that is historical, fictional, mythological, or religious, or an artist or artistic work. When readers recognize an allusion, they may make associations that contribute to their understanding of the text. For example:

- If a character is described as having a "Mona Lisa smile," an instant image will arise in the minds of most readers.
- Because allusions can be difficult to recognize, especially for young readers whose experiences are limited, teachers must provide instruction in how to recognize, research, and interpret unfamiliar references.

Clichés are common sayings that lack originality but are familiar and relatable to an audience. Though clichés are not necessarily beneficial to the author who is trying to write a wholly original work, they can be helpful for writers who are attempting to show that they can relate to an audience.

Dialect and **slang** are linguistic qualities that authors might incorporate into their writing in order to develop characters or setting. Dialect may reveal where a character is from; slang might be an indication of social, economic, and educational statuses.

Authors use **foreshadowing** to hint at events that are going to unfold in a story. Typically, foreshadowing is intended to create a sense of anticipation and suspense in the reader.

Irony describes using words to express something that is usually the opposite of a word's literal meaning. Irony comes in different forms:

- **Verbal irony** is used when a character or narrator says something that is the opposite of what is meant.
- **Situational irony** occurs when something happens that contradicts what the audience expects to happen.
- **Dramatic irony** occurs when the audience knows about something of which a character or characters are not aware.

> **Helpful Hint**:
> Figures of speech extend the meaning of words by adding emphasis to different aspects of their subjects and engaging the reader's imagination.

Practice Question

Question 5 refers to the poem "I'm Nobody! Who are you?" by Emily Dickinson.

> I'm nobody! Who are you?
> Are you nobody, too?
> Then there's a pair of us—don't tell!
> They'd banish us, you know.
> How dreary to be somebody!
> How public, like a frog!
> To tell your name the livelong day
> To an admiring bog!

5) What kind of figurative language is NOT used in the poem?
   A. simile
   B. personification
   C. hyperbole
   D. metaphor

Word Choice

Authors consider a number of factors when selecting words:

- **Denotation** is a word's meaning according to a dictionary.
- **Connotation** is a word's suggested or implied meaning and can be positive or negative, based on emotional associations with the word.

Writers choose words based on how effectively they convey the feelings, ideas, and associations they want to express; when it comes to word choice, precision is of the utmost importance. For example, Dr. Martin Luther King Jr. said, "I have a dream"; he didn't say "I have a plan."

The word *plan* suggests something practical and quotidian, while the word *dream* communicates a much larger desire, a more abstract idea, and a greater vision.

An author might also consider whether to write explicitly or implicitly about a subject based on the degree to which the writer wants the reader to think independently about the subject:

- **Explicit language** is clear, detailed, and exact; the wording is designed to prevent confusion and ambiguity.
- **Implicit language** allows for implied meanings; readers are left to draw their own conclusions.

If writers intend only to inform their readers, they may choose explicit language so that the readers can clearly understand the information being presented. On the other hand, if writers hope to change readers' behaviors, they might use implicit language with the goal of leading readers to their own conclusions.

> **Helpful Hint**:
>
> Mark Twain once said, "The difference between the almost-right word and the right word is really a large matter—it's the difference between the lightning bug and the lightning."

Practice Question

The following question refers to the excerpt from the poem "Ode to the West Wind," by Percy Bysshe Shelley.

O wild West Wind, thou breath of Autumn's being,

Thou, from whose unseen presence the leaves dead

Are driven, like ghosts from an enchanter fleeing,

Yellow, and black, and pale, and hectic red,

Pestilence-stricken multitudes:

O thou, Who chariotest to their dark wintry bed

The wingèd seeds, where they lie cold and low,

Each like a corpse within its grave, until

Thine azure sister of the Spring shall blow

Her clarion o'er the dreaming earth, and fill

(Driving sweet buds like flocks to feed in air)

With living hues and odours plain and hill:

Wild Spirit, which art moving everywhere;

Destroyer and Preserver; hear, O hear!

6) What is the connotation of the words *pestilence-stricken* in the poem?
   A. carrying a contagious disease
   B. full of color
   C. pathetic and sorrowful
   D. dead and decaying

Poetic Devices and Structures

Poets employ **poetic devices** to create aesthetic effects that impact readers and emphasize meaning. Most poetic devices—including rhyme, rhythm, meter, and repetition—create sound effects or provide structure in a poem.

Table 3.1. Poetic Devices	
Device Name	**Description**
Rhyme scheme	▪ Rhyme scheme is the arrangement of rhyming words in a stanza or poem. ▪ It usually appears at the end of a line, but it is possible for internal rhymes to be part of the scheme.

Table 3.1. Poetic Devices

Device Name	Description
	- A frequently used rhyme scheme is present in **quatrains**, in which the first and third lines rhyme and the second and fourth lines rhyme, creating an *abab* pattern: 　○ The repeating pattern of sound creates a sense of balance and musicality. 　○ It produces an aesthetic effect that allows readers to predict the upcoming sounds, thereby freeing them to focus on the ideas.
Slant rhyme	- Slant rhyme is not considered true rhyme. - The poet substitutes assonance or consonance (defined below) for real rhyme.
Internal rhyme	- Internal rhyme involves rhyming two or more words in the same line of poetry. - It affects the rhythm of the poem; it is the drumbeat or heartbeat of the poem. - It describes the pattern of accentuated sounds, which creates or heightens the emotional effect of the language.
Meter	- Meter is an established rhythm within a poem, in which accentuated syllables are repetitive and predictable. - Each unit of the meter, called a foot, has stressed and unstressed syllables. - It is often named by the type and number of feet in one line.
Iamb	- Iamb is a familiar poetic foot that occurs when an unaccented syllable is followed by an accented one, as in the word *contain* (con-TAIN).
Blank verse	- Blank verse is unrhymed poetry written in iambic pentameter. - Many English dramas, including Shakespeare's plays and Milton's *Paradise Lost* are written in blank verse.
Free verse	- This describes poetry without rhyme patterns or regular meter; unpredictable rhythms are found in the poem.
Repetition	- This device is used to emphasize important ideas and heighten the emotional effect of language. - Repetition can be of words themselves; a particularly important or charged word might be repeated to draw the reader's attention to it. - It can sometimes be found only in sounds, as when poets employ assonance or consonance.
Assonance	- Assonance is the inclusion of words with the same vowel sounds within one or two lines of poetry. - from "Stopping by Woods on a Snowy Evening" (Robert Frost): 　○ "The only other sound's the sweep / Of easy wind and downy flake" 　○ Here, assonance lends a musicality to the language in a poem.

Table 3.1. Poetic Devices

Device Name	Description
Consonance	<ul><li>Consonance is the repetition of the same consonant sounds at the end of a stressed syllable but following different vowel sounds in words that are fairly close together</li><li>from "Stopping by Woods on a Snowy Evening" (Robert Frost):<ul><li>"Whose woods these are I think I know."</li><li>Here, the poet uses consonance to highlight particular words; like the other sound devices, it creates a pleasing lyrical effect.</li></ul></li></ul>

In his poem "A Noiseless Patient Spider," Walt Whitman's speaker reveals the yearning of his soul using a combination of diction, repetition, and consonance. The repetition of the word *filament* emphasizes the amount of thread that is coming from the spider's body. The use of the words *tirelessly* and *ceaselessly* highlight the similarity between the spider's ongoing efforts to spin her web and the speaker's ongoing efforts to connect with the external world.

Helpful Hint:

A line with five iambs (ten syllables, beginning with an unstressed syllable and alternating for the rest of the line) is written in iambic pentameter. Shakespeare's verse is mostly written in this meter. From *Romeo and Juliet*: "But, soft! what light through yonder window breaks?" or "But, SOFT! what LIGHT through YONder WINdow BREAKS?"

The six present progressive verbs—the repetition of the *-ing* sound—enhance the reader's sense of the relentless efforts of the spider and the speaker to improve their situations.

Important Works

"Stopping by Woods on a Snowy Evening"

Author: Robert Frost

Publication Date: 1923

Summary: The speaker is driving a horse and carriage on a dark, snowy evening and stops to ponder the woods, which are owned by a villager who will not see the speaker stopping there. The speaker describes the actions of the horse, who shakes its harness, causing the bells on it to chime and perhaps signaling that stopping in such a remote area seems odd. The speaker describes the landscape and the evening itself—dark but lovely on the longest night of the year. The poem ends with the assertion that, though the time spent appreciating the woods and the evening is nice, the driver's journey must continue.

Themes, Motifs, and Symbols: nature, duty, choice, human isolation

"A Noiseless Patient Spider"

Author: Walt Whitman

Publication Date: 1868 (originally as stanza 3 from the larger poem "Whispers of Heavenly Death")

Summary: The narrator reveals his soul's yearnings to connect with the world and compares his continuous quest to find connections between himself and his surroundings with a spider's attempts to connect to the world by continuously creating and sending out threads.

Themes, Motifs, and Symbols: feelings of connection versus isolation; using creative means to connect with the world/surroundings

While some poets rely on established structures to organize their work, others prefer to create their own rules. **Closed-form poetry** follows a given form or shape; such poems usually have a specified number of lines and a designated number of feet in each line. This type of poetry also follows a consistent rhyme and meter; examples include blank verse, couplets, the villanelle, the quatrain, the sonnet, and the ballad.

Open-form poetry does not have restrictions and allows poets to create unique arrangements of words and lines that flow naturally or communicate a particular feeling. Authors of this type of poetry often use the lengths of the lines to emphasize ideas.

Poets design their poems according to the ideas they are communicating and the mood they hope to convey. Today, poets can choose any form they wish—open or closed. Some past and present poets reinforce their ideas using **pattern poems**. For example, in the seventeenth century, George Herbert wrote "Easter Wings." The first stanza follows:

> *Lord, who createdst man in wealth and store,*
>
> *Though foolishly he lost the same,*
>
> *Decaying more and more,*
>
> *Till he became*
>
> *Most poore:*
>
> *With thee*
>
> *O let me rise*
>
> *As larks, harmoniously,*
>
> *And sing this day thy victories:*
>
> *Then shall the fall further the flight in me.*

In addition to these poetic devices, poets employ many other types of figurative language that are common in literature, such as metaphors, similes, symbols, and analogies.

Practice Question

Question 7 refers to the following stanza from the poem "O, Fairest of the Rural Maids" by William Cullen Bryant.

The twilight of the trees and rocks

Is in the light shade of thy locks;

Thy step is as the wind, that weaves

Its playful way among the leaves.

7) What sound device is used in the lines "The twilight of the trees and rocks / Is in the light shade of thy locks"?
- A. internal rhyme
- B. consonance
- C. slant rhyme
- D. simile

Themes

Literary texts give concrete form to abstract, thematic ideas. Through a process of carefully examining the concrete details of a text, making evidence-based inferences, and thinking broadly about what these things suggest, readers can come to understand the **theme** of a literary work—the universal message that the authors hope to communicate through their artistic choices.

By tracing themes across time, location, and culture, students of literature can begin to recognize some of the common experiences that define humanity, such as love, loss, power, betrayal, growing old, and coming of age.

> **Helpful Hint**:
>
> A **theme** is an idea about some aspect of life or human nature.

To guide students through the process of determining a theme, effective teachers begin by providing instruction in how authors craft their ideas using the literary tools of plot, setting, character, figurative language, and point of view.

Through close reading and analysis of author's choice, students then infer what the author could be suggesting about life or human nature.

To direct student attention to the thematic ideas of a text, effective teachers might employ the following strategies:

- use **two-column response journals** to have students record interesting or memorable quotes and their reactions to them
- use **focus questions** that push students to make connections with the text (e.g., *How did the author's use of _____ affect your reaction to the story? Why would the author want you to react that way? What about this story can you relate to your own life?*)

> **Helpful Hint**:
>
> **Marxist literary theorists** examine how the experiences of—and relationships between—characters are influenced by socioeconomic class.

Reading Comprehension

- facilitate a discussion about the relationship between elements of the text, including the plot and character development, tone, and setting
- have students record words or images in their journals that are repeated and elements and ideas that are paired or contrasted
- take the time to not only explain figurative language to students but also to provide instruction in the thought processes that make analysis possible
- explicitly identify **signal words** or phrases, like *as a result*, and discuss their meanings with students

By asking students to use specific details to analyze the author's purpose, effective teachers push students to make connections, read closely, and improve their critical reading and thinking skills.

Practice Question

8) An ELA teacher is working with a small group of students on identifying theme. Which of the following self-guiding questions should the teacher have students ask themselves?
   A. What did I like best about this story?
   B. Why did I read this story?
   C. What is the author trying to teach me in this story?
   D. How is the author different from others I have read?

Literary Theory

Living in a diverse world makes the ability to recognize and empathize with multiple perspectives imperative. These abilities are also a powerful way to deepen one's understanding of art and literature. **Literary theory** means using a set of principles or a system of ideas to interpret literature from a unique angle:

- By viewing a single text through a variety of lenses, readers gain a depth of understanding that far exceeds that which can be developed based on straightforward analysis.
- Teaching literary theory allows instructors to highlight how the assumptions that people make can color their interpretations of literary works and the world as a whole.

Before thinking about a literary text from different theoretical perspectives, students must first have a general understanding of the text; in other words, teachers should engage students in the processes of literary criticism before introducing a particular theoretical framework. Specifically, teachers may have students engage in activities or discussions that prime their thinking to prepare them for the theory that they will be applying.

For example, an effective teacher might prepare students to analyze *The Great Gatsby* via a Marxist approach (discussed later in this chapter) to criticism by asking them to consider the relationship between financial wealth and social status.

Reader-response theory is centered on the idea that the audience experiences a transaction with the text as they read. The feelings and associations readers experience influence their interpretations of what they are reading:

- In the process of constructing meaning, the reader's responses blend with the author's intended meanings so that the reader ends up participating in the creative process.
- This means that there is no single correct interpretation of a text; understanding will be unique to each reader. (All interpretations, however, must still be grounded in textual evidence.)

Important Works

The Great Gatsby

Author: F. Scott Fitzgerald

Publication Date: 1925

Summary: Narrator Nick Carraway moves to Long Island in 1922, where his neighbor is the mysterious, self-made Jay Gatsby. Nick's cousin Daisy is trapped in a marriage with Tom, who is having an affair with a woman named Myrtle. Gatsby eventually invites Nick to one of his lavish parties and asks him to bring Daisy, with whom he had a past relationship. Daisy and Gatsby begin an affair, which enrages Tom. During an argument, Tom reveals that Gatsby's wealth comes from bootlegging, leading Daisy and Gatsby to angrily drive off with Daisy at the wheel. She accidentally hits and kills Myrtle. Myrtle's husband then kills Gatsby, believing he was the one responsible for his wife's death.

Themes, Motifs, and Symbols: social class/social hierarchy, love and marriage, the American dream

Feminist literary theory involves asking questions about the degree to which a literary text perpetuates the ideas that women are inferior to and dependent on men or that the perspective of a woman is not as interesting or significant as that of a man. One goal of feminist theory is to challenge the view that being female is the opposite of being male, that having characteristics of sensitivity or a desire to nurture others makes an individual "feminine" and weak. A related intention is to free both males and females from the rigid thinking perpetuated by traditional concepts of gender identity. Feminists maintain that, as students are confronted by feminist criticism, they will begin to recognize biases in their own thinking and in popular culture, making them more equipped to evaluate and challenge traditional gender roles.

Closely related to feminist theory is **queer theory**, which investigates texts by asking questions about both gender and sexuality. This lens of analysis involves recognizing and challenging all cultural assumptions related to sex and gender, especially those related to identity. One pillar of queer theory is that a person is not defined by sexuality and cannot be categorized in such terms because one's sexual identity is in a constant state of change. A queer analysis of a literary text challenges assumptions about the rigidity of sexuality and identifies alternative ways of thinking about the characters or their situations. For example, most commentary on Walt Whitman's poem "Song of Myself" points to Whitman's homosexual imagery; a queer analysis might come to the conclusion that Whitman finds all experiences to be erotic, even the undulating waves of the ocean, and that homosexuality constitutes only one small part of his sexual identity.

Deconstructionist literary criticism focuses on dissecting and uncovering the writer's assumptions about what is true and false, good and bad. Deconstructionists begin by examining language, which they consider a distortion of reality. They explain that meaning in language comes from differences:

- People understand good as the absence of bad; that is, one thing is understood as the absence of its opposite.

- By traditional thinking, reason or logic is the absence of emotion; by extension, if it is good to be rational, then it is not good to be emotional.

The goal of deconstructionism is to identify these binaries in language and thinking in order to inspire investigation into possible other alternatives. As deconstructionist critics read a literary text, they examine linguistic contradictions and ambiguities in order to uncover incongruities in the underlying reasoning. Deconstructionists argue that, because of these inconsistencies, no text can be reduced to one correct meaning or interpretation.

Important Works

"Song of Myself"

Author: Walt Whitman

Publication Date: 1855 (1881 when republished under its current title)

Summary: This poem is an ode to the author's self and an important work in the Transcendentalist movement. Whitman explains that humans have a transcendental understanding of themselves and, along with all other entities on Earth, have a "self" that contains part of the broader universe. Further, the self is united with God, which Whitman calls the "absolute self." Humans, therefore, have a sort of brotherhood with God and all things, as they, too, contain part of the entire universe.

Themes, Motifs, and Symbols: nature, self, identity, spirituality

Semiotic analysis is the study of signs, signals, visual messages, and gestures. In semiotics, a sign system is a set of behaviors or things which are analyzed as if they are symbols that represent ideas.

In Ernest Hemingway's novel *The Old Man and the Sea*, the sign system of the man's struggle with the fish and his determination to show the boy what a man can do signifies many ideas about human potential. To interpret a message using semiotic analysis, the following must be considered:

- Who created the message?
- For whom is the message created?
- What is the context of the message?

Marxist theory focuses on the economic systems that structure society and the ways in which human behavior is motivated by a desire for economic power. According to this theory, life cannot be understood through abstract principles or ideals but instead only in terms of the concrete, actual conditions that people experience.

Formalism or **New Criticism** emphasizes closely reading a text and analyzing how literary elements create meaning in it; it is unconcerned with the text's effect on the reader.

Important Works

The Old Man and the Sea

Author: Ernest Hemingway

Publication Date: 1952

Summary: Cuban fisherman Santiago has caught nothing in eighty-four days. His helper, Manolin, is forced to work on another boat, though he continues to check on Santiago and talk baseball with him. Santiago goes into the Gulf Stream and hooks a giant marlin. For three days, he struggles with the fish but also appreciates its strength and beauty. He eventually kills the marlin with a harpoon and sails back to shore. Sharks are attracted to the marlin's blood; though Santiago tries to fight them off, they consume all of his catch. He returns with only the marlin's carcass, angry at himself for fishing so far out and killing such a noble creature. Manolin and Santiago are reunited; Manolin agrees to return to Santiago's boat.

Themes, Motifs, and Symbols: friendship, man versus nature, defeat, perseverance

Practice Question

The following questions refer to this excerpt from the poem "In an Artist's Studio" by Christina Rossetti.

One face looks out from all his canvases,

One selfsame figure sits or walks or leans:

We found her hidden just behind those screens,

That mirror gave back all her loveliness.

A queen in opal or in ruby dress,

A nameless girl in freshest summer-greens,

A saint, an angel;—every canvas means

The same one meaning, neither more or less.

9) A critic comments that, in the poem, the famous artist's paintings of the woman suggest that he views her as an object to be admired and not as a real person. This critic asserts that the poem reveals a dangerous and biased assumption—that by portraying women in artistic ways, men are honoring them. The critic argues that, on the contrary, to make a woman the center of a piece of art is to objectify her. Which literary theory does this critic represent?
- A. Marxist
- B. feminist
- C. deconstructionist
- D. reader-response

Building Comprehension of Fiction

Readers of all ages enjoy fiction texts, thanks to relatable characters and well-developed plots. Teachers often use familiar stories as springboards to more in-depth comprehension because students are usually familiar with the literal meanings of such texts.

While there are many specific strategies to aid students in their comprehension of literary texts, some of the most common are listed below.

Graphic or Semantic Organizers

- storyboards or event sequence frames or timelines
- story maps (beginning, middle, end) or plot diagrams (rising action, climax, falling action, resolution)
- character maps (actions, feelings, appearance, dialogue)

- character trait identification charts

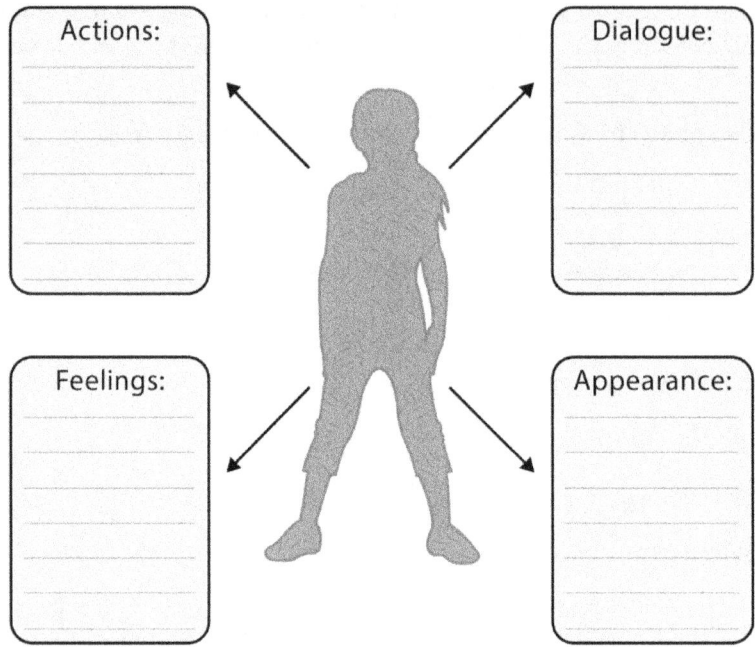

Guided Comprehension Questions

- those requiring students to underline, highlight, and locate the answer in the text
- those requiring a constructed response
- cloze exercises in which a portion of the text is removed and readers must fill in the blanks

Summarization and Main Idea Exercises

- written retellings that ask students to recall and write down important parts of the story in their own words
- exercises that ask students to create an outline of the story
- asking students to identify main or central ideas in the story
- asking students to identify themes or messages within the story

Specific Targeted Strategies

- **Directed Reading-Thinking Activity (DR-TA):** Students make predictions and read up to a preselected stopping point, and then they evaluate and refine predictions based on text evidence.
- The **Question-Answer Relationship (QAR) strategy** encourages students to identify the type of question and think about how to find the answer:
    - "Right there" questions are literal and require only the location of the relevant part.
    - "Think and search" questions require synthesis from multiple parts of the text.

- o "Author and you" questions require the text to have been read, but the answer is not directly in the text. These are typically inference and depth-of-knowledge (DOK) questions.
- o "On my own" questions require background knowledge and do not directly rely on text evidence.
- The **SQ3R strategy** was developed for reading textbooks, but it is useful for many different reading materials:
  - o **Survey:** previewing the text and taking note of graphics, headings, and so forth
  - o **Question:** generating questions about the text after previewing it
  - o **Read:** reading and looking for answers to the questions
  - o **Recite:** rehearsing or saying the answers to the questions
  - o **Review:** reviewing the text and answering or responding to any other questions
- **K-W-L charts** help students think about what they already know and what they want to know before reading as well as what they learned after reading:
  - o The **K** stands for "What I already know" about the topic.
  - o The **W** stands for "What I want to know."
  - o The **L** is completed after reading to state, "What I learned."

Group or Paired Strategies

- **Reciprocal teaching** assigns roles to groups of four students who work together to read and comprehend a text.
- **Think-pair-share** pairs students to answer comprehension questions about a text:
- o First, students think about their own answer by activating background knowledge.
- o They then pair with another student or a small group.
- o Students share their answer with their group or partner and then the entire class.
- **Peer-Assisted Learning Strategies (PALS)** require students to partner with a classmate; they then take turns providing each other assistance and feedback in reading comprehension.

Practice Question

10) Which strategy can be employed to help students activate background knowledge BEFORE they read a text?
   A. reciprocal teaching
   B. peer-assisted learning strategies
   C. plot diagrams
   D. K-W-L chart

Strategies for Developing Reading Comprehension

Before beginning each new text, teachers should model and practice pre-reading strategies throughout reading instruction. One such strategy is **previewing** a text, which involves identifying the author, the genre, and the general subject matter before reading. It also includes reading headings and chapter titles, examining related graphics, researching the author and the context of the work (as is age appropriate), and anticipating the author's purpose.

Previewing general information about a text allows an active reader to use another pre-reading strategy: **setting a purpose**. A teacher might introduce each new text with a guiding question (e.g., "What does it mean to be evil?") or a hypothetical situation that pushes students to examine their own value systems (e.g., "Imagine you are a business owner. Should you be required to hire a certain number of individuals with disabilities?"). After facilitating a discussion about the question or scenario, the teacher directs students to a particular text to examine how the author or characters would respond. By setting a purpose for students' reading, the teacher guides them toward the thematic elements of the text. Students are encouraged to draw connections between the author's choices and the overall message.

Before reading a new text, and throughout the reading process, students should also make predictions about what they are reading. A **prediction** is a kind of inference that is concerned with what is going to happen next. Making predictions is a valuable active reading skill because it requires readers to be constantly aware of what is going on in the text as well as what authors may be foreshadowing through their specific choices.

In addition to making predictions as they read, students should be thinking about their own levels of understanding, also known as **metacognition**. In metacognition, readers reflect on what they are thinking as they read. This helps to immediately identify any confusion or uncertainty. Readers who are aware of their thought processes are able to recognize and react when there is a breakdown in understanding. Part of metacognition in reading is using fix-up or fix-it-up strategies. Active readers apply these strategies when they realize they do not understand what they are reading. Common **fix-up strategies** include the following:

- slowing down the reading pace
- rereading the section in question
- reading beyond the text in question to see if confusion is cleared up
- using text clues
- observing illustrations/graphic elements
- identifying text features (bold words, italics, headings, relevant punctuation)
- figuring out the meaning of unfamiliar words
    - using context clues/words around the confusing word
    - using picture clues
    - using a resource to look up the word or words
    - asking a peer or teacher for assistance

Annotating is another important strategy that takes place during reading. To provide effective instruction in annotation and ensure that students are mastering the skill, teachers should set clear guidelines and expectations. For example, a teacher might ask students to make **VISA annotations:**

- interesting or new **V**ocabulary
- important **I**nferences
- helpful **S**ummaries
- brief **A**nalyses

Other annotating strategies include the following:

- underlining or highlighting main ideas or important information
- circling key words
- placing question marks next to confusing parts that might need further attention
- writing notes in the margins

Questioning is another way students can develop overall comprehension of a text. With this strategy, the reader asks and then answers questions about what has been read. Questioning occurs on three levels:

1. **Literal questions** are based on explicit information in the text and require only recall or identification of information from the text (e.g., On what day did Mark send the letter?).
2. **Inferential questions** are based on implicit information in the text. These questions require students to make an inference, prediction, or draw a conclusion (e.g., What will Mark most likely do after he sends the letter?).
3. **Evaluative questions** require readers to form an opinion on the text. Students will need to understand explicit information and then consider how they feel about this information (e.g., What do I think about Mark's action in sending the letter?).

Summarization is a strategy to help readers determine what is important in a text. Using their own words, readers reduce a text or section of text to its main points or central ideas. This is done by skipping insignificant details and redundancies and looking for general ideas rather than specific facts and examples. Student-produced summaries can provide valuable insight into comprehension levels:

- Students who actively comprehend what they read will produce accurate summaries.
- Those who struggle with comprehension may leave out important ideas or leave in unnecessary information.

Summaries should be used throughout the study of a text and in the post-reading process to gauge how well students understand the basic ideas of a work.

Teachers can encourage students to engage with the text using other post-reading strategies, such as having them reflect on their experiences with the text and write formal or informal responses. Teachers may also ask students to return to the guiding question, which synthesizes their understanding of the text and its thematic and cultural relevance.

> **Did You Know?**
>
> As readers consider textual evidence, they may change or expand their original interpretations.

Students can also make connections between the text, themselves (text-to-self), the world (text-to-world), and other literature (text-to-text). The use of text evidence should be encouraged in any post-reading exercise, even in students' personal responses.

It is important that the students' conclusions and understandings are fully informed and truly based in the text itself. Examination of textual evidence is an essential part of the process of constructing meaning.

Practice Question

11) What is an example of a metacognitive practice?
    A. a reader asking himself questions while reading
    B. a reader taking notes during a lecture about the historical background of a text that will soon be read
    C. a teacher providing pop quizzes to determine who has read a text
    D. a teacher explaining the characteristics of a given genre before students are asked to comprehend the genre

Answer Key

1) A: In this strategy, students listen to a lecture on a topic, read a text, and then discuss similarities or differences in the lecture versus the text.

2) D: Identifying specific evocative words will aid students in connecting word choice and tone.

3) D: The narrator is reporting the thoughts of the character, as the character's memory about not acting heroic in the past is revealed.

4) B: Option B describes an internal conflict in which Mrs. Dalloway struggles within her own mind to understand the meanings of her choices.

5) D: There is no metaphor in this poem. The line, "How public, like a frog" is a simile. The frog who can tell his name is personification. The line, "To tell your name the livelong day" is hyperbole.

6) D: The fall leaves are described as "leaves dead" and "like ghosts," so the connotations of the phrase *pestilence-stricken multitudes* is that the leaves are dead and decaying.

7) B: Consonance is repetition of the same consonant sounds at the end of a stressed syllable. *Twilight* ends with the same sound as *light*.

8) C: The theme is the message or lesson that the author is trying to teach.

9) B: This argument reflects feminist theory because it discusses popular perceptions of women and evaluates how those perceptions might be detrimental to the fight for gender equality.

10) D: The *K* stands for "What I already know" about the topic. The *W* is "What I want to know," and the *L* is completed after reading to state, "What I learned."

11) A: When readers ask themselves questions as they read, they are monitoring their own understanding.

Reading Literary Texts

Constructivism

In today's English classrooms, teachers are equipping students for success by devoting the bulk of their time to reading and discussing a variety of texts. This interactive approach to reading instruction (as opposed to a lecture-based approach, for example) is based on the theory of **constructivism:**

- As readers become involved with a text, they *construct* meaning through an active process of integrating what they are reading with their own reactions, knowledge, beliefs, and ideas.

- The constructivist perspective is linked to studies in cognition; constructivists are interested in the thinking processes readers use to comprehend and interpret text.

Many variables affect how people understand what they are reading, including prior knowledge of the subject of the text, mental schemas and assumptions, and motivation levels. For example, the extent of a reader's experience with narrative structures might determine how effectively the reader can follow the events of a new story:

- Those who are familiar with the logical structures of an argument may be better able to process the reasoning of persuasive text.

- Those who take time to understand, revisit, and reflect on the piece of writing will likely have a deeper understanding of it than a more casual reader.

Constructivism also places emphasis on how the social and cultural backgrounds of readers influence how they understand and experience a text. For example, when reading the introduction to Alice Walker's short story "Everyday Use," White, middle class students who have grown up in the urban areas of northern states may struggle to relate to a mom who wears overalls and kills hogs. Generally, students who have experiences that mirror the details of the text to some degree are better able to make meaningful personal connections with it.

> **Helpful Hint**:
>
> **Schemas** are cognitive connections that are molded in an individual's mind over time and shape a person's worldview. Knowledge is stored as a complex web of schemas; learning occurs when new information links to existing schematic networks.

Constructivists also emphasize that most learning and understanding occur in a social context. In other words, readers are better able to construct interpretations of and find meaning in a text when they have opportunities to engage in dialogue about it with others. For example, in an English classroom, a teacher might initiate a discussion with an open-ended, text-based question:

- Student A may answer with an assertion and simple explanation.

- Student B might disagree and explain her reasoning.

- Student A can then respond by elaborating on his original idea.

Important Works

"Everyday Use"

Author: Alice Walker

Publication Date: 1973

Summary: In this short story, Mama considers the past, including a fire that burned her daughter Maggie. She awaits the arrival of her other daughter, Dee, who has had a different life from her mother and sister after being sent away to school. Dee arrives with Hakim-a-barber, her boyfriend, and explains that she does not want to be called Dee anymore, saying that her oppressors gave her that name; she now goes by Wangero. Her mother explains that she was named after her grandmother and many others before her but agrees to call her Wangero. The family begins to eat, but Hakim-a-barber, a Muslim, cannot eat the collard greens and pork. After asking for some kitchen objects used to make butter, Dee finds two quilts made by her grandmother, aunts, and mother in Mama's trunk; she asks if she can have them. Mama says that they have already been promised to Maggie, but Dee advocates for the quilts, noting that she does not think Maggie—who is not as learned and worldly as she is—will know how to care for them. Though Maggie offers to give the quilts to her sister, Mama refuses. Dee suggests that her mother does not understand her heritage and that she and Maggie should make something better out of their lives. She drives off with her boyfriend, and Maggie and Mama stay in the yard enjoying the evening.

Themes, Motifs, and Symbols: family history and connectedness; heritage, race, and identity; education as a divisive force

Other students listening to this collision of thought can begin to examine the merits of each position and perhaps, after a prompt from the teacher, return to the text to look for evidence to contribute to the discussion. Students might even revise their original interpretations when they are confronted by the ideas of others.

During such open discussions, students not only deepen their understandings of the text but also practice critical thinking skills and effective ways of communicating ideas.

The main implication of constructivist theory for reading instruction is that teachers should design lessons that require students to both respond to and interact with text as they read as well as interact with each other through authentic discussions and debates. Activities that provide opportunities for students to process, share, and examine their thoughts about texts are essential.

Practice Question

1) Which of the following is NOT a way that class discussions support the constructivist theory of reading instruction?
   A. They offer students a chance to hear the ideas of their fellow students and increase their knowledge of diverse viewpoints.
   B. They provide students practice with social interaction by forcing them to listen to others and respect alternative opinions.
   C. They challenge students to use concrete evidence, which enhances their knowledge and memory of the text.
   D. They give students the opportunity to express their interpretations, consider any alternative viewpoints, and examine their ideas in terms of the evidence that is mentioned.

Literary Traditions

Not all texts can be classified as literature. In vague terms, creative writers write to entertain; however, the goal of authors, poets, and playwrights is rarely that simple.

Literary texts, especially when written well, have the capacity to create an experience for the reader by using language to reflect universal aspects of life or human nature. The power of language—in the form of literature—to elicit interpretive responses in readers has given rise to the field of **literary criticism**, the formal study, analysis, and evaluation of literary texts.

Helpful Hint:

Transactional reading, or **transactional reader-response theory**, was first developed by Louise Rosenblatt. This theory states that text on a page is nothing until it becomes a performance of meaning in the reader's mind. An individual's interpretation of a text gives it meaning.

The field of literary criticism continually shapes English literature courses. A critical approach to literature—which takes into account historical, philosophical, cultural, and social traditions—lends itself easily to valuable interdisciplinary instruction.

Effective teachers set clear purposes, some guiding questions, and logical structures for their courses; they also select texts purposefully, taking into account each text's origin, relevance, and canonicity.

American Literature

American literature includes works from the early colonial period through the present and is generally divided into five categories. The periods themselves, the specific range of years, and the authors associated with them continue to be debated among scholars, which is why some of them overlap. Many scholars consider the Civil War to be a turning point in American literature and a stand-alone era of literature; as such, this has been added as a sixth literary period to this list. Various subperiods exist loosely within these periods, each with its own characteristics:

- **The Colonial and Early National Period (seventeenth century – ca. 1830)**
    - The Revolutionary Period (ca. 1765 – ca.1790)
    - The Romantic Period (ca. 1830 – ca. 1870)

- o   Transcendentalism (late 1820s – early 1850s)
- **The Civil War Period (ca. 1855 – ca. 1870)**
- **Realism (ca. 1870 – ca. 1910)**
  - o   Naturalism (late nineteenth century; ca. 1880 – ca. 1915)
  - o   Regionalism (late nineteenth and early twentieth centuries; ca. 1865 – ca. 1920)
- **The Modernist Period (ca. 1910 – ca. 1945)**
  - o   Harlem Renaissance (ca. 1918 – ca. 1937)
  - o   The Lost Generation (ca. 1920 – ca. 1950)
- **The Contemporary Period (ca. 1945 – present)**

> **Helpful Hint**:
> In literature, a **canon** is a group of works that are considered to be culturally, artistically, or historically significant. **Canonicity**, therefore, refers to whether the work is considered important enough to be a part of the broad literature canon.

The Colonial and Early National Period (seventeenth century – ca. 1830)

Texts from this period represent the earliest American literature and center on exploration and life in the New World. Writings from this time often focus on the future, especially in the lead-up to the American Revolution and after the US declared its independence in 1776. The **Revolutionary Period** (ca. 1765 – ca. 1790), which is characterized by politically motivated writings, is included in this literary time frame. Writing styles from this period tend to be practical and straightforward.

Table 4.1. Important Writers of the Colonial and Early National Period and Its Subperiods	
Colonial and Early National Period (seventeenth century – ca. 1830)	
Author	Title(s)
William Bradford	*Of Plymouth Plantation*
Anne Bradstreet	*The Tenth Muse Lately Sprung Up in America,* various poetry
Jonathan Edwards	"Sinners in the Hands of an Angry God"
Olaudah Equiano	*The Interesting Narrative of the Life of Olaudah Equiano*
The Revolutionary Period (ca. 1765 – ca.1790)	
Author	Title(s)
Benjamin Franklin	*Poor Richard's Almanack*
Thomas Jefferson	*Notes on the State of Virginia,* various letters
James Madison	the "Federalist Papers" (with Alexander Hamilton and John Jay); most of the US Constitution
Thomas Paine	*Common Sense*; various essays

The Romantic Period (ca. 1830 – ca. 1870)

Did You Know?

The sermon "Sinners in the Hands of an Angry God" (Jonathan Edwards) is considered to be the catalyst for the First Great Awakening.

Writing from this period emphasizes individuals rather than groups and emotional experience rather than reason; value is placed on nature. Texts concerning both enslaved and free African Americans increased in the years up to, during, and following the Civil War. The Romantic Period also includes **Transcendentalism** (late 1820s – early 1850s), which describes a subperiod of literature based on the philosophy that all of creation is part of a unified whole. Transcendentalist writings value self-reliance and are marked by a belief in the inherent goodness of both people and the natural world around them.

Table 4.2. Important Writers of the Romantic Period and Its Subperiods	
The Romantic Period (ca. 1830 – ca. 1870)	
Author	Title(s)
James Fenimore Cooper	*The Last of the Mohicans*
Washington Irving	"The Devil and Tom Walker"
Edgar Allan Poe	"The Raven," "The Tell-Tale Heart," other various short stories and poetry
Sojourner Truth	"Ain't I a Woman"
Transcendentalism (late 1820s – early 1850s)	
Author	Title(s)
Ralph Waldo Emerson	*Self-Reliance* and *The American Scholar*
Henry David Thoreau	*Walden* and *Civil Disobedience*
Walt Whitman	"Song of Myself," "Oh Captain! My Captain!"

Civil War Period (ca. 1855 – ca. 1870)

Works from this time are considered by many scholars to signal a turning point in American literature. Ideals expressed during the Romantic Period were tested, and a new generation of writers emerged. Writings from this time are often narrative and include diaries and political speeches.

Table 4.3. Important Writers of the Civil War Period (ca. 1855 – ca. 1870)	
The Romantic Period (ca. 1830 – ca. 1870)	
Author	Title(s)
Mary Chesnut	*Diary of Mary Chesnut* (*A Diary from Dixie*)
Frederick Douglass	*My Bondage and My Freedom*
Abraham Lincoln	"The Gettysburg Address"

Realism (ca. 1870 – ca. 1910)

Inspired by the immense toll of the country's recent Civil War, authors during this period aimed to portray American life as it truly was. **Naturalism** (late nineteenth century) was considered an especially intense form of realism that supported ideas of determinism, scientific objectivism, and detachment. Regionalist authors are yet another subperiod. Also known as "local color," **Regionalism** (late nineteenth – early twentieth centuries) is characterized by a heavy focus on a region (e.g., dialect, history, customs). Increasing societal changes as a result of the Civil War and continued westward expansion helped fuel the Regionalist style of writing.

> **Did You Know?**
>
> Sojourner Truth delivered her speech "Ain't I a Woman" at the 1851 Women's Rights Convention in Akron, Ohio. It remains among the most notable women's rights and abolitionist speeches in US history.

Table 4.4. Important Writers of the Realism Period and Its Subperiods

The Realism Period (ca. 1870 – ca. 1910	
Author	Title(s)
William Dean Howells	writer and editor of the *Atlantic Monthly*
Mark Twain	*The Adventures of Huckleberry Finn*; various essays
Naturalism (late nineteenth century)	
Author	Title(s)
Kate Chopin	*The Awakening*
Jack London	*The Call of the Wild*
John Steinbeck	*The Grapes of Wrath*
Regionalism (late nineteenth century)	
Author	Title(s)
Willa Cather	*My Antonia*
William Faulkner	*Absalom! Absalom!*

The Modernist Period (ca. 1910 – ca. 1945)

The progress made possible by advancements in science and technology collided with the suffering brought about by World War I and the Great Depression, ushering in the **Modernist Period** of literature. This set the stage for the Modernist movement, defined as a radical break from the past. Characteristics of writings from this period include disillusionment and a sense of loss that range from destructive impulses to hope that change is imminent.

The **Harlem Renaissance** (ca. 1918 – ca. 1937), considered the most influential movement in African American literary history, is one subperiod of this time. Writings from this literary period are characterized by relationships to civil rights and reform organizations, with a goal of shifting how Black culture was represented. It includes literary as well as musical, theatrical, and visual arts.

Reading Literary Texts

The Lost Generation (ca. 1920 – ca. 1950) describes a generation of authors who largely came of age in the years leading up to and including World War I and the early 1920s. Characteristics of this subperiod include disillusionment, uncertainty about the future, and loss of identity.

Table 4.5. Important Writers of the Modernist Period and Its Subperiods	
The Modernist Period (ca. 1910 – ca. 1945)	
Author	Title(s)
E.E. Cummings	*The Enormous Room*; various poetry
Robert Frost	*A Boy's Will, North of Boston*
Sinclair Lewis Babbitt	*Main Street*
Margaret Mitchell	*Gone with the Wind*
Flannery O'Connor	*Wise Blood*; various short stories
Katherine Porter	*Ship of Fools*; various short stories
Ezra Pound	*Ripostes*; *Hugh Selwyn Mauberley*
Eudora Welty	*The Optimist's Daughter*
Edith Wharton	*The Age of Innocence*
Tennessee Williams	*A Streetcar Named Desire*; *The Glass Menagerie*; other plays
The Harlem Renaissance (ca. 1918 – ca. 1937)	
Author	Title(s)
Countee Cullen	"Yet Do I Marvel"; various poems
Langston Hughes	"Mother to Son"; various poems
Zora Neale Hurston	*Their Eyes Were Watching God*
The Lost Generation (ca. 1920 – ca. 1950)	
Author	Title(s)
T.S. Eliot	"The Love Song of J. Alfred Prufrock"; other poetry and plays
F. Scott Fitzgerald	*The Great Gatsby*, *Tender Is the Night*, other works
Ernest Hemingway	*The Old Man and the Sea*; *A Farewell to Arms*; *For Whom the Bell Tolls*; other works
Gertrude Stein	*The Autobiography of Alice B. Toklas*; *Tender Buttons*; other works

The Contemporary Period (1945 – present)

Writing during the **Contemporary Period** often reflects the political and cultural shifts of the times. The prospect of nuclear war, the Civil Rights Movement, women's rights, and a growing focus on equality shape this period of American literature.

Table 4.6. Important Writers of the Contemporary Period (1945 – present)	
Author	**Title(s)**
Sandra Cisneros	*The House on Mango Street*
Don DiLillo	*White Noise*
Nikki Giovanni	*Black Feeling; Black Talk; Black Judgement;* other works
Joseph Heller	*Catch-22*
Ursula K. Le Guin	*The Left Hand of Darkness*
Martin Luther King	"I Have A Dream"; various speeches and letters
Cormac McCarthy	*The Road, No Country for Old Men*
J.D. Salinger	*The Catcher in the Rye*
Amy Tan	*The Joy Luck Club*
John Updike	*Rabbit, Run*
Kurt Vonnegut	*Slaughterhouse-Five, Cat's Cradle*
Alice Walker	*The Color Purple*
August Wilson	*The Pittsburgh Cycle*
Richard Wright	*Black Boy*

Practice Question

2) This text provides a factually accurate account of the Civil War; while writing it, the author observed and recorded descriptions of and reactions to events of the war. The text is subjective, told from the first-person point of view, and filled with the details that impressed the writer. As it reveals the personal responses of a person in the midst of turmoil, it offers insights into the occurrences and effects of the Civil War. Which text does the passage describe?
- A. "Oh Captain! My Captain!" (Walt Whitman)
- B. The Diary of Mary Chesnut (Mary Chesnut)
- C. The Gettysburg Address (Abraham Lincoln)
- D. My Bondage and My Freedom (Frederick Douglass)

British Literature

British literature comprises the literary texts of the British Isles. The literature of Great Britain tends to reflect changes in culture and thinking over time and is therefore usually studied chronologically by period. Like American literature, subperiods with their own unique characteristics exist within these larger literary periods. The specific breakdown of these periods and the years associated with them continue to be debated among scholars:

- The Anglo-Saxon (Old English) Period (ca. 450 – ca. 1066)

- The Middle English (Medieval) Period (ca. 1066 – ca. 1500)
- The Renaissance (ca. 1500 – ca. 1660)
    - The Elizabethan Age (ca. 1558 – ca. 1603)
    - The Jacobean Age (ca. 1603 – ca. 1625)
    - The Caroline Age (ca. 1625 – ca. 1649); includes the Metaphysical poets (ca. 1600 – ca. 1690), who especially flourished during this time
    - The Commonwealth Period (ca. 1649 – ca. 1660)
- The Neoclassical Period (ca. 1600 – ca. 1785)
    - The Restoration (ca. 1660 – ca. 1700)
    - The Augustan Age (ca. 1700 – ca. 1745)
    - The Age of Sensibility (ca. 1745 – ca. 1785)
    - The Enlightenment (ca. 1600 – ca. 1800)
- The Romantic Period (ca. 1785 – ca. 1832)
- The Victorian Period (ca. 1832 – ca. 1901)
- The Modern Period (ca. 1901 – ca. 1945)
    - The Edwardian (ca. 1901 – ca. 1914) and Georgian (ca. 1910 – ca. 1936) Periods overlap with the Modern Period.
- The Postmodern Period (ca. 1945 onward)

The Anglo-Saxon (Old English) Period (ca. 450 – ca. 1066)

The first period of recorded texts is the **Anglo-Saxon Period**, also known as the **Old English Period**. Oral literature dominated the first half of this literary period until roughly the seventh century. Literature from this time is marked by epic poems about courageous heroes; their concerns were morality and goodness. Other works were often translations of legal, medical, or religious prose.

Table 4.7. Important Writers of the Anglo-Saxon (Old English) Period (ca. 450 – ca. 1066)

Author	Title(s)
Cædmon	"Cædmon's Hymn"
Cynewulf	*The Fates of the Apostles*
unknown/anonymous	*Beowulf*
unknown/anonymous	"The Wife's Lament"
unknown/anonymous	"The Seafarer"

The Middle English Period (ca. 1066 – ca. 1500)

The **Middle English (Medieval) Period** witnessed a major language, lifestyle, and culture shift that formed the foundation of the English language that is recognized today. Works from this period focus on religion, romance, diversity, and chivalry. Morality plays and folk ballads were also popular during this time.

Table 4.8. Important Writers of the Middle English (Medieval) Period (ca. 1066 – ca. 1500)

Author	Title(s)
Chaucer	*The Canterbury Tales*
Margery Kempe	*The Book of Margery Kempe*
Sir Thomas Malory	*Le Morte d'Arthur*

The Renaissance (ca. 1500 – ca. 1660)

The **Renaissance** is marked by a rebirth (the English translation of the French term *renaissance*) of Classical values and learning. It is divided into four subperiods, with authors and their works often overlapping. Political writings also began to appear during this period:

- The **Elizabethan Age** (ca. 1558 – ca. 1603) is known as the golden age of English drama and public theaters.
- The **Jacobean Age** (ca. 1603 – ca. 1625) describes literary and other arts under the reign of James VI of Scotland.
- **Metaphysical poets** (ca. 1600 – ca. 1690), whose works often focus on philosophical exploration, flourished during the **Caroline Age** (ca. 1625 – ca. 1649), which is often referred to as the "Age of Poetry."
- Finally, the **Commonwealth Period** (ca. 1649 – ca. 1660) marked the end of the English Civil War and the start of a Puritan-led Parliament during which public theaters closed in response to perceived transgressions—moral and otherwise.

> **Did You Know?**
>
> Many scholars consider *The Book of Margery Kempe* to be the first autobiography written in the English language.

Table 4.9. Important Writers of the Renaissance (ca. 1500 – ca. 1660)

The Elizabethan Age (ca. 1558 – ca. 1603)	
Author	Title(s)
Ben Jonson	*Every Man in His Humour*
Christopher Marlowe Dido	*Queen of Carthage*
William Shakespeare	*Romeo and Juliet, Hamlet, Macbeth*
Edmund Spenser	*The Faerie Queene*
The Jacobean Age (ca. 1603 – ca. 1625)	
Francis Bacon	*Advancement of Learning*
Robert Burton	*The Anatomy of Melancholy*

Table 4.9. Important Writers of the Renaissance (ca. 1500 – ca. 1660)	
Metaphysical Poets of the Caroline Age (ca. 1625 – ca. 1649)	
John Donne	"The Flea," various poems
George Herbert	"Easter Wings"
Andrew Marvell	"To His Coy Mistress," various poems
The Commonwealth Period (ca. 1649 – ca. 1660)	
Thomas Hobbes	*Leviathan*
John Milton	*Paradise Lost*

The Neoclassical Period (ca. 1600 – ca. 1785)

The **Neoclassical Period** comprises **The Restoration** (ca. 1660 – ca. 1700), the works of which gave birth to satire and "comedies of manner" and offered a response to the return of puritanism seen during the Commonwealth Period.

The Augustan Age (ca. 1700 – ca. 1745) sees female writers challenge gender stereotypes, especially concerning female roles. **The Age of Sensibility** (ca. 1745 – ca. 1785), also known as the "Age of Johnson," embraces ideas of neoclassicism (art inspired by classic antiquity) and the **Enlightenment** (ca. 1600 – ca. 1800), an outlook on the world shared by many intellectuals of the time that emphasizes logic, reason, and rules.

Table 4.10. Important Writers of the Neoclassical Period (ca. 1600 – ca. 1785)	
The Restoration (ca. 1660 – ca. 1700)	
Author	Title(s)
John Bunyan	*The Pilgrim's Progress*
Samuel Butler	*Hudibras*
William Congreve	*The Old Bachelor, The Way of the World*
John Dryden	*Absalom and Achitophel*
The Augustan Age (ca. 1700 – ca. 1745)	
Alexander Pope	*The Dunciad*
Jonathan Swift	*Gulliver's Travels*
The Age of Sensibility (ca. 1745 – ca. 1785)	
James Boswell	*Life of Johnson*; also known as *Life of Samuel Johnson*
Edmund Burke	*A Vindication of Natural Society*
Samuel Johnson	*The Dictionary of the English Language*
The Enlightenment (ca. 1600 – ca. 1800)	
John Locke	*A Letter Concerning Toleration; An Essay Concerning Human Understanding*

Table 4.10. Important Writers of the Neoclassical Period (ca. 1600 – ca. 1785)	
Montesquieu	*The Persian Letters*; various memoirs and discourses at the Academy of Bordeaux
Jean Jacques Rosseau	*The Social Contract*; *Discourse on the Arts and Sciences*

The Romantic Period (ca. 1785 – ca. 1832)

Works from the **Romantic Period** (ca. 1785 – ca. 1832) are diverse, arguably the most well-known, and characterized by a focus on feelings and the imagination. The French Revolution and the Industrial Revolution influenced many of the writers of this time, who believed that truth was found in nature and unrestrained imaginative experience. Many poems, lyrical ballads, and gothic horror novels were written during this time.

Table 4.11. Important Writers of the Romantic Period (ca. 1785 – ca. 1832)	
Author	**Title(s)**
Lord Byron	*Don Juan*
John Keats	*Hyperion*; "Isabella"
Percy Bysshe Shelley	"Ode to the West Wind"; "The Masque of Anarchy"
Mary Shelley	*Frankenstein*
William Wordsworth	"Lines Composed a Few Miles above Tintern Abbey"; "To the Cuckoo"

The Victorian Period (ca. 1832 – ca. 1901)

The **Victorian Period** (ca. 1832 – ca. 1901) was marked by social, religious, and economic turmoil; literature from this time often portrays idealized versions of life's struggles. Many scholars consider this period in writing as a bridge between the Romantic Period and the Modern Period. A growing middle class during this time benefited from the mass printing of novels and magazines; elegies were also popular. The **Victorian Period**, **Edwardian Period** (ca. 1901 – ca. 1914), and **Georgian Period** (ca. 1910 – ca. 1936)—the latter two of which overlap with the Modern Period—are all named for the reigning monarchs of the time; writings often center around cultural issues specific to each of these periods.

Table 4.12. Important Writers of the Victorian Period (ca. 1832 – ca. 1901)	
Author	**Title(s)**
Elizabeth Barrett Browning	"How Do I Love Thee?" (Sonnet 43 from *Sonnets from the Portuguese*)
Robert Browning	"The Pied Piper of Hamelin"; *Men and Women*
Charles Dickens	*A Tale of Two Cities*; *Oliver Twist*
Thomas Hardy	*The Return of the Native*; *Tess of d'Urbervilles*
Rudyard Kipling	*The Jungle Book*
Alfred Tennyson	*Ulysses*

Reading Literary Texts

The Modern Period (ca. 1901 – ca. 1945)

Writers of the **Modern Period** (ca. 1901 – ca. 1945) often focus on social issues in which characters experience epiphanies. Novelists were known to play with style during this time by writing in a stream of consciousness. As noted earlier, works from the Edwardian Period and the Georgian Period often overlap with the Modern Period.

Table 4.13. Important Writers of the Modern Period (ca. 1901 – ca. 1945)	
Author	Title(s)
Joseph Conrad	*Heart of Darkness*
T.S. Eliot	"The Waste Land"; various poems
D.H. Lawrence	*Women in Love*
Katherine Mansfield	"The Garden Party"; various short stories
George Orwell	*Animal Farm*
Bernard Shaw	*Pygmalion*
Dylan Thomas	"Do Not Go Gentle Into That Good Night"; various poems
Virginia Woolf	*Mrs. Dalloway*; various stories
William Yeats	"When You Are Old"; various poems

The Postmodern Period (ca. 1945 onward)

Some scholars note the emergence of the **Postmodern Period** (ca. 1945 onward) after World War II; it is often understood to be a response to modernism. By the late twentieth century, writers had become interested in psychology, criticism, and the close observation of human behaviors and relationships.

Table 4.14. Important Writers of the Postmodern Period (ca. 1945 onward)	
Author	Title(s)
Doris Lessing	*The Golden Notebook*
Penelope Lively	*The Road to Lichfield*; *A Stitch in Time*

> **Helpful Hint**:
>
> Samuel Beckett (*Waiting for Godot*, *Endgame*) was an Irish writer whose work straddles the Modern and Postmodern Periods. In his early years, he worked closely with the Modernist Irish writer James Joyce (*Portrait of the Artist as a Young Man*; *Ulysses*). Beckett's later works incorporate more Postmodern elements, such as fragmented narration and playful humor. Note that Joyce's *Ulysses*, a novel, is distinct from Tennyson's poem of the same name, described in Table 4.12.

Practice Question

3) Which of the following authors wrote during the Victorian Period? Select ALL that apply
    A. Charles Dickens
    B. Virginia Woolf
    C. Robert Browning
    D. John Donne
    E. William Wordsworth

World Literature

World literature can refer to all national literatures, but the term usually refers to a group of important representative literary works that are circulated and studied around the globe. These works come from a variety of areas including France, Africa, India, China, Japan, ancient Greece and Rome, and the ancient Middle East. The emphasis of study in a world literature course or unit is usually the cultural, philosophical, and historical context of the literary works. Sometimes, the works are grouped by commonalities, as in the study of lyrical poetry, creation myths, or hero tales; other times, selections are chosen to highlight how certain literary ideas have moved across cultures.

Non-Western literature describes works from countries other than the United States, those in Western Europe, or ancient Greece and Rome. Some examples of authors from non-Western countries are Isabel Allende and Gabriel García Márquez from Latin America, Bessie Head and Ngũgĩ wa Thiong'o from Africa, and Rumi of Persia. Usually studies of non-Western literature focus on the contrasts between Western and non-Western perspectives, with the goal of achieving familiarity with the rich histories, intellectual traditions, and cultural beliefs represented in the works. Studies on these works often emphasize both the interconnectedness and the diversity of cultures.

Table 4.15. Important Works in World and Non-Western Literature

Title (Author)	Country of Origin	Description
Things Fall Apart (Chinua Achebe)	Nigeria	depicts precolonial Nigeria and the impacts of European colonialism in the 19th century
Agamemnon (Aeschylus)	ancient Greece	one of three major Greek tragedies—a popular form of theater; describes how a family is punished by the gods for a series of murders; complex religious issues often addressed by the author
House of Spirits (Isabel Allende)	Chile	a family saga that follows four generations and is set against the backdrop of postcolonial Chile; uses magical realism to discuss the connections between politics, memory, and Chilean culture
The Epic of Gilgamesh (Anonymous)	ancient Mesopotamia	a story written as a poem on twelve clay tablets (standard Babylonian version) about a wild man created by the gods to prevent Gilgamesh from oppressing his people; Gilgamesh and his search for eternal life;

Table 4.15. Important Works in World and Non-Western Literature

Title (Author)	Country of Origin	Description
		considered as the foundation of heroic saga literature
The Blind Assassin *The Handmaid's Tale* (Margaret Atwood)	Canada	written with elements of science fiction, romance, and gothic suspense; a multilayered story concerning death and a family's history (*The Blind Assassin*); a dystopian novel that imagines a theocratic and totalitarian state in which handmaids are forced to bear children due to low reproduction rates (*The Handmaid's Tale*)
Labyrinths (Jorge Luis Borges)	Argentina	a collection of short stories and essays that feature magical realism and the use of symbolism and metaphors; many recurring themes, especially concerning the concept of time
The Good Earth (Pearl S. Buck)	United States (written in China by an American author; modeled after Chinese novels)	the story of a farmer and his family's life in 1920s China and the political and social upheavals of that time; winner of the Pulitzer Prize
Don Quixote (Miguel Cervantes)	Habsburg Spain	considered a prototype for the modern novel; revolves around the adventures of a young man who hopes to become a knight, serve his country, and usher in a return to chivalry
Three Sisters *The Seagull* (Anton Chekov)	Russia	a play concerning three sisters who must grapple with suffering and change in their own lives against the backdrop of real-world issues taking place around them (*Three Sisters*); a play in which the characters use subtext in dialogue; themes include unrequited love, artistic endeavors and the pursuit of fame, and ego versus self (*The Seagull*)
The Alchemist (Paulo Coelho)	Brazil	a novel about self-discovery and individuality; known for its use of allegory
The Divine Comedy *Inferno* (Dante)	Italy	a narrative poem that depicts Dante's travels in the afterlife and represents a soul's journey to God (*The Divine Comedy*); discusses the author's journey through Hell; the first part of The Divine Comedy (*Inferno*)
The Brothers Karamazov *Crime and Punishment* (Fyodor Dostoyevsky)	Russia	a philosophical novel revolving around patricide set against the backdrop of a modernizing Russia with themes of morality, faith, and doubt (*The Brothers Karamazov*);

Table 4.15. Important Works in World and Non-Western Literature

Title (Author)	Country of Origin	Description
		written after the author's exile in Siberia; depicts
		the moral dilemmas and mental anguish stemming from a murder (*Crime and Punishment*)
The Count of Monte Cristo (Alexandre Dumas)	France	an adventure novel that takes place during the Bourbon Restoration in France and tells the story of a man who escapes an unjust incarceration to seek revenge
Like Water for Chocolate (Laura Esquivel)	Mexico	a story of self-growth, love, tradition, rebellion, and family; employs the use of magical realism
Medea (Euripides)	ancient Greece	the second of the three major Greek tragedies; based on the myth of Medea and Jason, who
		leaves Medea for another woman; noted for its simplicity; examines themes of love, passion, and vengeance
The Tin Drum (Gunter Grass)	West Germany	the first book of Grass's *Danzig Trilogy*; narrated by a main character who lived through Nazi
		occupation; offers perspectives on German history and the human condition
Siddhartha: An Indian Poem (Herman Hesse)	Germany	a novel (not an actual poem) inspired by Hesse's visit to India; describes a young Brahman's search for self-realization
The Odyssey (Homer)	ancient Greece	epic poem divided into twenty-four books that explores themes of wandering, returning,
		"guest-friendship," omens, and being tested; tells the story of Odysseus, King of Ithaca, who tries to return home after the end of the Trojan War
The Kite Runner (Khaled Hosseini)	United States	takes place in Afghanistan (author's birthplace) in the midst of its turbulent history, including Soviet occupation and the rise of the Taliban; tells the story of friendship between a wealthy Afghan boy and a servant's son; themes of guilt, family, and redemption
The Hunchback of Notre Dame (Victor Hugo)	France	written to save Notre Dame cathedral and preserve French culture during an era of immense change; themes of determinism and

Table 4.15. Important Works in World and Non-Western Literature

Title (Author)	Country of Origin	Description
		architecture; original title: *Notre-Dame de Paris*
Peer Gynt (Henrik Ibsen)	Norway	a five-act play in verse; inspired by a fairy tale the author believed to be true; a story of youth, adventure, missteps, and eventual redemption
The Trial (Franz Kafka)	Germany	themes that examine the ideas of justice versus law, the absence of unequivocal truth, alienation, sexuality; considered to be a criticism of totalitarian authority
One Hundred Years of Solitude *Love in the Time of Cholera* (Gabriel García Márquez)	Colombia	an epic family saga spanning several generations and a century's worth of Latin American history (*One Hundred Years of Solitude*); a story of two lovers reuniting; woven with themes of aging, death, and love; set in a South American community affected by war and cholera outbreaks (*Love in the Time of Cholera*)
The Wind-Up Bird Chronicle (Haruki Murakami)	Japan	a story about a man who looks for his wife's missing cat and discovers a netherworld beneath Tokyo; examines themes of power, desire, and alienation
Cry, the Beloved Country (Alan Paton)	South Africa	takes place in the lead-up to Apartheid in South Africa; employs Biblical references; considered a social protest in response to a society that would eventually usher in Apartheid; showcases the consequences of fear
All Quiet on the Western Front (Erich Remarque)	Germany	written by a World War I veteran; describes the extraordinary mental and physical stresses endured by German soldiers during the war and the subsequent detachment they felt from civilian life; themes of blind nationalism and lost youth
Midnight's Children (Salman Rushdie)	United Kingdom	depicts the transition of India from colonial rule to independence and the country's eventual partition; employs a self-reflexive style that weaves history with fiction
The Tale of Genji (Murasaki Shikibu)	Japan	early 11th century work written by a noblewoman and lady-in-waiting at the peak of the Fujiwara clan's power; considered by

Table 4.15. Important Works in World and Non-Western Literature

Title (Author)	Country of Origin	Description
		some to be the world's first novel; depicts aristocratic lifestyles during the Heian Period through the lens of Hikaru Genji, the son of an emperor who is demoted to a commoner; themes include love, lust, and family loyalty
Antigone (Sophocles)	ancient Greece	the third of the three major Greek tragedies; describes the tale of a woman who buries her brother in defiance of an order from the king; examines themes of family loyalty, blindness versus sight, fate, free will, mortality, and civil disobedience
Anna Karenina *War and Peace* (Leo Tolstoy)	Russia	takes place during an age of liberal reform brought about by Emperor Alexander II of Russia; examines Imperial Russian society and themes of faith, betrayal, desire, and family (*Anna Karenina*); weaves history with philosophy; discusses the French invasion of Russia and the effects of the Napoleonic era on Tsarist society; includes themes of religion, patriotism, forgiveness, and pacifism (*War and Peace*)
Night *Dawn* (Elie Wiesel)	Buenos Aires, Argentina: Central Union of Polish Jews in Argentina (*Night*); France, US, UK (*Dawn*)	a memoir based on the author's experiences with his father in a Nazi German concentration camp; includes themes of lost faith, guilt, inhumanity, and the relationship between fathers and sons (*Night*); a novel about a Holocaust survivor who relocates to the British Mandate of Palestine, joins a paramilitary group, and is tasked with executing a British author; explores themes of past versus present and the internal struggle of becoming someone you despise (*Dawn*)

Practice Question

4) Which of the following texts could be included in a unit that explores the effects of colonialism from the perspectives of Indigenous peoples'? Select all that apply.
  A. Gunter Grass's *The Tin Drum*
  B. Chinua Achebe's *Things Fall Apart*
  C. Haruki Murakami's *The Wind-Up Bird Chronicle*
  D. Isabel Allende's *House of Spirits*
  E. Khaled Hosseini's *The Kite Runner*

Young Adult Literature

Young adult literature includes texts written for adolescent readers, youth, and young adults up to age twenty-five. Usually, the texts are fiction and include problem novels and romances; however nonfiction, poetry, graphic novels, and comics are popular as well. Young adult literature aims to be relevant to young people, to address their needs and interests, and to allow them to see themselves in the stories. Typical themes involve dealing with social issues, answering moral and ethical questions, relating to others, finding acceptance while maintaining uniqueness, and discovering one's individual identity.

Table 4.16. Important Young Adult Works		
Title (Author)	**Country of Origin**	**Description**
Tuck Everlasting (Natalie Babbitt)	United States	a story about immortality; a young girl discovers a family who drank from a spring that granted them eternal youth, prompting another character to attempt to exploit this knowledge; uses symbolism
Are You There, God? It's Me, Margaret (Judy Blume)	United States	the story of a sixth-grade girl who is seeking a single religion while dealing with the everyday experiences of being an adolescent girl
The Hunger Games (series) (Suzanne Collins)	United States	dystopian works that take place in a post-apocalyptic nation; themes include the origins and effects of war, distrust of authority, and class discrimination; told through the eyes of a teen protagonist
Lord of the Flies (William Golding)	United Kingdom	the tale of a group of British boys who are stranded on an island and their attempts to govern themselves; examines themes of individuality, groupthink, rational versus emotional, and morality versus immorality
The Outsiders (S.E. Hinton)	United States	written when the author was a teen; a story about rival gangs from different socioeconomic classes; explores themes of family dysfunction, identity, self-sacrifice, honor, and empathy

Table 4.16. Important Young Adult Works		
Title (Author)	Country of Origin	Description
Flowers for Algernon (Daniel Keyes)	United States	a short story turned novel about a lab mouse who has surgery to boost his intelligence; narrated as progress reports by the first human to undergo the same surgery; includes themes of the treatment of the mentally disabled, intellect versus emotion, and how the past affects the present; uses the science fiction theme of "uplift"
The Giver (Lois Lowry)	United States	a dystopian novel about a society that eradicates emotion and contention and the boy who is selected to store all of society's past memories; explores themes of individuality, memory, rules, control, freedom, and choice
Anne of Green Gables (L.M. Montgomery)	United States (published); Canada (written)	set on Prince Edward Island, Canada; the story of an orphaned girl mistakenly sent to live with her older siblings and the trials and tribulations she experiences as she grows up in her new town; examines themes of societal expectations versus imagination
Hatchet (Gary Paulsen)	United States	a wilderness survival novel; the first in a series; the story of a young teen who crash lands in the wilderness of Canada and his fight to survive; explores themes of man and nature, wisdom versus knowledge, transformation, family, and perseverance
Harry Potter (series) (J.K. Rowling)	United Kingdom	a fantasy series; the life and times of a young wizard and his friends who study at a school for witchcraft and wizardry and their struggles against a dark wizard; themes include death, loss, love, corruption, and prejudice

Table 4.16. Important Young Adult Works

Title (Author)	Country of Origin	Description
The Catcher in the Rye (J.D. Salinger)	United States	a coming-of-age novel about a teen who has been expelled from his prep school; takes place over the course of about three days; themes include identity, alienation, sex, and the author's perception of phoniness in the world around him

Practice Question

5) The book introduces a world without color, joy, or fear, in which a single person holds the memories of the community's history. When a young boy is selected to become the new Receiver of Memory, he must decide if he wants his community to know the truth. Which book is being described here?
   A. Lois Lowry's *The Giver*
   B. Gary Paulsen's *Hatchet*
   C. William Golding's *Lord of the Flies*
   D. Suzanne Collins's *The Hunger Games*

Literary Context

Context refers to both the historical and cultural times during which a text is written. The critical emphasis on context is based on the theory of **situated cognition**, which suggests that human activity is socially situated and unavoidably influenced by its social and cultural surroundings; therefore, the choices humans make—including those that authors make about their works—must be understood in light of the circumstances that frame them. To truly understand a text, students must be aware of the social and cultural components that influenced the author.

Cultural context refers to the literary, artistic, and musical movements that were going on at the time a work was written. *Civil Disobedience* (Henry David Thoreau) exemplifies the point that an author's purposes are culturally responsive to some degree. Thoreau, a Romantic Transcendentalist, was influenced by Ralph Waldo Emerson's idea of self-reliance. He was profoundly disturbed by the concepts of majority rule and mandatory conformity to unjust laws; thus, his purpose in writing *Civil Disobedience* was to persuade his readers to be self-reliant by following their own senses of right and wrong, even when that meant disregarding the law.

Historical context refers to the time during which the author was writing. Students must be able to distinguish historical context from the setting of the story itself. For example, the setting of *The Scarlet Letter* (Nathanial Hawthorne) is seventeenth-century Boston, a Puritan village of the Massachusetts Bay Colony in which conformity is expected as a way of preventing sin. To truly understand the author's work, however, students must know that Hawthorne actually wrote his novel in 1849. Like Thoreau, he was reacting to the ideas of Emerson and the Romantic Transcendentalists and was interested in the early Women's Rights Movement, which asserted that women can be self-reliant, must have individual rights, and must not conform to practices that subjugated them. Unlike Thoreau, Hawthorne was a

Romantic Anti-Transcendentalist: he recognized the human capacity for individuality but also its capacity for darkness, sin, and evil. Hawthorne created a story that explores the admirable but lonely lifestyle of self-reliance, nonconformity, and individualism.

In planning reading instruction, teachers can implement a few context-related best practices in order to ensure students are getting as much as they can from their studies. Effective teachers frame the study of a literary work with information about its context and may incorporate a number of different techniques for teaching context:

- They may begin a context-based lesson by having students activate prior knowledge through revisiting previous English or history lessons that might contribute to their understanding of the text.

- If time permits, teachers might assign a short research activity about the historical, cultural, and geographical contexts of a literary text to help students form the habit of making their own inquiries about background information.

- Alternatively, if pressed for time, the didactic approach of giving a short lecture on the context of a text can also be time well spent.

Teachers may integrate some essential or life question that would make the study of the text more personally meaningful to students:

- Example: If the text is *Civil Disobedience*, an essential question of the unit of study could be, "When is nonconformity the right alternative?"

- Teachers may also include additional content-related guiding questions related to context, such as, "How were the author's artistic choices influenced by the cultural-historical issues of the time period?"; "How are the characters responding to and forming relationships within the social situation of the text?"; "How does this reflect the author's perspective on society?"

Finally, teachers will return to discussions of context as their studies with the class progress: students look for familiar historical or cultural ideas as well as any intertextual references that may help them gain a deeper understanding of the work.

Important Works

Civil Disobedience

Author: Henry David Thoreau

Publication Date: 1849

Summary: The work is a critique of the American government's response to slavery and the Mexican War. Thoreau explains that government itself is not necessarily a good thing, and the majority, who rules any government, may be wrong. He notes that people are not required to obey unjust laws and must follow their own senses of morality. He calls on people to refuse to participate in the unjust US government lest they further perpetuate its evils. He argues that attempting to enact change via voting or legislation is largely futile since those operating within a vile government cannot understand how terrible it is. He calls on people to reject the government by avoiding any interactions with it, just as he did by not paying taxes, which caused him to be jailed.

Themes, Motifs, and Symbols: rejection of government, individual conscience, unjust laws

The Scarlet Letter

Author: Nathaniel Hawthorne

Publication Date: 1850

Summary: Hester Prynne is a young mother living in a puritanical New England village who is forced to wear a red letter *A* on her clothing to reveal her adultery to the public. Her husband, who she believed was dead, comes to the village in disguise and with a new name—Roger Chillingworth—to meddle in its affairs. Hester refuses to name the father of her child, Pearl, despite the villagers' pressures to do so. Chillingworth discovers that Arthur Dimmesdale, a young minister and the village leader, is the father and confronts him. Unable to handle his guilt, Dimmesdale becomes ill and reveals his paternity before dying. Having lost her love, Hester moves to Europe with Pearl but eventually returns to New England. Upon her death, she is buried next to Dimmesdale.

Themes, Motifs, and Symbols: conformity, guilt, judgment and lack of belonging (the letter *A* itself), revenge

Practice Question

Question 6 refers to the first stanza of "The Sun Rising" by John Donne, 1572 – 1631.

Busy old fool, unruly Sun,

Why dost thou thus,

Through windows, and through curtains call on us?

Must to thy motions lovers' seasons run?

Saucy pedantic wretch, go chide

Late school-boys and sour prentices,

Go tell court-huntsmen that the king will ride,

Call country ants to harvest offices,

Love, all alike, no season knows nor clime,

Nor hours, days, months, which are the rags of time.

6) What can the reader infer from knowing that "The Sun Rising" is a metaphysical poem?
   A. The poem is about philosophical questions.
   B. The poem is using literal language to address questions about human nature.
   C. The poem reflects the concerns of twentieth-century society.
   D. The poem is mocking religion and faith.

Literary Genres and Instructional Strategies

Literature can be classified into **genres** and **subgenres**, categories of works that are similar in format, content, tone, or length. Most works fall into one of four broad genres:

- nonfiction
- fiction
- drama
- poetry

As students experience each genre, they should receive instruction that integrates all aspects of literacy. In other words, students should experience not only reading practice in the genre, but also receive plentiful writing practice and numerous discussion opportunities to deepen their knowledge of the genre they are studying. Objectives for lessons in genre studies should integrate all levels of Bloom's taxonomy with the goal of equipping students with the abilities to understand, interpret, discuss, and create works in various genres.

Nonfiction

Nonfiction is a genre of prose writing that uses information that is true and accurate to the best of the author's knowledge. This quality, however, does not mean that nonfiction is dry or uninspiring; in fact, nonfiction writing comes in many forms, most of which lend themselves to a degree of creativity and originality in terms of how the factual information is presented. For example, **literary nonfiction**, or **creative nonfiction**, is a mix of expressive and informative writing that tells a true, verifiable, or documented story in a compelling, artistic way. Nonfiction texts are written to inform, reflect, and entertain and may take any of the following forms:

> **Helpful Hint**:
>
> **Bloom's taxonomy** is a framework for understanding how humans learn. The first level of the taxonomy is **remembering**. Once students have mastered basic recall, they can be pushed toward **understanding** and **applying** new information; eventually, they can move on to **analyzing**, **evaluating**, and **creating** texts using their knowledge.

- **essay:** a short work about a particular topic or idea
- **speech:** a short work with a specific purpose, intended to be presented orally in front of an audience
- **news article:** a short recounting of a particular story
- **biography:** a detailed, creative, textual representation of another person's life
- **autobiography:** an account of an individual's life, told by the individual

Students should be given opportunities to respond to nonfiction texts both in writing (e.g., a research report) and with interactive activities (e.g., debates and discussions).

When working with nonfiction texts, students should pay particular attention to voice and tone, text structures, and thoughts and ideas. Through guided readings, group discussions, and independent reflection, students should discover that these elements, when taken together with context, can reveal the author's purpose. In successful classrooms, the author's purpose is a guiding question, where the study of nonfiction is partly dedicated to helping students recognize and understand bias in literature.

Direct instruction of nonfiction should include the following:

- identifying the rhetorical strategies used in a nonfiction text

Reading Literary Texts

- summarizing a nonfiction text by stating the format, the author's purpose, the intended audience, and the central idea or argument
- evaluating the writer's assumptions, claims, appeals, and evidence

As students gain familiarity with the nonfiction genre, they should begin writing their own nonfiction pieces, applying their understanding of the author's purpose, and using published texts as models for effective voice, tone, and organization.

Practice Question

7) Comparing a fiction and nonfiction text on the same topic can help students do which one of the following?
   A. understand the difference between a biography and an autobiography
   B. develop skills in identifying logical fallacies
   C. recognize differences among genres
   D. modify the expressiveness of their reading based on the audience

Fiction

Fiction is a prose genre made up of narratives whose details are not based in truth but are instead the creations of the author. Fiction is typically written in the form of novels and short stories. It includes many subgenres; subcategories can be found within some of these subgenres.

Table 4.17. The Subgenres of Fiction and Their Subcategories

Subgenres and Descriptions	Subcategories and Their Descriptions
Folklore • a set of beliefs and stories of a particular people that are passed down through generations; includes many forms/subcategories	• **fables:** short stories intended to teach moral lessons • **fairy tales:** stories that involve magical creatures, such as elves and fairies • **myths:** stories, often involving gods or demigods, that attempt to explain certain practices or phenomena • **legends:** unverifiable stories that seem to have a degree of realism about them • **tall tales:** stories that take place in realistic settings but include characters with wildly exaggerated capabilities
Science fiction • Writers tell imaginative stories that are grounded in scientific and technological theories or realities; often explores ideas involving the future of humanity and its relationship with the universe or with technology	• **dystopian fiction:** explores social, cultural, and political structures in the context of an imagined world or society
Horror • intended to impact the reader via the experiences of fear, paranoia, or disgust;	**mysteries and thrillers:** may also arouse fear or paranoia; tend to be fast-paced and outcome-driven; often focus on human behaviors or relationships

Table 4.17. The Subgenres of Fiction and Their Subcategories

often involves paranormal or psychological content	
Realistic fiction	
▪ includes stories that are meant to be relatable for readers; possesses a degree of verisimilitude, especially in the dialogue between characters	**historical fiction:** relies on realistic settings and characters from an earlier time to tell new stories
Satire	
▪ uses critical humor to reveal vice and foolishness in individuals and institutions; aims to improve the individual or institution being ridiculed ▪ employs rhetorical devices such as sarcasm, irony, mockery, exaggeration, understatement, as well as an honest narrative/speaking voice that is dismayed or appalled by the object of the satire ▪ shows a subject to be ludicrous or wrong while simultaneously appealing to the reader's reason and sense of virtue	

In planning and facilitating fiction studies, teachers should emphasize important literary elements like plot, character, setting, and figurative language. (See "Literary Elements" in Chapter 3 for more information on these elements.)

To encourage metacognition (discussed in Chapter 3), teachers should engage students with fiction in a variety of ways:

- Effective teachers might have their students record personal responses to a text in a journal.
- Students might also be prompted to compare plot development across a few different texts to illustrate the importance of various plot elements.
- A speaking and listening activity might require students to present interviews with the characters: one student may interview another (who is acting as one of the characters) and ask about the character's perspectives and motivations.
- Teachers should also make time for students to write fiction; a meaningful assignment might parallel a text read in class.
  - For example, if a class reads a story about a character maturing, students can write narratives about personal experiences that left them more mature.

Practice Question

8) Which answer option BEST describes a myth?
   A. a story that includes a magical creature who teaches children a lesson
   B. a story that uses humor to reveal vice or foolishness
   C. a story set in a realistic historical time period
   D. a story that attempts to explain a specific worldview or a natural phenomenon

Drama

Drama is expressive writing that tells a story to an audience through the actions and dialogue of characters, which are brought to life by actors who play the roles on stage. Dramatic works, called **plays**, are written in poetic or lyrical verse, or in regular prose. Along with the dialogue between the characters, authors rely on stage directions to describe the sets and to give instructions to the actors about what they are to do.

> **Helpful Hint**:
>
> **Prosody** is the overall liveliness and expressiveness of reading. It includes appropriate pauses and changes in pitch and intonation based on punctuation and the overall meaning of the piece.

In some plays, actors perform long speeches in which the characters explain their thinking about philosophical ideas or social issues. Known as **monologues**, these speeches can be directed toward other characters. A monologue delivered as if nobody were listening is called a **soliloquy** (as in Shakespeare's famous "To be or not to be" soliloquy from *Hamlet*).

Important Works

Hamlet

Author: William Shakespeare

Publication Date: 1603

Summary: Prince Hamlet of Denmark is mourning the death of his father, the king. He also ponders how quickly his mother, Gertrude, married Claudius, his father's brother. The king's ghost visits Hamlet, telling him that Claudius poisoned him and that Hamlet must avenge his father's death. To cover up his plans, Hamlet purposely begins to act strangely. This worries Claudius, who hires Hamlet's friends to spy on him. Hamlet eventually becomes suspicious of everyone around him, including his love interest, Ophelia.

To discover if the ghost's message is true, he stages a play in which a man's brother poisons him to marry his wife. Claudius is clearly upset by the play, so Hamlet confronts his mother. Polonius, Ophelia's father, is hiding in the curtains during this confrontation; thinking he is Claudius, Hamlet stabs and kills Polonius.

Claudius banishes Hamlet to England, but he eventually returns to find Ophelia dead. Her brother Laertes challenges Hamlet to a duel; both die. In the fray, Hamlet also stabs and kills Claudius. Gertrude, who accidentally drinks a cup of poison meant for Hamlet, also dies.

Themes, Motifs, and Symbols: madness, doubt, betrayal, revenge

Sometimes characters in drama (or fiction) have very unique attributes, such as catchphrases or particular manners of speech or dress. Such devices, known as **character tags**, make characters memorable to readers.

Using drama in the classroom is a great way to get students interested in different types of texts. Building on students' innate curiosity and imagination, the possibilities are endless. Acting out dramas helps students work on expressive reading (prosody) and reinforces social and emotional learning as students analyze the emotions and actions of characters.

It is important to have older students think about how both the stage directions and the dialogue contribute to a play's meaning. To jog student interest, especially in linguistically complex dramas like those of Shakespeare, teachers might have students watch video clips of actual performances.

Comparing specific scenes performed by different actors stimulates interest and can be used to discuss the different ways in which a scene can be interpreted.

Students may also benefit from acting out scenes or giving speeches, which allows them to express their own interpretations of the characters or actions. To engage students in writing activities, a teacher may prompt them to write their own scripts or research reports on a play's context, author, characters, or subject matter.

Practice Question

9) Drama is a genre well suited for helping students understand which one of the following?
   A. literary context
   B. prosody
   C. figurative language
   D. concepts of print

Poetry

Poetry is imaginative, expressive verse writing characterized by rhythm, unified and concentrated thought, concrete images, specialized language, and the use of patterns:

- A **line** is a unit of poetry and can be separated by some sort of punctuation, meter, and/or rhyme.
  - Although a line may be a unit of attention, it is usually not a unit of meaning.
- A **stanza** is a group of lines followed by a space.
  - Each stanza may have a specific number of lines; the lines are sometimes arranged in a pattern created by meter and/or a rhyme scheme.
  - The **pattern** is often repeated in each stanza of the poem, although the pattern can be varied for effect.
  - A stanza with two lines is a **couplet**; three lines, a **tercet**; four lines, a **quatrain**; five lines, a **cinquain**; and so on.
  - Modern poems may have stanzas with varying lengths or none at all.

Different poetic forms utilize techniques and structures in unique ways. A **ballad** is a short narrative song about an event that is considered important; it is intended to be recited. Ballads are characterized by a dramatic immediacy, focusing on one crucial situation or action that often leads to a catastrophe. They are frequently about courage, love, political disputes, or military battles. The narrator in a ballad tends to be the public voice, speaking without personal judgment until it is interrupted by dialogue. Often, repetition is used to express emotion and reinforce the facts. Though the language of folk ballads is plain—usually without descriptive and figurative qualities—the emotional effect of the forceful language is nevertheless impactful. Literary ballads, like *The Rime of the Ancient Mariner* by Samuel Taylor Coleridge, are distinguished by rhythmic, poetic language and stanzas.

A **sonnet** is a lyrical poem composed of fourteen lines, usually written in iambic pentameter. (For more information on iambic pentameter and meter, see the Chapter 3 section "Poetic Devices and Structures.") There are two main structural patterns that sonnets follow:

- The **Italian**, or **Petrarchan**, pattern has eight lines (an **octave**) that follow an *abba abba* rhyme scheme, followed by six lines (a **seste**) that follow either a *cde cde* or a *cd cd cd* rhyme scheme.
    - Usually, the octave in an Italian sonnet poses a question, describes a problem, or tells a story; the seste, then, answers the question, solves the problem, or comments on the story.
- The **English**, or **Shakespearean**, pattern has three groups of four lines (called **quatrains**) and ends with a rhyming couplet.
    - The rhyme scheme of the English sonnet is *abab cdcd efef gg*.
    - The quatrains present variations on a single theme; the couplet is a concluding remark.

A **haiku** is a short poem format, created in Japan, that consists of three lines and seventeen syllables divided into five, seven, and five syllables on the three lines, respectively.

Finally, a **villanelle** is usually nineteen lines long; contains five stanzas, each with three lines; and a final stanza of four lines. It also includes a **refrain**—two lines that repeat throughout the poem following a specific pattern. Dylan Thomas's "Do Not Go Gentle into That Good Night" is a common example of a villanelle.

When delivering poetry lessons, teachers should incorporate opportunities into their lesson plans that allow students to respond to both the effect the poem has on them personally as well as the aesthetics of the poem itself. To introduce poetry and build interest for a poetry unit, an effective teacher might select an especially forceful poem, read it dramatically, and invite students to share their responses in a discussion forum.

When having students analyze poetry, it is best to promote multiple readings, model with a think-aloud of an analytical reading, provide copies of poems that students can annotate, and perhaps establish a process to follow for the collaborative and independent reading of poems. The following steps may be included in such a process:

- an initial reading to experience the mood of the poem and the musicality of the language
- a second reading to delineate the pauses and thought units and to identify the speaker
- a third, close reading to take marginal notes on the structure of the poem, the denotation and connotations of unfamiliar words, the impact of imagery and figurative language, and the meaning of confusing lines or phrases
- a final reading to formulate some thematic ideas, drawn from the details

In conjunction with analyzing poems, students should have opportunities to present their original poetry in classroom "coffee houses." Depending on the literature course, students might also be taught the different poetic forms, like sonnets and ballads, in addition to the characteristics of the different types of poetry (e.g., Metaphysical and Romantic).

Important Works

The Rime of the Ancient Mariner

Author: Samuel Taylor Coleridge

Publication Date: 1798

Summary: An old mariner tells a story of his youth to a man traveling to a wedding. The mariner's ship was stuck in ice when an albatross, believed to be good luck, visited. The bird follows the ship after it becomes unstuck. Things start to go wrong after the mariner shoots and kills the bird: there is no wind, no water to drink, and the crew begins to experience nightmares. As penance, they hang the dead bird around the neck of the mariner. The crew members then see a ship in the distance and hope it is their savior, but it is only a ghost ship that brings more bad fortune. Everyone on the ship—except the mariner—drops dead. The mariner remains on the ship with the corpses for seven days but is unable to pray for forgiveness. Eventually, moved by the beauty of the sea creatures, he is able to pray, and the dead albatross suddenly drops from his neck. Although he is rescued, he must atone for his slaughter of the albatross by telling his story as he wanders the world.

Themes, Motifs, and Symbols: nature, dreams, prayer, good versus evil, the albatross as a symbol of sin

Practice Question

Question 10 refers to the poem "The Harlem Dancer" by Claude McKay, seen below in its original format:

Applauding youths laughed with young prostitutes

And watched her perfect, half-clothed body sway;

Her voice was like the sound of blended flutes

Blown by black players upon a picnic day.

She sang and danced on gracefully and calm,

The light gauze hanging loose about her form;

To me she seemed a proudly swaying palm

Grown lovelier for passing through a storm.

Upon her swarthy neck black, shiny curls

Luxuriant fell; and, tossing coins in praise,

The wine-flushed, bold-eyed boys, and even the girls,

Devoured her with their eager, passionate gaze;

But, looking at her falsely-smiling face,

I knew her self was not in that strange place.

10) What kind of poem is "The Harlem Dancer"?
   A. a ballad
   B. a villanelle
   C. a sonnet
   D. a satire

Answer Key

1) C: A strong familiarity with the exact details of the text, while valuable, is less important to constructivists than an individual's personal understanding of the text.

2) B: In her diary, Mary Chesnut records her observations about the Civil War, which took place during the years in which she chronicles her thoughts. The work is also published under the title *A Diary from Dixie*.

3) A, C: Charles Dickens and Robert Browning both wrote during the Victorian Period (ca. 1832 – ca. 1901).

4) B, D, E: *Things Fall Apart*, *House of Spirits*, and *The Kite Runner* all explore the effects of colonialism on Indigenous populations.

5) A: *The Giver* tells the story of a boy in a dystopian society who must decide what to do with the memories he has been given.

6) A: Philosophical concerns are often the subject of Metaphysical poetry.

7) C: Comparing fiction and nonfiction texts on the same topic can help students understand how the genres differ.

8) D: A myth is a story, often involving gods or demigods, that attempts to explain a practice, worldview, or natural phenomenon.

9) B: Drama is particularly useful in helping students develop oral reading skills and prosody.

10) C: "The Harlem Dancer" is a sonnet. The poem develops a theme about the dancer, contains fourteen lines (three quatrains with an *abab*, *cdcd*, and *efef* rhyme scheme), and ends with a rhyming couplet.

Reading Informational and Argumentative Texts

In today's information-rich world, students benefit from having solid understandings of the goals and structures of informational texts. In fact, it is just as important for students to know the format of a current event article, editorial, or speech as it is for them to know the structure of a sonnet or short story. To interpret informational texts, students benefit from making connections between texts; an effective teacher might therefore assign multiple articles on the same subject and ask students to make comparisons.

Author's Purpose

The authors of **nonfiction texts** usually have one of the following purposes for writing:

- to persuade
- to inform
- to explain
- to entertain
- to describe

Authors who write to **persuade** try to convince the reader to act or think a certain way. They may use specific reasons and supporting evidence to do this. Persuasive writers also use **rhetoric**, which is language chosen specifically for its particular effect, to influence readers.

Writing to **inform** is as straightforward as the term suggests: the author sets out simply to communicate information to the reader. Purely informative writing is found in many textbooks and news articles. Some informational writing may also **instruct** the reader; types of this writing include lists, steps to be followed, and information presented in a sequential order. Similar to informing, some writing explains. It might define a term, discuss how things are similar or different, or **explain** a problem and its solution.

Nonfiction may also entertain. Typically, this type of writing will **narrate**, or tell a (true) story. Like fiction, **narrative nonfiction** (sometimes referred to as **literary nonfiction**) will include a setting, characters, and a plot. The writer may also use figurative language and other devices to entertain the reader. Finally, nonfiction texts may describe something, such as a detailed description of an event, person, place, or even inanimate object.

The acronym *PIEED* helps students think about the author's purpose. Figure 5.1. illustrates each of the PIEED purposes:

- Persuade
- Inform

- **E**xplain
- **E**ntertain
- **D**escribe

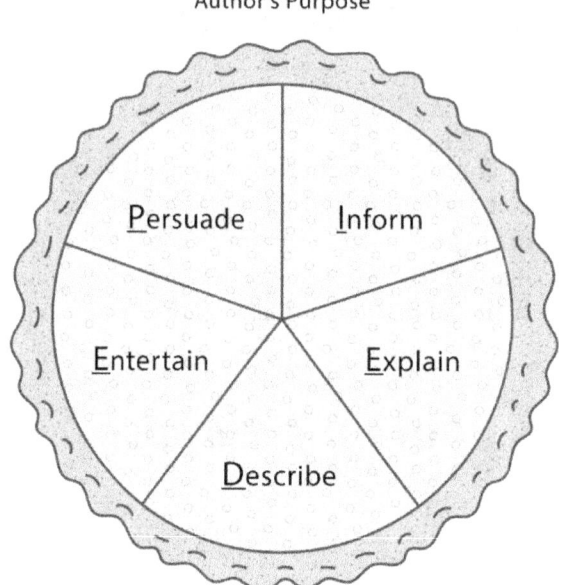

Author's Purpose

Nonfiction takes many forms, as described in Table 5.1. The form of a work of nonfiction is often related to the author's purpose. To **identify the purpose of a text**, many educators use the following step-by-step process:

> **Helpful Hint**:
>
> A **purpose statement** aims to summarize the specific goals or topics of a written work; it is a declarative sentence.

- **Step one:** While reading the text, think of the question "Why did the author write this?"
- **Step two:** After reading, complete the statement "The author wrote this mainly to _____."
- **Step Three:** Find important details in the text that support the statement; if no such details exist, the purpose statement might need to be modified.

Table 5.1. Forms of Nonfiction

Form	Description
Essay	a short work about a particular topic or idea
Speech	a short work with a specific purpose, intended to be presented orally in front of an audience
News article	a short recounting of a particular story
Biography	a detailed, creative textual representation of a person's life
Autobiography	an account of an individual's life, told by the individual

Practice Question

1) A high school teacher is working with students to identify the purpose of a science article in preparation for similar questions on the SAT/ACT. Which advice should he give students to help them determine the author's purpose?
   A. to ask whether the author achieved her purpose for writing the text
   B. to look for specific text evidence that supports an assertion about the author's purpose
   C. to tell them that the purpose will generally be revealed explicitly in the introductory paragraph
   D. to tell them that a "call to action" never gives possible clues to the author's purpose

Text Structure

Authors organize nonfiction texts with structures that suit their purpose. A structure may be a sequence of events (e.g., a news story about the days leading up to an important event), or it could be a thorough description of something (e.g., the opening paragraph of an essay describing a person or place in detail).

Many historical texts use a **cause-and-effect** pattern in which the cause is presented first, and the result is discussed next. A chapter in a social studies text about the Industrial Revolution, for example, might follow this pattern, citing the Industrial Revolution as the cause for a change in working and living conditions in many cities.

Other works are organized in a **problem-solution** structure, in which a problem is presented and then a possible solution is discussed. Teachers might introduce this structure through a collaborative activity in which students identify a problem in the classroom, school, or community. They can then write a letter to a decision-maker about the issue and a possible solution. Finally, students can read other problem-solution texts to see how other authors structure their arguments.

Students can use a **compare and contrast** structure to explain how two things from their everyday experiences are similar and different. Charts and other graphic organizers can help them organize their thoughts and understand this structure. A teacher might ask students, for example, to use a **Venn diagram** (Figure 5.2.) to determine the similarities and differences presented in a text.

It is helpful to integrate reading and writing nonfiction/expository texts that use the same structure. This approach is used in many textbooks and curricular resources based on the Common Core State Standards.

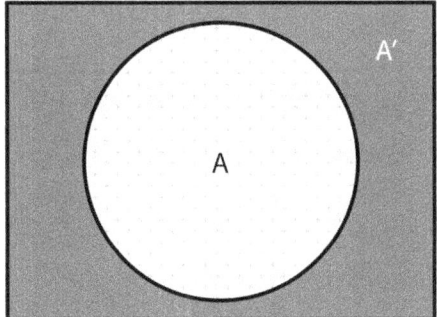

Figure 5.2. Venn Diagram Example

Important Works

Nature

Author: Ralph Waldo Emerson

Publication Date: 1836

Summary: Emerson describes the foundational principles of Transcendentalism, a philosophical movement that esteems nature and dislikes formal religion. He explains how humans can find solitude in nature, which allows them to experience God free from the constraints of the modern world. He further explains how humans can use nature for societal advancements, such as those of the Industrial Revolution. He elaborates on the true beauty in natural things, the role of language in human existence and the description of the world, and how language can be corrupted. He argues that nature is a path to truth and morality. Linking nature and God, Emerson argues that nature is a way humanity can experience the act of creation. He criticizes strict empiricism as reductionist and instead encourages a focus on the whole of the natural world.

Themes and Rhetorical Strategies: nature, problems with modern society, unity, religion, modern science

Practice Question

Question 2 refers to the following excerpt taken from Chapter IV of the essay *Nature* by Ralph Waldo Emerson:

Words are signs of natural facts. The use of natural history is to give us aid in supernatural history: the use of the outer creation, to give us language for the beings and changes of the inward creation. Every word which is used to express a moral or intellectual fact, if traced to its root, is found to be borrowed from some material appearance. *Right* means straight; *wrong* means twisted. *Spirit* primarily means wind; *transgression*, the crossing of a line; *supercilious*, the raising of the eyebrow. We say *the heart* to express emotion, *the head* to denote thought; and *thought* and *emotion* are words borrowed from sensible things, and now appropriated to spiritual nature. Most of the process by which this transformation is made, is hidden from us in the remote time when language was framed; but the same tendency may be daily observed in children. Children and savages use only nouns or names of things, which they convert into verbs, and apply to analogous mental acts.

2) How does Emerson structure the information in this section of text?
  A. from general to specific
  B. sequentially
  C. chronologically
  D. using spatial details

Identifying Central Ideas

Nonfiction texts each contain a **central**, or **main idea**. Identifying this idea is an important—though sometimes challenging—skill for students. When being taught to look for the main idea, students should start with simple texts and identify the topic of each. For example, the topic of a text might be "horses." Students then ask themselves a question such as, "What is the author saying about horses?" The answer to that question is the central idea of the text. For example, the answer might be "Horses are animals that have helped humans throughout history."

An **implicit main idea**—which is not explicitly stated in the text—is more difficult to identify. Students must synthesize information and details from many parts of the text. The following process can help students identify the main idea:

- Identify the main idea of each paragraph first.
    - It might be stated explicitly as a topic sentence, or it might be implied.
    - If the idea is implied, students will need to summarize the paragraph in a single sentence in their own words.
- After determining the main idea of each paragraph, students can think about what these main ideas have in common or make a "summary of summaries."

Students should check their main idea statements to make sure they have no specific details or examples and that they encapsulate only the most important points. Because identification of the central idea and summarization are similar thought processes, these skills are often taught together. Teachers might also introduce the central idea as the most important idea within the summary.

Helpful Hint:

When stated explicitly, the main idea is referred to as a **thesis**, or **thesis statement**.

Practice Question

When a fire destroyed San Francisco's American Indian Center in October of 1969, American Indian groups set their sights on the recently closed island prison of Alcatraz as a site of a new Indian cultural center and school. Ignored by the government, an activist group known as "Indians of All Tribes" sailed to Alcatraz in the early morning hours with eighty-nine men, women, and children. They landed on Alcatraz, claiming it for all the tribes of North America. Their demands were ignored, and so the group continued to occupy the island for the next nineteen months, its numbers swelling up to 600 as others joined. By January of 1970, many of the original protestors had left, and on June 11, 1971, federal marshals forcibly removed the last residents.

3) What is the main idea of this passage?
  A. The government refused to listen to the demands of American Indians.
  B. American Indians occupied Alcatraz in protest of government policy.
  C. Few people joined the occupation of Alcatraz, weakening its effectiveness.
  D. The government took violent action against protestors at Alcatraz.

Textual Evidence

The goal in courtrooms, science labs, and classrooms is not just to arrive at conclusions, but to come to evidence-based conclusions. Within the constructivist framework, students are urged to formulate responses to and interpretations of the texts they read, and then they must cite specific evidence to support their conclusions.

In the early grades, students begin by referring to the text when looking for answers to teacher-provided questions. When they get older, students move to asking their own questions and quoting text to articulate their answers. By middle school, students should be able to cite details in the text in order to explain and justify their thinking.

In addition to using evidence themselves, students must also be able to identify and interpret an author's use of evidence in the context of an informational text.

They must then learn how to evaluate arguments based on the evidence and claims made in support of those arguments. Students should learn how to identify **supporting details**—the evidence provided by the author to support the main idea. They can then evaluate the reliability of an article by exploring the effectiveness and suitability of the supporting details provided by the author.

An effective teacher might have students first identify the claims of an article, and then look for the evidence the writer includes to substantiate the claim. Evidence can then be evaluated based on its source. Supporting details are often introduced by **signal words** that explain to the reader how one idea is connected to another. Table 5.2. provides a list of some of the most common signal words and their associations.

Table 5.2 Common Signal Words and Their Associations	
Association/Reason for Use	**Signal Words**
Adding information	*additionally, also, in addition, furthermore, too*
Providing an example	*for example, for instance, in other words, in particular*
Showing cause and effect	*because, so, therefore, consequently*
Comparing	*in the same way, like, likewise, similarly*
Contrasting	*alternatively, conversely, instead of, otherwise, unlike*
Providing sequence	*first, second, next, after, before, then, finally*

Students should learn to differentiate between facts and opinions in order to effectively analyze an author's argument:

- **Facts** are based in truth and can usually be proven; they are pieces of information that have been confirmed or validated.
- **Opinions** are judgments, beliefs, or viewpoints that are not based on evidence and are often stated in descriptive, subjective language that is difficult to define or prove.

Students should be aware that, even when reading informational texts, they will have to draw their own inferences in order to fully make sense of what they are reading. Readers draw **inferences** when they use their own knowledge in combination with details from the text to understand the meaning of a sentence, paragraph, or passage.

> **Helpful Hint**:
>
> While opinions can be included in informative texts, they often offer little impact unless they are supported by some kind of evidence.

Practice Question

Question 4 refers to the following passage.

Increasingly, companies are turning to subcontracting services rather than hiring full-time employees. This provides companies with many advantages. For example, subcontractors offer greater flexibility, reduced legal responsibility to employees, and a lower possibility of unionization within the company. However, it has also led to increasing confusion and uncertainty over the legal definition of employment. Recently, the courts have grappled with questions about the hiring company's responsibility in maintaining fair labor practices. Companies argue that they delegate that authority to the subcontractors, while unions and other worker advocate groups argue that companies still have a legal obligation to the workers who contribute to their businesses.

4) According to the passage, which of the following is NOT an advantage of using subcontracting services?
   A. greater flexibility
   B. uncertainty about the legal definition of employment
   C. reduced legal responsibility to employees
   D. lower possibility of unionization within the company

Argumentation

A written argument begins with a proposition, thesis, or assertion that will be defended throughout the work. A set of assumptions may then be established. Next, research and evidence are presented in an organized way; opposing arguments are often mentioned and countered. In learning to evaluate arguments, students should receive plentiful instruction about critical thinking as well as practice on how to use it.

Critical thinking involves asking questions about the quality of reasoning or the validity of beliefs or assumptions. Rather than accepting information as necessarily true, students should be taught to ask questions and formulate responses to arguments presented in any text. Effective teachers provide questions to guide critical thinking:

- What are the conclusions the author is making and what evidence is being provided?
- What assumptions are being made in order for this reasoning to work?
- Is there any fallacious reasoning?
- Is there any deceptive, ambiguous, or omitted information?
- Is the evidence accurate and reliable?
- What other causes or conclusions are possible?

Students must be able to evaluate evidence, identify errors in reasoning, and recognize the rhetorical strategies that are being used in a given piece of informative writing. In evaluating evidence, students should ask questions about its relevancy and reliability. **Evidence relevancy** depends on how closely the evidence is related to the argument and how recently the information was established:

- Evidence must be **representative**, meaning that it speaks directly to the situation or claim being discussed.
- Evidence that is irrelevant or too dated should be viewed with a skeptical eye.

- Evidence must also come from a reliable source, the definition of which will vary depending on the topic and the kind of evidence that is being gathered.

Part of assessing an argument is understanding its logical construction. With **deductive reasoning**, the argument begins with a general statement or premise that is proven. Then, by applying the premise to a set of circumstances, specific conclusions can be drawn. If the initial premise is not valid, the reasoning is not sound or logical.

With **inductive reasoning**, facts are gathered and conclusions are drawn from these facts. If there are enough facts to prove a conclusion, the conclusion is supported. Reasoning breaks down when there is contradictory or incomplete evidence. A **logical fallacy** is an error or breakdown in logical reasoning. Students should learn to recognize logical fallacies in order to evaluate the effectiveness of evidence in informative texts. Some of the most common logical fallacies are discussed in Table 5.3.

Table 5.3. Common Logical Fallacies

Logical Fallacy	Description
Slippery slope	The main argument is based on the assumption that if one particular thing happens, a series of other specific things will follow.
Hasty generalization	An individual comes to a conclusion based on prior experiences or assumptions without enough evidence.
Circular argument	The argument is simply restated repeatedly with no inclusion of new evidence.
Red herring	Distracting information is introduced, moving the focus away from the most important points of the argument.
False analogy	This describes an argument based on an incorrect or misleading analogy.
Non sequitur	This is the introduction of an argument that does not logically flow from the preceding arguments.
False dilemma (either/or **fallacy** or dichotomy **fallacy**)	The argument is constructed so that it appears there are only two possible options from which to choose.
Dichotomous thinking	An argument is set up in dichotomies—pairs of opposing terms (good/evil, true/false)—so that people can only see the extremes of a situation rather than its complexities and subtleties.
Ad hominem fallacy	*Ad hominem* (Latin for "aimed at the man") describes a type of fallacy that focuses on the character or attributes of an opponent or speaker; it appeals to the emotions and prejudices of readers and listeners and ignores the actual focus of the main argument.

Practice Question

5) Which logical fallacy is represented in the argument below?

Why should I care about the corruption on the school board? The property taxes are of far greater concern.
   A. hasty generalization
   B. false analogy
   C. red herring
   D. slippery slope

Rhetorical Strategies

Rhetoric is the powerful use of language and the purposeful expression of ideas meant to command the reader's attention. In rhetoric, a deliberate effort is made to show the connection between points, to relate each point to the central idea, and to use words that will elicit a response from an audience.

In addition to giving careful thought to the words chosen, writers consider how to position words in a sentence in order to make the biggest impact. For example:

- To emphasize a word, a writer might repeat the word and place it at the end of a sentence.

- Parallel sentence construction might be used to accentuate the key facets of an issue.

- Figures of speech may be used to engage the reader's attention and connect new ideas to those that are familiar.

- A series of vivid images may be included to describe events in more detail.

- Writers might also include personal anecdotes to illustrate their points.

In a speech to Americans after the assassination of Martin Luther King Jr., Robert Kennedy said: "We can move in that direction as a country, in greater polarization—Black people amongst Blacks, and White amongst Whites—filled with hatred toward one another. Or we can make an effort, as Martin Luther King did, to understand, and to comprehend, and replace that violence, that stain of bloodshed that has spread across our land, with an effort to understand, compassion, and love."

Kennedy uses several rhetorical strategies to convince his audience to change their approach to the issue of race. He contrasts the words *hate* and *hatred* with the words *love* and *compassion*. He uses a vivid image—the "stain of bloodshed"—to describe the approach of the past. To define the concept of polarization, he repeats the word *understand* and creates a parallel between the verbs *understand*, *comprehend*, and *replace* in order to emphasize his goals for race relations in the United States.

Important Works

"Statement on the Assassination of Martin Luther King, Jr."

Speaker: Robert Kennedy

Date: April 4, 1968

Summary: Kennedy learns of King's assassination after landing in Indianapolis, Indiana, where he planned a campaign stop in a predominantly African American neighborhood in his bid for the Democratic presidential nomination. He realizes that those listening likely had not yet heard of King's assassination. In this impromptu speech, Kennedy explains that there are two paths: one filled with hatred and bitterness and one filled with compassion and love. He notes that he understands loss—having lost his brother to murder—though his brother was killed by a fellow White man. He calls for White and Black Americans to try to understand each other and continue the work that King began. He concedes that the path forward will not be easy, and they must pray for the nation and for the compassion needed to handle such a tragedy without violence or further hatred or divisiveness.

Themes and Rhetorical Strategies: appeals to ethos and pathos, unity, compassion/understanding

To provide **rhetorical support** is to support generalizations, claims, and arguments with examples, details, and other evidence. Because these rhetorical appeals are present in nearly all kinds of informative texts, students should receive significant instruction in, and practice at, identifying various appeals and their purposes in context. In rhetoric, writers can appeal to the audience in three main ways:

- logical appeals (**logos**)
- emotional appeals (**pathos**)
- ethical appeals (**ethos**)

Helpful Hint:

The goal of rhetorical instruction is to equip students with the skills to recognize, interpret, and evaluate rhetoric so that they can make informed decisions that are not clouded by the subtle influences of others.

In Kennedy's speech quoted above, the young politician relies heavily on pathos—emotional appeal—to remind his audience that violence is unnecessary and that compassion and love can overcome it. As consumers of popular media, students need to understand that they do not have to be convinced by rhetoric: they can withhold their judgments and are free to disagree with some or all of what they read or hear. In fact, an audience can appreciate the craft, artistry, or power of a rhetorical text and still choose to not be persuaded by it.

Practice Question

Question 6 refers to the speech "Tribute to the Dog" by George Graham Vest.

The one absolutely unselfish friend that man can have in this selfish world, the one that never deserts him, the one that never proves ungrateful or treacherous is his dog. A man's dog stands by him in prosperity and in poverty, in health and in sickness. He will sleep on the cold ground, where the wintry winds blow and the snow drives fiercely, if only he may be near his master's side. He will kiss the hand that has no food to offer. He will lick the wounds and sores that come in encounters with the roughness of the world. He guards the sleep of his pauper master as if he were a prince. When all other friends desert, he remains. When riches take wings, and reputation falls to pieces, he is as constant in his love as the sun in its journey through the heavens.

6) Which rhetorical device does George Graham Vest use?
  A. humor
  B. pathos
  C. allusion
  D. rhetorical question

Audience Appeal

The principles that guide rhetorical practice rely heavily on a writer's understanding of the audience. To appeal to a particular audience most effectively, a writer must understand the audience's **perspective**—their point of view, frame of reference, position, or attitude toward an idea or occurrence. The writer has to appeal to the audience in ways that will be most appropriate for their unique perspectives.

For example, a congressperson addressing a group of campaign supporters will appeal very differently to that audience as opposed to a congressional committee that the congressperson is trying to persuade. Good writers will select rhetorical strategies that appeal to their desired audiences. For example, the writer may include an expert opinion from an authority whom he knows a particular audience will respect. Writers may also use **testimonials**—statements about the quality or value of a person, idea, or thing. When someone with a good reputation supports something, it strengthens an argument or claim.

> **Helpful Hint**:
>
> An **argument from authority** or **appeal to authority** is a logical fallacy in which a person uses the opinion of an expert to support a claim without providing other evidence.

Students should learn to identify expert opinions and testimonials and the reasons writers might employ these when trying to convince an audience of a particular idea. The language used by the writer should also be crafted to appeal to the technical knowledge of the audience. **Technical language** is related to a specific field of study and has a wide range, from computer technology to mechanics, engineering, and beyond. **Nontechnical language**, however, does not require specialized knowledge. Students should learn to identify technical and nontechnical language in an informative text; these can provide insight into the author's intended purpose and audience.

For example, a scientist writing for a group of peers might rely heavily on technical language since doing so will enhance the scientist's credibility as a professional in the field. On the other hand, if the scientist is writing to a popular audience, technical language might be a hindrance to the reader's understanding and will therefore be left out.

In all cases, students should be aware that writers of informative texts have a heightened awareness of their audiences. This awareness allows them to shape their writing to be most effective for their intended purposes. By considering an author's specific choices, students can likely identify the author's audience and, subsequently, the author's purpose in writing.

Practice Question

Question 7 refers to the following email.

To: All Employees

From: Dennis Frazier, Manager

Date: 08/28/24

Re: Email Communication

This is a reminder of our email policy. Please refrain from sending company-related emails through personal email accounts. Use company-assigned email accounts for all professional correspondence. Please email managers and team leaders about time off at least three days in advance. Last-minute emails or phone calls are not acceptable. Please respond to emails within forty-eight hours, as some are time sensitive. Thank you in advance for helping us all work better together!

7) Who is the intended audience of the memo?
- A. customers
- B. managers
- C. employees
- D. clients

Nonfiction Instructional Strategies

Many of the comprehension strategies discussed in Chapter 3 for literary texts can also be used for nonfiction texts, but there are additional considerations. Nonfiction texts might be less predictable in purpose and structure. For example, **expository texts** aim to teach the reader, or *expose* the reader to something. This means that students are learning something new from a factual perspective while also analyzing the rhetorical techniques used by the author.

Students will encounter nonfiction texts more often than fiction texts both across the curriculum and in their everyday lives. They should therefore be given plenty of strategies for overall comprehension of nonfiction texts. Students must draw connections between the text and what they already know; it is therefore constructive for teachers to help students tap into or activate **background knowledge**. Some effective methods to accomplish this include the following:

- A **brainstorm web** is used by writing the subject of the text in the center and encouraging students to fill in the rest of the web with information they already know about the topic.

- An **ABC brainstorm** can be done in small groups or as a class. Students write one word or phrase they already know about the topic for each letter of the alphabet.

- In **free brainstorm**, students are asked to freely write down (or draw) what they already know about a topic.

Students should be taught to use various annotation strategies and encouraged to mark up the text, write in the margins, or use sticky notes. **Text coding** can help students develop metacognition skills:

- I = I already know this.
- X = This is not what I expected.
- * = This is important.
- ? = I have a question about this.
- ?? = I am really confused by this.
- ! = This is surprising.
- L = I learned something new.
- RR = This section needs to be reread.

Helpful Hint:
Collaborative learning strategies are effective in tackling challenging nonfiction texts. Students can be divided into pairs for reading activities or placed in larger groups where each member works on a different part of the text.

In addition to annotating, students can be prompted to use **systematic note-taking strategies**:

- completing a full or partial outline of the text from a template
- using two-column notes where students put main ideas on one side and important details on the other (known as the **split-page method**, or **two-column method**)
- using the **Cornell method** of note-taking whereby each page is divided into keywords, notes, and a summary (see Figure 5.3)

Finally, students will benefit from a toolbox of fix-up strategies to use when comprehension breaks down. These might be similar to strategies used for fiction texts:

- Students should know when and how to use the glossary in each textbook.
- Students should have access to dictionaries that are appropriate for their ages and skill levels so that they can consult them as needed.
- Students should know to whom to go and how to ask for assistance when they have exhausted all of their independent strategies.

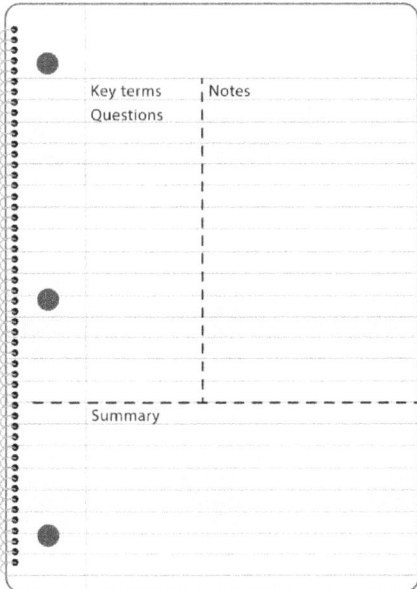

Reading Informational and Argumentative Texts

Practice Question

8) An eighth-grade teacher wants to activate students' background knowledge before reading a nonfiction passage on space exploration. Which of the following activities BEST meets this goal?
  A. asking students to freewrite a story set in outer space with extraterrestrial characters
  B. having students construct a Milky Way galaxy out of construction paper and glitter
  C. asking students to think about careers of the future that may be possible because of space exploration
  D. asking students to write down three things they know about space exploration

Selecting Texts

Finding a balance between the complexity of a text and a student's level of literacy development can be challenging. Many programs recognize this challenge and structure goal-setting and student assessments in a growth-over-time approach. Regardless of the milestones laid out by a school or district, teachers should encourage students to tackle ever-more sophisticated texts as they develop the foundational skills they need to take on new challenges. This, however, does not mean pushing students beyond what they can decode.

Giving students developmentally inappropriate texts may lead to a lack of confidence and less interest in, and enthusiasm for, reading. It can also lead to bad habits, such as guessing at or skipping unfamiliar words instead of trying to decode them or asking for help. Many factors contribute to a text's complexity. In determining appropriateness, educators should evaluate texts based on both qualitative and quantitative measures and their matches to the reader.

Quantitative measurements include anything for which a number can be calculated, such as the following:

- word frequency
- the lengths of words and sentences
- average syllables per word

Helpful Hint:
MetaMetrics also offers Lexile measures for Spanish language texts.

Quantitative measurements can help calculate a range or score that is assigned to a text. For example, MetaMetrics is a company that uses word frequency and sentence length in an equation to yield a score. Scores are assigned to both readers and texts. Scores assigned to readers typically come from standardized tests and measure current levels of reading ability; these are called **reader measures**.

Helpful Hint:
Lexile measures are only effective for texts that follow a typical structure. They are not effective for poetry and drama; these types of texts must be measured for complexity using other methods.

MetaMetrics also assigns Lexile ranges to texts; these are called "Lexile text measures" or "Lexile measures." While these ranges do not have direct correlations to grade levels, educators can use charts created by MetaMetrics and/or a state or district to find the typical Lexile ranges for a given grade.

Table 5.4. Lexile Reader and Text Measures for Grades 1 – 12

Grade Reader Measures, Midyear* 25th to 75th Percentile	Text Measures**
1 BR120L to 295L	190L to 530L
2 170L to 545L	420L to 650L
3 415L to 760L	520L to 820L
4 635L to 950L	740L to 940L
5 770L to 1080L	830L to 1010L
6 855L to 1165L	925L to 1070L
7 925L to 1235L	970L to 1120L
8 985L to 1295L	1010L to 1185L
9 1040L to 1350L	1050L to 1260L
10 1085L to 1400L	1080L to 1335L
11 and 12 1130L to 1440L	1185L to 1385L

NOTES:

*The **Grade Reader Measures, Midyear** column is the typical range of reading ability for students in each grade. These measures are designed to help compare a student's level to a typical range; they are not intended to be standards.

**The Text Measures column describes text measures that have been revised from previous measures to better align with the Common Core State Standards for English Language Arts to ensure that students will meet these standards and be "college and career ready" by the end of high school.

Other metrics for measuring the readability of a text include scales such as the **Flesch-Kincaid Grade Level**, the **Gunning Fog Index**, and the **SMOG Index**. A specific program or school may also use another proprietary tool, such as the **Accelerated Reader Bookfinder** or **Scholastic's Guided Reading Leveling Resource Chart**.

Beyond the quantitative measures are **qualitative measures**, which examine the following types of components of a text and are best evaluated by readers themselves (i.e., not through the use of a formula based on various metrics):

- the layout of the text (illustrations, text size)
- the overall text structure (simple narrative chronology, more advanced argumentative essay)
- sentence structure (prevalence of simple or more complex sentences)
- levels of meaning (whether ideas are communicated explicitly or implicitly)
- knowledge demand (the cultural knowledge or other ideas that the reader must already know)

No single measure of any text, however, can determine appropriateness for all students. For example, Lexile ranges do not account for mature subject matter. Teachers also need to differentiate literacy instruction in the classroom. For whichever strategy a program uses to address individualization of reading instruction, teachers must find just the right level of text complexity where students are challenged but not frustrated. Text complexity is highly individualized and should be matched to the instructional task:

- Texts at the independent reading level (for independent reading) require students to read with 99 percent accuracy and 90 percent comprehension. These are generally texts just "below" a student's reading level.

- Instructional reading level texts are used for teacher-guided instruction and are typically read at 85 percent accuracy with over 75 percent comprehension. These texts are usually "at" the student's reading level.

- Frustration-level texts are those read at less than 85 percent accuracy and less than 50 percent comprehension. These texts are generally "above" a student's reading level and are not recommended. New research, however, suggests that such texts might be effective in paired reading activities with proficient readers.

In addition to selecting texts based on text measures, educators should consider other factors that depend on age. The following questions should guide the selection of texts for students:

- Are texts aligned to instructional goals?
- Are texts at the appropriate level (instructional or independent) for the planned activity?
- Are texts relevant and aligned to student interests?
- Do texts promote deep comprehension or analysis?
- Do texts contain highly specialized or nuanced vocabulary with which students may not be familiar?
- Do texts offer multimodal elements (appealing to different modes of communication such as written text, spoken language, and visual images) that might be relevant for instructional objectives?

When students are self-selecting texts or choosing something to read based on their own interests, they may still need scaffolding from educators. Knowing a student's personality, interests, and independent reading level can be helpful in this regard; however, even independent reading levels can evolve. Some students may seek out and enjoy more challenging texts, while others become frustrated at that level. Knowledge of the individual student should always guide suggestions.

Practice Question

9) What is one disadvantage of relying on Lexile level as the sole indicator of text appropriateness?
    A. It is only applicable to students whose first language is English.
    B. It fails to account for qualitative text features.
    C. It does not encourage the reading of rigorous texts.
    D. It can only be used to measure fiction texts.

Answer Key

1) B: Supporting text evidence is key to confirming both the author's purpose as well as answers on the SAT/ACT.

2) A: Emerson begins by making a general assertion about language and then goes on to provide specific examples of words that support his assertion.

3) B: The author states, "Ignored by the government, an activist group known as 'Indians of All Tribes' sailed to Alcatraz in the early morning hours with eighty-nine men, women, and children." The author goes on to describe the nineteen-month occupation of the island.

4) B: Options A, C, and D are listed as advantages of using subcontracting services (introduced after the signal words *for example*). Uncertainly about the legal definition of employment is given later as one of the disadvantages of using subcontracting services.

5) C: This is a red herring—a totally unrelated issue is being brought up.

6) B: The author is using pathos to appeal to the audience's feelings of love and appreciation toward devoted dogs.

7) C: The memo addresses "All Employees" in the heading segment.

8) D: Having students write down what they already know about the topic (in this case, space exploration) will help them retrieve background information to set them up for more successful comprehension of the passage.

9) B: Lexile measures only account for quantitative text features like word and sentence lengths; they do not measure content, knowledge demands, and so on.

Composition

At its most basic level—the sentence—the use of effective language is essential to effective communication. Beyond these basics, however, students must spend a significant amount of time both inside and outside of school developing the writing, speaking, and listening skills that will allow them to succeed in the adult world. An ELA classroom emphasizes building students' written communication skills, which extend far beyond the basics of grammar and vocabulary: producing meaningful writing is a task that requires extensive planning and revising.

The Recursive Writing Process

Students should understand that writing is a process—even professional writers put their work through several phases before releasing their finished products. A **recursive writing process** means that writers may return to a previously completed part of the process. Also known as the **authoring cycle**, this process includes several phases in which ideas are transformed into written form to effectively communicate meaning:

1. **Phase one:** plan
2. **Phase two:** draft
3. **Phase three:** revise
4. **Phase four:** edit
5. **Phase five:** publish

The first step in planning is to **brainstorm** ideas; this can take many forms. For example, teachers might have the class generate ideas for topics and write them on the board or screen. Students can then create their own **webs** or **outlines** to organize their ideas. This initial planning can help students formulate their overall points and supporting details. If students struggle with the outline format, graphic organizers are useful tools for helping students understand text organization visually.

Brainstorming activities can be based on a book the students have read; their opinions of the work; (e.g., "I liked the book," "I did not like the book," "My favorite/least favorite part was …"); and the reasons for their opinions. Students might also write a simple expository piece that introduces a topic and then uses supporting details to inform the reader. Brainstorming activities can also help students organize the events they want to describe when writing narratives.

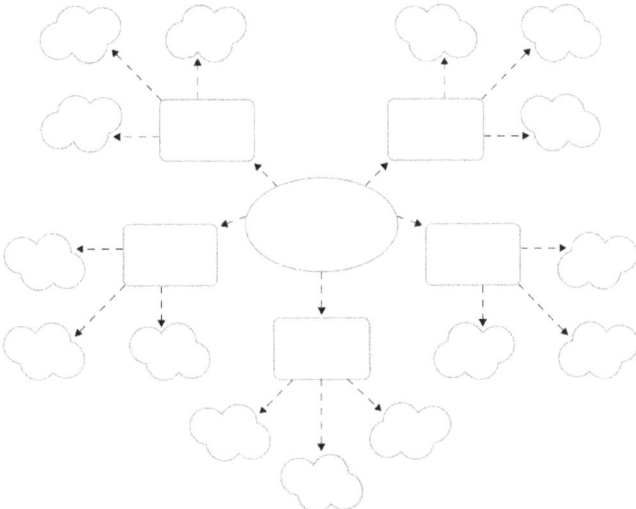

After brainstorming, students **draft** their pieces and connect their ideas with an introductory statement followed by the supporting and concluding sections. A **thesis statement** (discussed in greater detail in the next section) is central to the structure and meaning of an essay: it uses a one- or two-sentence statement to present the writer's argument or position on an issue. With scaffolding, students then go through a **revision** process where they address weaknesses in the writing, such as adding more details to support the thesis, or connecting words (*because, also, then*) to improve clarity. Students can then edit for capitalization, punctuation, and spelling.

I. The first paragraph introduces the reader to the topic (e.g., *Cats make better pets than dogs.*).
   A. An anecdote may get a reader's attention; here, the writer could relate a personal story about an experience with a dog or a cat.
   B. Thesis statement: While dogs are loyal and protective, cats are smarter, more affordable, independent, and cuter, so they make better pets.
II. Cats are smarter than dogs.
   A. Dogs often get sick from eating foreign objects, incurring costly vet bills; cats rarely eat such items.
   B. If dogs are left outside alone, they may get lost and are at risk of injury or death due to traffic; cats are able to protect themselves better and almost always find their way home.
III. Cats are easier to care for than dogs.
   A. Cats are smaller and lazier; they do not require walks.
   B. Cats can be left alone for several days with ample food, water, and litter; dogs require daily attention and thus a dog sitter.
IV. Cats are more pleasant to live with than dogs.
   A. Cats have softer fur and are therefore cuddlier.
   B. Cats are quieter than dogs; they meow, while dogs bark.
V. The final paragraph concludes the essay and discusses the broad implications of the issue.
   A. Restatement of Thesis: Even though dog ownership has many benefits, the convenience, affordability, and enjoyment cats offer make them the superior pet.
   B. With so much to offer, cats will surely become even more popular than they are today.

Teachers can also use **peer and teacher feedback** as part of the revision process. Receiving feedback helps students understand that the main purpose of writing is to communicate ideas; having other readers offer their perceptions and suggestions is therefore an important part of revision.

Students should **publish** their work after the final copy is created, particularly if the writing project is significant in scope. Having students read their work aloud is one simple and immediate way to publish a piece (as well as a way to link reading and writing), as is posting the written work on a classroom or school bulletin board. Teachers may have students organize and bind their work into a simple book using string or fasteners, or they may collect student work into a class-wide literary sampler.

> **Helpful Hint**:
>
> Teachers can support students in the revision process by giving them a simple checklist to help ensure they have met certain criteria. One such checklist is the **COPS mnemonic**, which stands for **C**apitalization, **O**rganization, **P**unctuation, and **S**pelling.

If a teacher uses student portfolios in the classroom, students can prepare their pieces for inclusion in a digital or physical folder. This may involve transcribing the piece digitally, adding illustrations, or matting it on construction paper.

Teachers should also emphasize that sharing work with others is an important part of publishing. This is also a great way to build a connection between home and school: students should be encouraged to share their work with parents or guardians. Teachers should also show student work samples or portfolios at parent conferences to further build the home-school connection.

Practice Question

1) A high school English teacher sponsors a creative writing club that meets weekly after school. He asks the reading specialist for advice on a high-impact way to publish student work and share it with the school community. What should the specialist suggest?
   A. invite administrators to attend one of the club meetings and listen to students read their work
   B. encourage students to read their pieces at home to their family members
   C. plan a digital or print literary journal that can be shared across the school
   D. teach students to use publishing and graphic design software to format their pieces

Organizing Writing

All students should know how to develop a thesis statement and organize their nonfiction writing to include an introduction, body, and conclusion. The **thesis**, or **thesis statement**, is central to the structure and meaning of an essay: it presents the writer's argument or position on an issue, concisely packaged into a one- or two-sentence statement. A strong, direct thesis statement is key to the organization of any essay and introduces its central idea and the main points that will be used to support that idea.

> **PROMPT:** Many high schools have begun to adopt 1:1 technology programs, meaning that each school provides every student with a computing device, such as a laptop or tablet. Educators who support these initiatives say that the technology allows for more dynamic collaboration and that students need to learn technology skills to compete in the job market. On the other hand, opponents cite increased distraction and the dangers of cyberbullying or unsupervised internet use as reasons not to provide students with such devices.

In your essay, take a position on this question. You may write about either one of the two points of view given, or you may present a different point of view on this question. Use specific reasons and examples to support your position.

Possible Thesis Statements

1) Providing technology to every student is good for education because it allows students to learn important skills such as typing, web design, and video editing; it also gives students more opportunities to work cooperatively with their classmates and teachers.

2) I disagree with the idea that schools should provide technology to students because most students will simply be distracted by the free access to games and websites when they should be studying or doing homework.

3) By providing each student with a laptop or tablet, schools can help students apply technology to work more effectively with other students, communicate with teachers and classmates, and conduct research for class projects.

The purpose of an **introduction** is to set the stage for the essay. This is accomplished by capturing the reader's interest, introducing and providing context for the topic, and stating the central idea and main points of the essay. Usually, the introductory paragraph ends with a thesis statement.

Introduction Example

Technology has changed massively in recent years, but today's generation barely notices—high school students are already experienced with the internet, computers, apps, cameras, cell phones, and more. It is inevitable that these technologies will begin to make their way into classrooms. Opponents of 1:1 technology programs might argue that students will be distracted or misuse the technology, but that is exactly why schools must teach them to use it. Students need to know how to navigate technology safely and effectively, and schools have a responsibility to ensure they learn these skills. By providing each student with a laptop or tablet, schools can help students learn how to apply technology to work more effectively with other students, communicate with teachers and classmates, and conduct research for class projects.

The **body** of the essay should consist of paragraphs that present the details that support the main idea. Each paragraph should be structurally consistent, beginning with a topic sentence to introduce the main idea, followed by supporting ideas and examples. No extra ideas unrelated to the paragraph's focus should appear. Transition words and phrases can be used to connect body paragraphs and improve the flow and readability of the essay.

Body Paragraph Example

Technology can be a powerful tool for collaboration. When all of the students in a classroom have access to reliable laptops or tablets, they are able to share information and work together on projects more effectively. Students can communicate quickly via email, share files through a cloud service, and use a shared calendar for scheduling. They also have the opportunity to teach each other new skills since each student may bring to the group unique knowledge about particular apps or programs. When the availability of technology is limited or inconsistent, these opportunities are lost.

Composition

To end an essay smoothly, the author must compose a conclusion that reminds the reader of the importance of the topic and then restates the essay's thesis and supporting details. The writer should revisit the ideas in the introduction and thesis statement, but these ideas should not be simply repeated word-for-word. Rather, a well-written conclusion will reinforce the argument using wording that differs from the thesis statement but conveys the same idea. The conclusion should provide the essay with a sense of closure and leave the reader with a strong impression of its main idea.

> **Helpful Hint:**
>
> The acronym **RENNS** can be used to recall the kinds of details that writers can use to support their main ideas: **R**easons, **E**xamples, **N**ames, **N**umbers, and **S**enses. By varying the types of details they use, writers can make text more interesting and convincing.

Conclusion Example

As technology continues to change and become more incorporated into everyday life, students will need to adapt to it. Schools already teach young people myriad academic and life skills, so it makes sense that they would also teach students how to use technology appropriately. When technology is incorporated into schoolwork, students will learn to collaborate, communicate, and research more effectively. Providing students with their own devices is one part of this important task, and schools that do so should be supported.

Practice Question

2) What is the purpose of a thesis statement?
   A. to effectively conclude an essay
   B. to summarize the supporting details of an argument
   C. to present the writer's main argument
   D. to introduce the topic of an essay

Writing Well

In addition to learning how to craft an argument, students should learn how to effectively use language to present their ideas. Writing well means that the language and tone are appropriate for the purpose and audience of the writing task, the flow of ideas and the relationships among them are logical and clear, and the sentences are varied enough to keep the reader interested.

Transitions are words and phrases that help connect ideas throughout a text between sentences and paragraphs. They can be used to imply a range of relationships, including cause and effect, sequence, contradictions, and continuance of an idea. The consistent and creative use of transitions helps essays flow logically from one idea to the next and will make the content easier for the reader to follow.

Table 6.1. Transitional Expressions

Meaning	Expressions
Addition	*and, furthermore, moreover, too, also, in addition, next, besides, first, second*
Contrast	*although, in contrast, but, conversely, nevertheless, however, on the contrary, on the other hand*

Table 6.1. Transitional Expressions

Meaning	Expressions
Time	*later, earlier, when, while, soon, thereafter, meanwhile, whenever, during, now, until now, subsequently*
Location	*nearby, adjacent to, beyond, above, below*
Comparison	*similarly, in the same manner, in like manner, likewise*
Cause	*because, since, on account of, for that reason*
Illustration	*specifically, for instance, for example*
Effect	*therefore, consequently, accordingly, as a result*
Summation	*in summary, in brief, to sum up*
Conclusion	*in conclusion, finally*
Referring back to an object or idea	*this, that, these, those* (The pronoun reference must be clear and near the antecedent to avoid a pronoun reference error.)
To replace a noun	Use personal pronouns for coherence to avoid unnecessary redundancies.

Varied syntax is an important component of good writing. A variety of well-written sentences helps maintain the reader's interest in the essay. Writers should use sentences that differ in length and begin with varying words, rather than repeating the same word at the start of each new sentence. It is also important for writers to use a mix of different sentence structures, including simple, complex, compound, and compound-complex sentences.

Teachers should instruct students on how to choose words and tone that are appropriate to the task. For instance, a formal essay on an academic topic may benefit from complex sentences and an expansive vocabulary. On the other hand, a first-person essay on a personal topic may use more casual organization and vocabulary. Students should also be instructed to use clear, direct vocabulary and avoid using vague, general words (e.g., *good, bad, very,* or *a lot*). While varied word choice can help improve an essay, it is better to use more familiar vocabulary than to try to impress the reader with unfamiliar words or those that do not fit the context of the essay.

Overwriting occurs when writers try to imbue their work with inappropriate and awkwardly ornate language or complex, technical terms. Not only might this kind of writing seem disingenuous to the audience, but it will also likely become difficult to follow.

> **Helpful Hint**:
>
> Transitions between paragraphs can be polished by starting paragraphs with references to ideas mentioned previously in the text or by concluding them with a transition to the next topic, which helps guide the reader from one paragraph to the next.

Practice Questions

Use the following text to answer questions 3 – 5.

(1) For centuries, artists and philosophers have long debated about the relationship between life and art. (2) While some argue that art is an imitation of life, others believe that, just as often, life ends up imitating art. (3) In no other genre is the impact of art on our real lives more visible than in the realm of science fiction. (4) Great minds of science fiction, such as Jules Verne; Gene Roddenberry; H.G. Wells; and Stanley Kubrick have introduced ideas that, though fantastical at the time of their inception, eventually became reality. (5) Many of these artists were dead before they ever saw their ideas come to life. (6) Some of humanity's biggest accomplishments were achieved first in science fiction. (7) Jules Verne wrote about humanity traveling to the moon over a century before it happened. (8) Scientists Robert H. Goddard and Leo Szilard both credit his work—on liquid-fueled rockets and atomic power, respectively—to the futuristic novels of H.G. Wells. (9) Gene Roddenberry, the creator of Star Trek, dreamed up replicators long before 3-D printers were invented. (10) Jules Verne's work, for example, was the inspiration for both the submarine and the modern-day helicopter. (11) H.G. Wells wrote about automatic doors long before they began to turn up in almost every grocery store in America. (12) Roddenberry's Star Trek is even credited as the inspiration for the creation of the mobile phone. (13) Kubrick's HAL from *2001: A Space Odyssey* represents voice control at its finest, long before virtual assistants were installed in all the new smartphone models.

3) In context, which of the following is the BEST version of the underlined portion of sentence (1), which is reproduced below?

. . . artists and philosophers have long debated about the relationship between life and art.
  . . . artists and philosophers have examined the facts and debated about the relationship between life and art.
  . . . artists and philosophers have hemmed, hawed, and debated about the relationship between life and art.
  . . . artists and philosophers have debated about the relationship between life and art.
  . . . artists and philosophers have hemmed and hawed about the relationship between life and art.

4) Which of the following introductory phrases should be inserted at the beginning of sentence (6), which is reproduced below?

Some of humanity's biggest accomplishments were achieved first in science fiction.
   A. Therefore,
   B. In fact,
   C. However,
   D. In addition,

5) In context, which of the following would provide the BEST introduction to the final paragraph?
   A. Transportation was of particular concern to science fiction writers, who dreamed up new ways for humanity to get around the world.
   B. These same authors had other interesting ideas as well.
   C. Sometimes science fiction is so much like life it is incredible.
   D. Many of the ideas life borrows from science fiction have infiltrated our everyday lives and our world to an even greater degree.

Strategies for Writing Instruction

Research concerning writing instruction has resulted in a number of empirically tested, outcome-driven strategies that ELA teachers employ to continuously teach and assess their students. Some of the most commonly practiced strategies are described below.

Writing workshop is an approach that integrates instruction, practice, and assessment in a consistent, daily schedule:

- Writing workshop time is first signaled by a particular sound, image, announcement, or environmental change.
- The teacher then provides a mini-lesson on a particular skill or segment of the writing process (beginning with idea generation and ending with publication and celebration).
- Next, students have time to work on their writing independently or in small groups while the teacher circulates to conduct one-on-one and small group conferences.
- Finally, students share their work from the day, especially if they have applied knowledge from the mini-lesson.

Writing teachers might also employ models or modeling in their instruction. **Models** are exemplary examples of writing, which the teacher uses to highlight certain qualities or characteristics. Students view and discuss the model and then attempt to apply this knowledge to their own writing. The teacher may also model a particular skill by practicing it, along with the thought process, aloud in front of students.

Collaborative writing is especially useful when students—or the entire class—are new to a particular skill or process and may lack confidence. Collaborative writing occurs when partners or small groups of students work together to complete the full writing process or segments of it. This strategy allows students to share ideas and build confidence; it also provides an avenue by which students can practice how to review writing and provide feedback. Process writing involves teaching students a clear process for writing and how to use techniques and strategies for completing each part of the process. The writing process typically includes the following steps:

- planning (brainstorming, outlining, mapping)
- drafting (writing)
- revising (adding and deleting, rewriting, reorganizing)
- editing (editing and proofreading)

Teachers can also use specific activities and exercises to help students develop strong writing skills throughout the writing process. Some of these strategies are discussed in the "Planning" section below and grouped by their stage in the writing process.

Planning and Drafting

Data dump is an informal prewriting method. Students write down a topic and then any words that immediately come to mind. For example, a student might write the word *environmentalism* and then list terms like *climate change*, *pollution*, and *endangered animals*. After a data dump, students select only the words that most closely pertain to their chosen topic.

In **guided prewriting**, the class (or a group of students) comes up with ideas and/or a writing structure. The teacher helps by visually projecting ideas or writing them on a board. Mapping, outlining, webbing, and listing are common strategies for guided prewriting. **RAFT** is a prewriting method that encourages students to consider their purpose, audience, and organization pattern. Students think about the following questions:

- **R**ole of writer: What perspective will you, as the writer, take?
- **A**udience: Who will read the piece?
- **F**ormat: How will you communicate your message (story, essay, drama, and so forth)?
- **T**opic: What will you write about?

Media or tech-enabled planning involves students watching a video, looking at images, or searching for ideas online. This can be a useful strategy for students who are stuck or who do not have an opinion on an issue or a clear topic to write about.

Framed paragraphs, a type of scaffolding technique, are fill-in-the-blank templates used to help students write paragraphs. For example, an "empty" frame for a persuasive paragraph might look something like this:

I think that _____. The first reason I think this is because _____.
The second reason I think this is because _____. Lastly, I
believe that _____. For these reasons, _____ should _____.

Paragraph or essay hamburgers encourage students to plan a paragraph or essay with the topic sentence or introduction as the top "bun" and the concluding sentence or concluding paragraph as the bottom "bun." The supporting details, or body paragraphs, are the middle parts of the "hamburger."

Shared or interactive writing is a process in which writers are scaffolded by "experts," usually teachers. In shared writing, the teacher scribes for the students, who must give explicit direction concerning what to write. This can be an effective method for students who have difficulty with the physical task of writing. In interactive writing, students compose the written piece, but the teacher serves as the subject matter expert who facilitates the process. Both shared and interactive writing processes help students see and participate in an effective model for writing, which can give them confidence and strategies to use in independent writing assignments. In both methods, the teacher helps scaffold learning as needed. This might involve the following:

- asking leading questions ("What should happen after_____?")
- offering ideas for transitions or breaks ("Let's start our next sentence with 'Additionally,'")
- providing more explicit instruction to reinforce concepts ("Now, we need to add supporting details. What supporting details can we add?")

Practice Question

6) Ms. Johnson wants to teach a simple introduction to the process of revising for coherence by adding transitional words and phrases. Which instructional method would be the MOST appropriate?
   A. collaborative writing
   B. writing workshop
   C. process writing
   D. modeling

Revision and Editing

Modeling or **think-alouds** can be used with a sample piece, which can be authored by the teacher or a student (with the student's permission and name removed as requested), and should involve whole-class input. The piece can be projected on a screen and edited through a "track changes" feature in a word processing program or even copied onto a transparency and written on. Teachers can encourage input from the class and model strategies to revise writing, such as reading aloud, identifying and refining thesis and topic sentences, and so on. This process is helpful since it allows students to participate in and experience the revision and editing processes.

Conferencing or **peer review** can also be used after first modeling the process and then providing guidelines to students. Research proves that the most successful writing conferences are structured and occur when students have a clear idea of what type of feedback they should provide and how to give feedback in a constructive way. **Self-assessment** should also be taught as part of the revision process: students can be given a checklist or rubric from which to assess their own drafts and make necessary revisions.

Practice Question

7) A ninth-grade student has completed a data dump prewriting exercise with the topic of "autonomous vehicles." What should she do NEXT?
   A. use her word list to prepare an outline
   B. think of synonyms for each of the words
   C. draft her essay using all the words
   D. select the best words from the list

Rules and Guidelines of English Language Usage

The importance of verbal communication skills cannot be overstated: email communication, professional reports, court documents, business memos, and all other forms of written correspondence require a certain level of language expertise in order to be most effective.

While the many rules and guidelines of English language usage may be challenging for writers, the study of these structures can increase confidence in verbal communication—a benefit that will extend to nearly all areas of life.

Grammar

Grammar refers to the structures and systems that make up a language. The parts of speech play unique roles in the context of a sentence and are the building blocks of sentences, paragraphs, and entire texts. Though some words fall easily into one category or another, many can function as different parts of speech based on their usage within a sentence. There are eight parts of speech that are typically defined by grammarians:

- nouns
- pronouns
- verbs
- adverbs
- adjectives
- conjunctions
- prepositions
- interjections

> **Helpful Hint**:
>
> **Prescriptivism** encourages language usage that observes grammatical correctness and adheres strictly to time-honored rules. Descriptivism argues that language should be taught in a way that mirrors how it is used in a day-to-day social context.

Syntax is the study of how words are combined to create sentences. In English, words are used to build phrases and clauses, which are combined to create sentences. By varying the order and length of phrases and clauses, writers can create sentences that are diverse and interesting. The term *mechanics* describes those rules that govern the minutiae of written English: punctuation, capitalization, and spelling. **Usage conventions** guide writers and speakers more broadly in the area of word choice to ensure accuracy and agreement within a sentence.

Practice Question

8) Which term BEST describes the rules that govern the finer details of written English?
   A. grammar
   B. mechanics
   C. usage conventions
   D. syntax

Nouns and Pronouns

Nouns are people, places, or things; the subject of a sentence is typically a noun. For example, in the sentence "The hospital was very clean," the subject, *hospital*, is a noun because it is a place. Nouns can be divided into many categories:

- common nouns (*chair, car, house*)
- proper nouns (*Julie, David*)
- abstract nouns (*love, intelligence, sadness*)
- concrete nouns (*paper clip, bread, person*)
- compound nouns (*brother-in-law, roller coaster, toothpaste*)
- noncountable nouns (*money, water*)
- countable nouns (*dollars, cubes*)
- verbal nouns (*writing, diving*)

Pronouns stand in for nouns and can be used to make sentences sound less repetitive. For example, in the sentence, "Sam stayed home from school because Sam was not feeling well," the name *Sam* appears twice in the same sentence. Instead of repeating the name *Sam*, the author can use the pronoun *he*:

Sam stayed home from school because <u>he</u> was not feeling well.

Based on their roles in a sentence, pronouns can be divided into different categories, as described in Table 6.2.

Table 6.2. Categories of Pronouns

Category	Function	Example
Personal pronouns	act as subjects or objects in a sentence	<u>She</u> received a letter.
Possessive pronouns	indicate possession	The car is <u>mine</u>.
Reflexive/intensive pronouns	intensify a noun or reflect back upon a noun	I made the dessert <u>myself</u>.

Table 6.3. Personal, Possessive, and Reflexive/Intensive Pronouns

Case	First Person		Second Person		Third Person	
	singular	plural	singular	plural	singular	plural
Subject	*I*	*we*	*you*	*you (all)*	*he, she, it*	*they*
Object	*me*	*us*	*you*	*you (all)*	*him, her, it*	*them*
Possessive	*mine*	*ours*	*yours*	*yours*	*his, her, its*	*theirs*
Reflexive/intensive	*myself*	*ourselves*	*yourself*	*yourselves*	*himself, herself, itself*	*themselves*

Composition

Relative pronouns begin dependent clauses. Like other pronouns, they may appear in subject or object case, depending on the clause:

Charlie, <u>who</u> made the clocks, works in the basement.

Table 6.4. Relative Pronouns

Pronoun Type	Subject	Object
Person	*who*	*whom*
Thing	*which, that*	*which, that*
Possessive	*whose*	*whose*

Interrogative pronouns begin questions:

<u>Who</u> worked last evening?

Table 6.5. Interrogative Pronouns

Interrogative Pronoun	Example
Who	<u>Who</u> lives there?
Whom	To <u>whom</u> shall I send the letter?
What	<u>What</u> is your favorite color?
Where	<u>Where</u> do you go to school?
When	<u>When</u> will we meet for dinner?
Which	<u>Which</u> movie would you like to see?
Why	<u>Why</u> are you going to be late?
How	<u>How</u> did the ancient Egyptians build the pyramids?

Demonstrative pronouns (*this, that, these, those*) point out or draw attention to something or someone. They can also indicate proximity or distance:

<u>This</u> is my apartment

Give <u>those</u> to me later.

Because pronouns take the place of nouns, they need to agree in number with the noun they replace.

The <u>teachers</u> are going to have a pizza party for <u>their</u> students.

Traditionally, pronouns must also agree in gender with the noun they are replacing; however, this rule has become less stringent in recent years as ideas about gender identification continue to shift. The intentional use of *they* when referring to a singular noun is becoming more commonplace and accepted. Alternatively, sentences can be rewritten to avoid the use of gender-specific pronouns.

Traditional: If a student forgets his or her homework, he or she will not receive a grade.

Use of singular *they*: If a student forgets their homework, they will not receive a grade.

Rewritten with a plural antecedent: Students who forget their homework will not receive a grade.

Pronouns should also be used carefully to avoid ambiguity in sentences. In the example below, it is unclear to whom the pronoun *she* refers. The sentence needs to be rewritten for clarity:

Incorrect: After the teacher spoke to the student, she realized her mistake.

Correct: After Mr. White spoke to the student, she realized her mistake.

(*She* and *her* refer to the student.)

Correct: After speaking to the student, the teacher realized her own mistake.

(*Her* refers to the teacher.)

Practice Questions

Questions 9 and 10 refer to the following sentence:

I have lived in Minnesota since August, but I still don't own a warm coat or gloves.

9) Which list includes all of the nouns in the above sentence?
   A. coat, gloves
   B. I, coat, gloves
   C. Minnesota, August, coat, gloves
   D. I, Minnesota, August, warm, coat, gloves

10) In which of the following sentences do the nouns and pronouns NOT agree?
    A. After we walked inside, we took off our hats and shoes and hung them in the closet.
    B. The members of the band should leave her instruments in the rehearsal room.
    C. The janitor on duty should rinse out his or her mop before leaving for the day.
    D. When you see people in trouble, you should always try to help them.

Verbs

Helpful Hint:

Helping verbs include: *is, am, are, was, were; be, being, been; has, had, have; do, does, did; should, would, could; will*.

Verbs express action (*run, jump, play*) or states of being (*is, seems*). Verbs can stand alone, or they can be accompanied by helping verbs, which are used to indicate tense. **Verb tense** indicates the time of the action. The action may have happened in the past, may be occurring in the present, or might take place in the future. The action may have been **simple** (occurring once) or **continuous** (ongoing). The **perfect tense** and the **perfect continuous tense** describe when actions occur in relation to other actions.

Table 6.6. Verb Tenses

Tense	Past	Present	Future
Simple	I answered the question.	I answer your questions in class.	I will answer your question.
Continuous	I was answering your question when you interrupted me.	I am answering your question; please listen.	I will be answering your question after the lecture.

Composition

Table 6.6. Verb Tenses

Tense	Past	Present	Future
Perfect	I had answered all questions before class ended.	I have answered the questions already.	I will have answered every question before the class is over.
Perfect continuous	I had been answering questions when the students started leaving.	I have been answering questions for thirty minutes and am getting tired.	I will have been answering students' questions for twenty years by the time I retire.

Changing the spelling of a verb and/or adding helping verbs is called **conjugation**. In addition to tense, verbs are conjugated to indicate person. **Person** describes the relationship of the speaker to the subject of the sentence:

- first (*I*, *we*)
- second (*you*)
- third (*he*, *she*, *it*, *they*)

Number refers to whether the subject of the sentence is singular or plural. Verbs are conjugated to match the person and number of the subject; the conjugation of the verb must therefore agree with the subject of the sentence. A verb that has not been conjugated is called an **infinitive** and begins with the word *to* (*to swim*, *to be*).

Table 6.7. Verb Conjugation (Present Tense)

Person	Singular	Plural
First person	I answer	we answer
Second person	you answer	you (all) answer
Third person	he/she/it answers	they answer

Sometimes, the subject and verb are separated by clauses or phrases. In the example below, the subject *cars* is separated from the verb by the relatively long phrase "that had been recalled by the manufacturer," making it more difficult to determine how to correctly conjugate the verb:

Incorrect: The cars that had been recalled by the manufacturer <u>was</u> returned within a few months.

Correct: The cars that had been recalled by the manufacturer *were* returned within a few months.

Verbs can also be classified by whether they take a **direct object**, which is a noun that receives the action of the verb. **Transitive verbs** require a direct object. In the sentence below, the transitive verb *throw* has a direct object (the ball):

The pitcher will throw <u>the ball</u>.

Intransitive verbs do not require a direct object. Verbs like *run*, *jump*, and *go* make sense without any object:

He will run.

Many sets of similar verbs include one transitive and one intransitive verb, which can cause confusion. Some troublesome verb combinations include *lie/lay*, *rise/raise*, and *sit/set*. The exam may test your understanding of these. Some commonly confused intransitive and transitive verbs are listed in Table 6.8.

Table 6.8. Intransitive and Transitive Verbs

Intransitive Verbs	Transitive Verbs
lie: to recline	lay: to put (lay something)
rise: to go or get up	raise: to lift (raise something)
sit: to be seated	set: to put (set something)
Intransitive Verbs	**Transitive Verbs**
Hint: These intransitive verbs have *i* as the second letter. The word *intransitive* begins with *i*.	Hint: The word *transitive* begins with a *t*, and it takes an object.

Practice Questions

11) Which of the following sentences contains an incorrectly conjugated verb?
    A. The brother and sister runs very fast.
    B. Neither Anne nor Suzy likes the soup.
    C. The mother and father love their new baby.
    D. Either Jack or Jill will pick up the pizza.

12) Which of the following sentences contains an incorrect verb tense?
    A. After the show ended, we drove to the restaurant for dinner.
    B. Anne went to the mall before she headed home.
    C. Johnny went to the movies after he cleans the kitchen.
    D. Before the alarm sounded, smoke filled the cafeteria.

Adjectives and Adverbs

Adjectives modify, or describe, nouns and pronouns. In English, adjectives are usually placed before the word they modify, although they can also come after a linking verb such as *is* or *smells*:

The <u>beautiful blue</u> jade necklace will go perfectly with my dress.

I think that lasagna smells <u>delicious</u>.

The suffixes *–er* and *–est* are used to modify adjectives in a comparison. The suffix *–er* is used when comparing two things, and the suffix *–est* is used when comparing more than two items:

Anne is taller than Steve, but Steve is more coordinated.

Of the five brothers, Jordan is the funniest, and Alex is the most intelligent.

Composition

Adjectives longer than two syllables are compared using *more* (for two things) or *most* (for three or more things). *More* and *most* should not be used with *–er* and *–est* endings. For example:

Incorrect: Of my two friends, Clara is the smartest.

Correct: Of my two friends, Clara is smarter.

Incorrect: My most warmest sweater is made of wool.

Correct: My warmest sweater is made of wool.

Adverbs, which are often formed by adding the suffix *–ly*, modify any word (or set of words) that is not a noun or pronoun:

Adverbs typically answer the following questions:

- Where?
- When?
- Why?
- How?
- How often?
- To what extent?
- Under what conditions?

He quickly ran to the house next door.

(*Quickly* modifies the verb *ran*.)

Practice Questions

13) Which list includes all of the adjectives used in the following sentence?

The new chef carefully stirred the boiling soup and then lowered the heat.
- A. new, boiling
- B. new, carefully, boiling
- C. new, carefully, boiling, heat
- D. new, carefully, boiling, lowered, heat

14) Which of the following sentences contains an adjective error?
- A. The new red car was faster than the old blue car.
- B. Reggie's apartment is in the tallest building on the block.
- C. The slice of cake was tastier than the brownie.
- D. Of the four speeches, Jerry's was the most long.

Other Parts of Speech

Prepositions set up relationships in time ("*after* the party") or space ("*under* the cushions") in a sentence. A preposition will always function as part of a **prepositional phrase**, which includes the preposition and the object of the preposition:

I ran <u>over the river</u> and <u>*through* the woods</u>.

Table 6.9. Common Prepositions	
Prepositions	**Compound Prepositions**
along, among, around, at, before, behind, below, beneath, beside, besides, between, beyond, by, despite, down, during, except, for, from, in, into, near, of, off, on, onto, out, outside, over, past, since, through, till, to, toward, under, underneath, until, up, upon, with, within, without	according to, as of, as well as, aside from, because of, by means of, in addition to, in front of, in place of, in respect to, in spite of, instead of, on account of, out of, prior to, with regard to

Conjunctions join words to phrases, clauses, and sentences. There are three main types of conjunctions: coordinating, correlative, and subordinating. **Coordinating conjunctions** join together two independent clauses (complete thoughts). These can be remembered using the acronym *FANBOYS*:

- **F**or
- **A**nd
- **N**or
- **B**ut
- **O**r
- **Y**et
- **S**o

The following sentences use coordinating conjunctions:

> I will order lunch, <u>but</u> you need to go pick it up.

> Make sure to get sandwiches, chips, <u>and</u> sodas.

Correlative conjunctions (*whether/or, either/or, neither/nor, both/and, not only/but also*) work together to join items:

> <u>Both</u> the teacher <u>and</u> the students needed a break after the lecture.

Subordinating conjunctions join dependent clauses—thoughts that cannot stand alone as sentences—to the related independent clause. They usually describe a relationship between the two parts of the sentence, such as cause-effect or order and can appear at the beginning or in the middle of a sentence:

> We treat ourselves during football season to several orders <u>because</u> we love pizza.

> <u>Because</u> we love pizza, we treat ourselves during football season to several orders.

Composition

Table 6.10. Subordinating Conjunctions	
Time	after, as, as long as, as soon as, before, since, until, when, whenever, while
Manner	as, as if, as though
Cause	because
Condition	although, as long as, even if, even though, if, provided that, though, unless, while
Purpose	in order that, so that, that
Comparison	as, than

Helpful Hint:

A preposition acts as an adverb when it provides more information about a verb: *Several days ago, we took the turkey bones <u>outside</u> because of the smelly garbage.* Here, the preposition explains where the bones were taken.

Interjections, like *wow* and *hey*, express emotion and are most commonly used in conversation and casual writing. They have no grammatical attachments to the sentence other than to add expressions of emotion. They may be punctuated with commas or exclamation points and may appear anywhere in a sentence. For example:

<u>Ouch</u>! He stepped on my toe.

Practice Questions

Choose the word that BEST completes the sentence.

15) Her love _____ blueberry muffins kept her coming back to the bakery every week.
    A. to
    B. with
    C. of
    D. about

16) Christine left her house early on Monday morning, _____ she was still late for work.
    A. but
    B. and
    C. for
    D. or

Syntax

In English, words are used to build phrases and clauses, which are then combined to create sentences. Phrases and clauses are made up of a subject, a predicate, or both:

- The **subject** is what the sentence is about. It is usually a noun that performs the main action of the sentence, and it may be accompanied by modifiers.

- The **predicate** describes what the subject is doing or being. It contains the verb(s) and any modifiers or objects that accompany it.

A **phrase** is a group of words that communicates a partial idea and lacks either a subject or a predicate. Phrases are categorized based on the main word in the phrase. A **prepositional phrase** (discussed above) begins with a preposition and ends with an object of the preposition.

The dog is hiding <u>under the porch</u>.

A **verb phrase** is composed of the main verb and its helping verbs.

The chef <u>would have created</u> another soufflé, but the staff protested.

A **noun phrase** consists of a noun and its modifiers:

The big, red barn rests beside the <u>vacant chicken house</u>.

Clauses contain both a subject and a predicate and can be either independent or dependent. An **independent** (or **main**) clause can stand alone as its own sentence:

<u>The dog ate her homework</u>.

Dependent (or **subordinate**) **clauses** cannot stand alone as their own sentences. They start with a subordinating conjunction, relative pronoun, or relative adjective, which will make them sound incomplete:

<u>because the dog ate her homework</u>

Table 6.11. Words That Begin Dependent Clauses

Subordinating Conjunctions	Pronouns and Adjectives
after, although, as, because, before, even if, even though, if, in order that, once, provided, since, so, so that, than, that, though, unless, until, when, whenever, where, whereas, wherever, whether, while	how, that, when, where, which, who, whoever, whom, whomever, whose, why

Table 6.12. Types of Clauses

Sentence Type	Number of Independent Clauses	Number of Dependent Clauses	Example
Simple	1	0	San Francisco in the springtime is one of my favorite places to visit.
Compound	2 or more	0	The game was canceled, but we will still practice on Saturday.
Complex	1	1 or more	I love listening to the radio in the car because I can sing along.
Compound-complex	2 or more	1 or more	I wanted to get a dog, but I have a fish because my

Composition

Table 6.12. Types of Clauses			
Sentence Type	Number of Independent Clauses	Number of Dependent Clauses	Example
			roommate is allergic to pet dander.

Sentence errors fall into three categories:

- fragments
- comma splices (comma fault)
- fused sentences (run-on)

A **fragment** occurs when a group of words lacks both a subject and verb as needed to construct a complete sentence or thought. For example:

Incorrect: Why am I not going to the mall? Because I do not like shopping.

Correct: Because I do not like shopping, I will not plan to go to the mall.

A **comma splice** (**comma fault**) occurs when two independent clauses are joined with only a comma to "splice" them together. To fix a comma splice, a coordinating conjunction can be added, or a comma can be replaced with a semicolon:

Incorrect: My family eats turkey at Thanksgiving, we eat ham at Christmas.

Correct: My family eats turkey at Thanksgiving, and we eat ham at Christmas.

Correct: My family eats turkey at Thanksgiving; we eat ham at Christmas.

Fused (**run-on**) sentences occur when two independent clauses are joined with no punctuation. Like comma splices, they can be fixed with a comma and conjunction or with a semicolon. For example:

Incorrect: My sister lives nearby she never comes to visit.

Correct: My sister lives nearby, but she never comes to visit.

Correct: My sister lives nearby; she never comes to visit.

Practice Questions

17) Which of the following is a simple sentence?
    A. Elsa drove, while Erica navigated.
    B. Betty ordered a fruit salad, and Sue ordered eggs.
    C. Because she was late, Jenny ran down the hall.
    D. John ate breakfast with his mother, brother, and father.

18) Which of the following would NOT be an acceptable way to revise and combine the underlined portion of the following sentences?

They receive an <u>annual pension payment. The amount of the pension</u> has been reviewed and changed a number of times.
- A. annual pension payment, the amount of which
- B. annual pension payment; the amount of the pension
- C. annual pension payment, the amount of the pension
- D. annual pension payment; the amount of each payment

Punctuation

The main punctuation marks are periods, question marks, exclamation marks, colons, semicolons, commas, quotation marks, and apostrophes. There are three terminal punctuation marks used to end sentences:

- The **period** ends declarative (statement) and imperative (command) sentences:

    Sarah and I are attending a concert.

- The **question mark** ends interrogative sentences:

    How many people are attending the concert?

- **Exclamation marks** indicate that the writer or speaker is conveying intense emotion or energy:

    That was a great concert!

The colon and the semicolon, though often confused, each have a unique set of rules about their respective uses. Both punctuation marks are used to join clauses, but the construction of the clauses and the relationships between them are different.

The **semicolon** is used to show a general relationship between two independent clauses (IC; IC):

The disgruntled customer tapped angrily on the counter; she had to wait nearly ten minutes to speak to the manager.

Helpful Hint:

Exclamation points have impact only in contrast to their frequency of usage: If the exclamation point is used frequently, each exclamation will be less impactful. If it is used sparingly, it will effectively draw the reader's attention.

Coordinating conjunctions (FANBOYS, discussed above) cannot be used with semicolons; however, conjunctive adverbs can be used following a semicolon:

She may not have to take the course this year; however, she will eventually have to sign up for that specific course.

The **colon**, somewhat less limited than the semicolon in its usage, is used to introduce a list, a definition, or a clarification. The clause preceding the colon must be an independent clause, but the clause that follows does not have to be:

Incorrect: The buffet offers three choices that include: ham, turkey, or roast beef.

Correct: The buffet offers three choices: ham, turkey, or roast beef.

Composition

Correct: The buffet offers three choices that include the following: ham, turkey, or roast beef.

Note that neither the semicolon nor the colon should be used to set off an introductory phrase from the rest of the sentence:

Incorrect: After the trip to the raceway; we realized that we should have brought earplugs.

Incorrect: After the trip to the raceway: we realized that we should have brought earplugs.

Correct: After the trip to the raceway, we realized that we should have brought earplugs.

The **comma** is a complicated type of punctuation that can serve many different purposes in a sentence. Comma placement is often an issue of style, not mechanics, meaning there may be more than one correct way to write the sentence. There are, however, a few important hard-and-fast comma rules, which are outlined in Table 6.13.

Table 6.13. Rules for Comma Usage

Rule	Example Sentence(s)
Commas should be used to separate two independent clauses along with a coordinating conjunction (FANBOYS).	Khalid ordered the steak, but Bruce preferred the ham.
Commas should be used to separate coordinate adjectives (two different adjectives that describe the same noun).	The shiny, regal horse ran majestically through the wide, open field.
Commas should be used to separate items in a series.	The list of groceries included cream, coffee, doughnuts, and tea.
Commas should be used to separate introductory words, phrases, and clauses from the rest of the sentence.	<ul><li>Slowly, Nathan became aware of his surroundings after the concussion.</li><li>Within an hour, the authorities will descend on the home.</li><li>After Alice swam the channel, nothing intimidated her.</li></ul>
Commas should be used to set off **appositive phrases**—descriptors that are not needed for the sentence to make sense grammatically.	<ul><li>Estelle, our newly elected chairperson, will be in attendance.</li><li>Ida, my neighbor, watched the children for me last week.</li></ul>
Commas should be used to set off titles of famous individuals.	Charles, Prince of Wales, visited Canada several times in the last ten years.
Commas should be used to set off the day and month of a date.	I was born on February 16, 1958, in Minnesota.
Commas should be used in numbers of more than four digits.	We expect 25,000 visitors to the new museum.

Quotation marks are used for many purposes, including enclosing direct quotations in a sentence. **Terminal punctuation** that is part of the quotation goes inside the marks; terminal punctuation that is part of the larger sentence goes outside. For example:

She asked him menacingly, "Where is my peanut butter?"

What is the original meaning of the phrase "king of the hill"?

In American English, commas are used to set quotations apart from the surrounding text and are placed inside the marks:

"Although I find him tolerable," Arianna wrote, "I would never want him as a roommate."

While titles of longer works, like novels and anthologies, are italicized, quotation marks enclose titles of short, or relatively short, literary works such as short stories, chapters, and poems (excluding epic poems):

For English class, we read "The Raven" by Edgar Allan Poe.

Quotation marks also set off words used in a special sense or for nonliterary purposes:

The shady dealings of his Ponzi scheme earned him the ironic name "Honest Abe."

Apostrophes (sometimes referred to as **single quotation marks**) have a number of different uses:

- They show possession.
- They replace missing letters, numerals, and signs.
- They form plurals of letters, numerals, and signs in certain instances.

Like commas, there are a number of rules for the correct usage of apostrophes, some of which are described in Table 6.14.

Table 6.14. Rules for Apostrophe Usage

Rule	Examples
To signify possession by a singular noun not ending in *s*, add *'s*.	boy → boy's
To signify possession by a singular noun ending in *s*, add *'s*.	class → class's
To signify possession by an indefinite pronoun not ending in *s*, add *'s*.	someone → someone's
To signify possession by a plural noun not ending in *s*, add *'s*.	children → children's
To signify possession by a plural noun ending in *s*, add only the apostrophe.	boys → boys'
To signify possession by singular, compound words and phrases, add *'s* to the last word in the phrase.	everybody else → everybody else's
To signify joint possession, add *'s* only to the last noun.	John and Mary's house
To signify individual possession, add *'s* to each noun.	John's and Mary's houses
To signify missing letters in a contraction, place the apostrophe where the letters are missing.	do not → don't

Composition

Table 6.14. Rules for Apostrophe Usage	
Rule	Examples
To signify missing numerals, place the apostrophe where the numerals are missing.	1989 → '89
To demonstrate possession or form a contraction with a numeral, add 's; only use for pluralization when the absence of an apostrophe would create confusion.	<ul><li>Music from the 1980s is my favorite.</li><li>Mind your p's and q's.</li><li>The class earned a total of four As and sixteen Bs on the exam.</li></ul>

Important Works

"The Raven"

Author: Edgar Allan Poe

Publication Date: 1845

Summary: A man passes the time by reading in his room while grieving his dead love interest, Lenore. He hears a knock at the door and calls out to her, but no one is there. A knock on the window follows, so the man opens it, and a raven flies in and perches atop a bust of the Greek goddess Athena. The man asks the raven his name, and the raven replies, "nevermore." The raven continues this utterance, and the man wonders if the bird is trained to say this word. Still thinking of Lenore, the man asks the bird if his grief will end and if he will see her again in heaven, but the raven says again, "nevermore." He angrily demands that the bird leave, but it refuses and stays upon the bust forever.

Themes, Motifs, and Symbols: the raven as a symbol of loss/grief, supernatural, futility, death

Practice Questions

19) Which of the following sentences contains an error in punctuation?
    A. I love apple pie! John exclaimed with a smile.
    B. Jennifer loves Adam's new haircut.
    C. Billy went to the store; he bought bread, milk, and cheese.
    D. Alexandra hates raisins, but she loves chocolate chips.

20) Which punctuation mark correctly completes the following sentence?

Sam, why don't you come with us for dinner_
    A. period (.)
    B. semicolon (;)
    C. question mark (?)
    D. colon (:)

Capitalization

The most important rules for capitalization are listed in Table 6.15.

Table 6.15. Rules for Capitalization	
Rule	Example
The first word of a sentence is always capitalized.	We will be having dinner at a new restaurant tonight.
The first letter of a proper noun is always capitalized.	We're going to Chicago on Wednesday.
Titles are capitalized if they precede the name they modify.	Kamala Harris, the vice president, met with President Biden.
Months are capitalized but not the names of the seasons.	Snow fell in March even though winter was over.
The names of major holidays should be capitalized. The word *day* is only capitalized if it is part of the holiday's name.	We always go to a parade on Memorial Day, but on Christmas day we stay home.
The names of specific places should always be capitalized; general location terms are not capitalized.	We're going to San Francisco next weekend so I can see the ocean.
Titles for relatives should be capitalized when they precede a name but not when they stand alone.	Fred, my uncle, will make fried chicken, and Aunt Betty is going to make spaghetti.

Helpful Hint:

The comma before the conjunction in a series of items is called the **Oxford comma (serial comma)**. It is optional and will not appear on the exam.

Practice Question

21) Which of the following sentences contains an error in capitalization?
    A. My two brothers are going to New Orleans for Mardi Gras.
    B. On Friday we voted to elect a new class president.
    C. Janet wants to go to Mexico this Spring.
    D. Peter complimented the chef on his cooking.

Answer Key

1) C: A school-wide literary journal is an effective way to publish and distribute creative writing in a high school.

2) C: A thesis statement presents the writer's main argument.

3) C: This version of the sentence is the clearest, most concise option for communicating this idea.

4) B: *In fact* can be used correctly in this instance to draw attention to interesting information that builds on the previous sentence.

5) D: This option provides a brief but interesting overview of the information to come.

6) D: When introducing a new skill, teachers should first model it for students in order to demonstrate confidence and eliminate confusion.

7) D: After a data dump, students can refine their lists by circling the most closely associated words or crossing out unrelated words.

8) B: The term *mechanics* is used to describe the finer details, or minutiae, of English. Such details include punctuation, capitalization, and spelling. *Grammar* refers to the structures and systems that make up a language. *Usage conventions* guide writers and speakers more broadly in the area of word choice in order to ensure accuracy and agreement within a sentence. Syntax describes the study of how words are combined to create sentences.

9) C: *Minnesota* and *August* are proper nouns, and *coat* and *gloves* are common nouns. *I* is a pronoun, and *warm* is an adjective that modifies *coat*.

10) B: "The members of the band" is plural, so the plural pronoun *their* should be used instead of the singular *her*.

11) A: Option A should read "The brother and sister run very fast." When the subject contains two or more nouns connected by the word *and*, the subject is plural and requires a plural verb.

12) C: Option C should read "Johnny will go to the movies after he cleans the kitchen." It does not make sense to say that Johnny does something in the past ("went to the movies") after doing something in the present ("after he cleans").

13) A: *New* modifies the noun *chef*, and *boiling* modifies the noun *soup*. *Carefully* is an adverb modifying the verb *stirred*. *Lowered* is a verb, and *heat* is a noun.

14) D: Option D should read "Of the four speeches, Jerry's was the longest." The word *long* has only one syllable, so it should be modified with the suffix *–est*, not the word *most*.

15) C: The correct preposition is *of*.

16) A: In this sentence, the conjunction joins together two contrasting ideas, so the best answer is *but*.

17) D: Option D contains one independent clause with one subject and one verb. Options A and C are complex sentences because they each contain both a dependent and independent clause. Option B contains two independent clauses joined by a conjunction and is therefore a compound sentence.

18) C: This option creates a comma splice; the other options are all correct.

19) A: Option A should use quotation marks to set off a direct quote: "I love apple pie!" John exclaimed with a smile.

20) C: The sentence is a question, so it should end with a question mark.

21) C: Spring is the name of a season and should therefore not be capitalized.

Inquiry, Research, and Media

Research Resources

Forming a specific and answerable research question provides the focus of the writer's research and is a crucial component of the planning process for students learning how to write research papers or essays. For example, the topic "education" is too broad to result in meaningful research findings. Writers must therefore narrow the topic to "higher education" or, even further, to "higher education in the twenty-first century." From there, writers must further narrow their focus by formulating a specific question to explore: "What are some of the changes that institutions of higher education must address to stay relevant in the twenty-first century?" After formulating a research question, the writer searches for relevant, impactful information from credible sources.

With today's students relying heavily on the internet for information, teachers have the responsibility to not only guide students in the appropriate use of digital resources but also ensure that they understand the value of print resources and how to utilize them. Most importantly, teachers must equip students with the following knowledge:

- how to evaluate the credibility of a text based on its source
- how to evaluate **contemporaneity** (how up-to-date the research is)
- how to determine the purpose of the research

Print resources may generally be more credible because they go through numerous reviews before arriving in the hands of the researcher. Print resources include books, magazines, newspapers, and journals.

Digital and online resources, on the other hand, may pose a bigger challenge for young researchers since the internet provides limited—if any—oversight regarding who can post information online or its reliability. Students must therefore be taught to remain particularly aware of inaccuracies and bias when using the internet for research.

Students should be directed toward reliable online sources and how to locate these. **Credible sources** provide research that is trustworthy because the information has been fact-checked. Such sources include **peer-reviewed journals** (journals that ask other subject matter experts to review content before it is published) and websites from reputable institutions, such as the World Health Organization or the American Academy of Pediatrics.

It is critical for students to learn the skills needed to evaluate online sources on their own. Some questions they may ask include the following:

- *Is the article from a peer-reviewed journal?*
    - Most research journals identify themselves as peer-reviewed on their website or in the journal itself.

- It is recommended to limit library database searches to include only peer-reviewed research.
- *Is the article recent?*
    - Articles that are over a decade old may contain information that is out of date or that has since been proven inaccurate.
- *Is the author trustworthy?*
    - Is the author of the article listed?
    - Does the author have academic credentials (such as a PhD) or hold an academic post?
    - Is the author free from bias, or does the author seem to promote a particular political view or personal agenda?

Helpful Hint:
Less credible online sources include personal blogs, opinion pieces, and online message boards.

When conducting research, students should understand the differences between primary and secondary sources:

- A **primary source** is an unaltered piece of writing that was composed during the time the events being described took place.
    - Books written by political candidates to inform people about their stands on various issues are examples of primary sources.
- A **secondary source** might address the same topic as a primary source but provides extra commentary or analysis.
    - An online article written by a journalist analyzing how candidates' positions will affect the election is a secondary source.

Helpful Hint:
Primary sources are usually written by people who have directly experienced an event. Secondary sources are written by people who did NOT experience the event themselves.

Practice Questions

1) Which of the following would NOT be a good choice for an authoritative print source in a research project?
   A. a book published by the NRA that cites statistics from Canada to support a pro-gun agenda
   B. a recent magazine article from *Psychology Today* that reviews mental health assessment tools
   C. a dissertation explaining new research on the use of sentence diagramming with adult learners
   D. a sacred text that discusses the basic tenets of a religion

2) The students in Professor Johnson's class are searching for secondary sources for a paper on the polio vaccine. Which one of the following might they consult?
   A. an interview with a person who has been diagnosed with polio
   B. pictures of patients who have received the polio vaccine
   C. a journal article on the rate of polio inoculation in the United States
   D. an interview with a doctor who specializes in the treatment of polio

Citing Sources

In discussing the use of reference materials, teachers must also understand and address the topic of **source integration**—how a resource is used effectively without overwhelming the writer's own voice and ideas. Some general guidelines for resource use include the following:

- Resources should not be overused or underused.

- Resources should support the writer's ideas appropriately without overshadowing them or replacing them altogether.

- Whenever possible, writers should avoid beginning and/or ending paragraphs with cited material; this ensures that the resources are truly integrated and that the ideas that are shaping the paragraphs via the topic sentences are the writer's own.

Sources can be integrated into a research paper in three different ways:

- quoting
- paraphrasing
- summarizing

A **quotation** is an exact (or near exact) transfer of content and punctuation from a resource into a research paper. Quotations should be less than four lines long and denoted directly in the text using quotation marks and a parenthetical citation. Sometimes, longer quotes are included if they are especially impactful; such quotes should be offset to represent a significant break from the writer's own words. Quotes are most effective when integrated completely into sentences and paragraphs of a research text, which is why bracket and ellipses rules exist to clarify any sections of a quotation that the writer might have altered in order to lend coherence to the sentence or paragraph.

A **paraphrase** is not simply a synchronistic syllable replacement of words; to paraphrase something involves changing both the wording and the syntax used to express an idea. In other words, when paraphrasing, writers use their own unique voices to restate specific information from a source.

Summaries are similar to paraphrases in that they require authors to use their own voices; however, summaries usually cover much more material. While writers may paraphrase a particular point or idea from an article, for example, they may summarize the article as a whole.

All three types of source integration—quotations, paraphrases, and summaries—require citation according to the appropriate style manual, or guide. Proper **citations** have two parts:

1. The original source must be credited within the document itself (**in-text citation**).

2. The source must then be credited at the end of the document using a reference page, a bibliography page, or a **works cited** page.

Style manuals function as guidebooks for the documentation of sources within a written document. Some style manuals that apply more narrowly to specific technical fields may be used. For instance, the ***Publication Manual of the American Psychological Association (APA)*** is used for the fields of education, psychology, and other social sciences. Many word processing programs have tools and references to assist writers in adhering to various writing styles and their citation formats. Numerous websites and applications are also available to assist in the easy formation of accurate citations. The most common style guides and examples of their preferred citation formats are discussed below.

APA In-Text Citation

The general trend in the early 1900s was to consult the student, an action that had, up to that time, been looked upon as "soft pedagogy" (Tolman, 1902, p. 159).

APA References Page

Tolman, A. (1902). The revival of English grammar. *The School Review*, 10(2), 157 – 165.

The ***Modern Language Association Style Manual and Guide to Scholarly Publishing (MLA)*** is used in the arts, humanities, and literature.

MLA In-Text Citation

The popularity of fantasy opened up "other worlds" to readers: "He was a faun. And when he saw Lucy he gave such a start of surprise that he dropped all of his parcels" (Lewis 114).

MLA Works Cited Page

Lewis, C.S. *The Chronicles of Narnia*. New York: Harper Collins, 1994. Print.

***The Chicago Manual of Style* (CMOS or Chicago)** is widely used in the sciences, history, literature, and art.

Chicago In-Text Citation

The power of the naval forces could not be underestimated. "So great was the force of the big naval guns that surgeons swore they had seen men killed by the wind of a passing shot."[1]

Chicago Footnote

[1]Toll, Ian W. *Six Frigates: The Epic History of the Founding of the U.S. Navy*. New York: W. W. Norton & Company, 2006.

A Manual for Writers of Research Papers, Theses, and Dissertations by Kate Turabian (Turabian) is used for history and theological studies. Turabian is very similar to Chicago style. The main difference between the Chicago and Turabian styles is the largely stand-alone nature of Turabian. Readers of an article written in Chicago style may have to reference other materials to fully understand what they are reading. Readers of an article written in Turabian style will find stand-alone information within the text itself.

Turabian In-Text Citation

It is difficult to understand Hoekema's "new-self." For example, Hoekema acknowledges the difficulty of differentiating between the objective and subjective parts of sanctification.[25]

Turabian Footnote

[25]The objective or definitive part of sanctification is that which is finished at salvation. Hoekema explains this in the Reformed view in pages 73 – 74 of the *Five Views on Sanctification*. He terms progressive sanctification as "subjective."

Turabian Bibliography

Hoekema, Anthony A. "Reformed Perspective." In *Five Views on Sanctification*, ed. Stanley N. Gundry, 59 – 90. Grand Rapids: Zondervan, 1987.

Electronic sources are those which are primarily accessed online. With the rapid development of electronic communication and publishing, style manuals have had to evolve quickly to accommodate new reference formats: websites, online books, journal articles, DVDs, online magazines and newspapers, interviews, and more. While many style guides have turned away from requiring URLs and other complicated details, some citations still require a **DOI (Digital Object Identifier)**. Writers must therefore consult specific style manuals for instructions and details on how and when to incorporate a DOI. When citing electronic sources, writers should take note of the following elements:

- the author(s), compiler(s), or editor(s) of a text, keeping in mind that the authors may be a corporation or group
- the title of the book, article, website posting, or blog, especially if it differs from the name of the website or the website sponsor
- the name of the website, often revealed in the URL (www.apa.studies)
- the sponsor of the website or an associated organization, institution, or company
- the date on which the electronic source was posted (as in website articles) or published (as in articles from online periodicals)
- the date that the researcher accessed the source
- the format of the source (Note: If a resource is a PDF, it may be because this source is actually a print source; otherwise, online reference materials fall under the web format.)

The following is an example of how to cite an electronic source with a DOI:

Kuh, G. (1999). How are we doing? Tracking the quality of the undergraduate experience, 1960s to the present. *The Review of Higher Education, 22(2), 99 – 120*. doi: 10.1353/rhe.1999.0003

When research writers summarize, paraphrase, or quote the ideas or conclusions of others but neglect to credit the original sources, they are committing **plagiarism**. Whether the result of malice or ignorance, plagiarism is a serious offense with serious consequences. Academic, professional, and even legal consequences can arise from the improper and unethical use of another person's work. It is therefore imperative that teachers instruct students on the proper methods for citation.

Helpful Hint:

When in doubt as to whether information is considered common knowledge, it is always "safer" to credit a relevant source or consult a style manual.

One type of information that does not need to be cited, however, is **common knowledge**, which refers to frequently reiterated sets of facts and information that is assumed to be true among a group or within a culture. In the general public, common knowledge is broad: it is information that the typical person can be expected to know. Within a group of medical professionals, on the other hand, common knowledge takes on a different meaning—one in which a basic understanding of medical terminology is assumed.

Practice Questions

3) Which of the following would be an effective way to introduce and integrate a source into a research paper?
   A. Some people think ". . .
   B. This quotation says it well: ". . .
   C. I don't know how to say this, but this author says it best: ". . .
   D. Dr. Philip Stern, professor at Iowa State University, concluded after his experiment that ". . .

4) Which of the following answer options accurately paraphrases the following quotation?

"Eighty-eight percent of the adult learners in the control group scored below the adult learners in the experiment group."
   A. Lots of folks did well in the experiment group.
   B. Eighty-eight percent of the adults in the control group did better than the adults in the experiment group.
   C. Hooray for the experiment group; they did super fantastic!
   D. After the researcher had administered the final test, the control group scored eighty-eight percent worse than the group that received the intervention.

Media Literacy

Types of Media

Media has rapidly evolved over the last century. **Radio** was once the primary media outlet for news and entertainment. Although it is still used, its popularity has been supplanted by other types of media as technology has become more advanced.

Movies became popular with the invention of film in the early twentieth century. **Television** became a mainstream product in the 1950s, bringing broadcast media into people's homes. The **internet**, which became popular in the late 1990s and early 2000s, quickly led to the creation of many new genres of media, including podcasts, social media, and video/music streaming. Today, media is usually categorized into four types:

- **print media** (physical magazines and newspapers)
- **broadcast media** (film, TV, and radio)
- **outdoor media** (billboards and banners)
- **digital media** (websites, social media, and podcasts)

Media—regardless of the type—will always influence society, and some of these influences are negative. For example, media can allow people to easily disseminate false information and spread harmful stereotypes or biases. It can also desensitize people to violence and suffering through repeated exposure. However, not all of the impacts of media are negative. The internet can spread information much more quickly than other types of media and allows people from all over the world to collaborate. It also gives people access to news that was not traditionally available through radio, newspapers, or television. The internet can be particularly useful to populations who historically have not been able to produce traditional broadcast media.

Media is also the primary way through which businesses advertise their products or services. Advertisements are found in all types of media, and are often the main way that media content is funded. For example, ads may be shown before or during streaming videos, and news websites usually sell ad space to raise revenue.

In many types of media, the line between ads and content can become blurred. This is especially true for digital media, wherein **sponsored content**—ads paid for by businesses—might be integrated into social media accounts or websites. As part of media literacy, students should be taught how to identify ads or sponsored content in all types of media.

Practice Question

5) Which one of the following is an example of broadcast media?
   A. a social media account
   B. a newspaper
   C. a radio show
   D. a billboard

Analyzing Media

Media literacy is the ability to find and effectively analyze media content. All types of media—from magazines to movies to podcasts—can be analyzed in much the same way as traditional texts. Students should learn to assess both the content and context of the media they consume. Important aspects of media analysis include the following:

- the message or main idea of the content
- the intent or purpose of the people who produce the content
- the effect the media has on the audience
- the techniques used to produce this effect

Teachers often begin the process of analyzing media by explaining to students that no media is completely neutral: every piece has a message. Students should be able to identify the key information communicated in a piece of media and understand how it builds the message. To place media's message in the proper context, students must look for the intent of its producers—who made this piece of media and why?

Every piece of media has a purpose. Like informational texts, media can inform, persuade, or entertain. To identify the purpose of a piece of media, students should first identify the person or organization behind it. Knowing this information allows students to assess the producer's bias so they can evaluate the strength of the content. Asking the following types of questions can help students determine bias:

- Is the producer a person or company with a vested interest in the subject matter?
- Are the producers experts in their fields, or do they have any professional qualifications?
- Is the producer a magazine or news organization with a known political bias?
- How are the producers funded and how might this affect their biases?

Once the creator is identified, the intent of the media can be analyzed. For example, if a notable scientific study is being covered in media, the intent of the media creator will determine how that study is presented:

- The university that did the study may promote it with an upbeat article on its website.
- A news site may drive traffic to its site by focusing on sensationalized aspects of the study.
- A company may use the study to advertise its own products.
- Social media accounts may use the study to promote a specific political agenda.

Media can have many different effects on the consumer and can affect an individual's knowledge, attitudes, beliefs, and behaviors. These effects might change the way an individual thinks or behaves or reinforce existing beliefs and behaviors.

There is debate in media studies about the strength of media effects. Older theories, such as the **direct effect theory**, were based on the belief that people passively consume media and are strongly and directly affected by it. Newer theories, some of which are discussed below, emphasize that people's relationship to media is more complex:

> **Helpful Hint**:
> Advances in technology have allowed businesses to target very specific groups of customers. As part of a media literacy program, students can study how their online habits shape the types of ads they see.

- **agenda-setting theory:** The media has the ability to influence which topics people think are important but has less effect on what people think about those topics.
- **framing theory:** A person's understanding of the world is influenced by how media presents topics, including the media's use of language and chosen point of view.
- **cultivation theory:** People who consume media, particularly TV, are likely to perceive the world as it is depicted in the media.
- **uses and gratifications theory:** People actively seek out and consume media to meet specific needs.
- **spiral of silence:** Media shapes which views are perceived as "minority positions," and people who perceive themselves as holding minority views are less likely to voice these.

> **Helpful Hint**:
> **Propaganda** is communication designed to influence public opinion, often through partial truths—or even total falsehoods. Students should learn to identify propaganda and become familiar with the various logical fallacies it often uses.

To help students develop skills in evaluating various types of media, they should be exposed to multiple sources of information and learn how to compare and contrast them. For example, an informational article or podcast could be compared to a documentary film on the same topic. Similarly, advertisements across various platforms like radio, print, and film—both past and present—could be compared to identify techniques used and how those impact the viewer, reader, or listener.

Along with comparing media representations of various topics, students should be taught to confirm facts from a variety of sources and spot examples of media messages that contain lies or claims that cannot be verified through other sources. Again, the availability of technology can be a help. For example, in the past, the public often had to rely on word of mouth to confirm the claims of advertisers about a product or service; now, online reviews can reveal much and help consumers make informed purchases.

Helpful Hint: As part of a media literacy program, students should learn how advertising drives content in digital media. Often, the intent of producers is simply to attract viewers and raise ad revenue.

Important Works

"Day of Infamy" speech

Speaker: Franklin Delano Roosevelt

Date: December 8, 1941

Summary: The speech was delivered the day after the Japanese attacked Pearl Harbor. Roosevelt begins by explaining that the attack was unprovoked and that Japan and the US were in peaceful negotiations at the time; however, because of the distance between Hawaii and Japan, he concludes that the attack had been planned for some time, which he sees as an intentional deception. FDR explains that many lives were lost and that Japanese forces subsequently attacked Malaya, Hong Kong, Guam, the Philippines, Wake Island, and Midway Island. He says that the US will use force to defend itself and that it will be victorious. He concludes by formally asking Congress to declare war on Japan.

Themes and Rhetorical Strategies: appeal to emotion, anger, betrayal, war

Practice Questions

6) Students are watching a news clip in which a police officer talks about the destruction of a homeless camp. The teacher then asks the students how the story would be different if the presenter interviewed a homeless person. Which media effect is this lesson highlighting?
   A. agenda-setting theory
   B. spiral of silence
   C. framing theory
   D. uses and gratifications theory

7) A middle school teacher wants to design an activity to help students confirm the accuracy of information in an online video about a historical topic. Which activity is MOST appropriate?
   A. having students compare the information in the video to multiple photographs covering the same topic
   B. assigning students the task of creating their own videos on the same topic
   C. encouraging students to use the information in the video to create a multimedia presentation on the same topic
   D. asking students to compare the information in the video with that in multiple print sources

Creating Media

The use of varied media often makes a message clearer and more engaging. Many national and state standards require students to work on media projects such as presentations, videos, posters, charts, graphs, and audio recordings. Often, these types of projects promote curricular integration as students use media skills to analyze and present information across content areas.

Teachers should help students learn to create high-quality and engaging multimedia projects. Effective presentations should have the following elements:

- contain an appropriate balance of media elements
- use sound, images, and video aligned with the overall message of the presentation
- offer opportunities for audience participation, if possible
- be aligned with the project purpose and audience

Students should strive to use media in their work for a specific purpose—often to elaborate on a point or help the audience visualize something. The use of media elements as "decoration" or "fluff" is generally not a best practice. Students should therefore be taught to recognize and evaluate effective presentations, both those they make themselves and those made by others. Rubrics customized for specific types of media can be very helpful for both teacher and student evaluation of media.

With the increased use of media comes more responsibility. Students should use appropriate online etiquette and must learn to navigate fair-use issues in the digital space.

Students creating and posting media must follow basic **netiquette protocols**, meaning they should use a communication style appropriate to the online environment. Most schools and districts have netiquette policies, which might include the following:

- keeping the people behind digital communications in mind at all times
- remembering that nothing posted online is private or temporary
- using an appropriate tone for the audience
- maintaining the privacy and confidentiality of others
- avoiding the use of all caps, emojis, or slang

When creating media, students must also learn how to correctly use and cite media sources (described earlier in this chapter). **Copyright** is the legal ownership of a work of art. Copyrighted works can only be reproduced or repurposed under specific conditions.

Fair use refers to the legal use of copyrighted work without the permissions of the rights-holder in certain circumstances. Fair use doctrine follows four main guidelines:

1) Purpose and character of use: Education and nonprofit use of copyrighted works is usually permitted. Works that are transformative—meaning they add something substantially new—are also usually able to use copyrighted materials.

2) Nature of the work: Personal, creative works of art are less likely to be considered for fair use.

3) Amount and substantiality of the work: Using small portions of copyrighted works is often permitted.

4) Effect of the use on the market for copyrighted material: Reproduction of copyrighted materials that substantially affects the ability of the original creators to market their products is not allowed.

Classroom use of copyrighted content often falls under fair use guidelines because it is for educational purposes; however, the principles of fair use must still be considered. For example, it may be appropriate for students to use properly cited images in a slide presentation given to the class. It would not, however, be appropriate for students to use those copyrighted images on their personal websites without the copyright-holder's permission. In these cases, the material has two different purposes: one is a limited educational setting; the other is the broad online dissemination of someone else's work.

> **Helpful Hint**:
>
> Types of art that CAN be copyrighted include written works, paintings, photographs, musical compositions, movies, and sound recordings. Things that CANNOT be copyrighted include recipes/formulas, ideas, slogans, and common knowledge.

Of course, not all media is copyrighted. Work that is in the **public domain** is free for use because its copyright has expired, was forfeited, or never existed. Students can be directed to sites that offer photos and images in the public domain. Additionally, some work falls under a Creative Commons license. **Creative Commons (CC)** is a nonprofit organization that helps content creators designate how their work may be used. All CC content must be attributed to its creator. Further, there are multiple types of CC licenses that dictate how the work may be used. Some require that the content only be used for noncommercial purposes or that it only be reused if the new work will also fall under a Creative Commons license.

Students and teachers should also be aware of liability before using images or videos featuring other students. Schools and districts will typically have a media release policy and associated forms that parents must sign. Without such documentation, photos and videos of students should not be posted on any online platforms, including class websites or social media pages.

Practice Question

8) A high school teacher assigns an activity wherein student groups create a website highlighting the life and work of a well-known author of the past. What should the teacher advise students BEFORE they begin?
   A. They can use any type of media on the site because it is for educational purposes and thus falls under fair use.
   B. They should avoid the use of any images on their website because of the risk of copyright infringement.
   C. They should seek out image sources that are in the public domain or that have certain types of CC licenses.
   D. They can use most types of media on the site but should provide links to the original sources for proper citation.

Answer Key

1) A: A book written by a special interest group may be biased and would therefore not be a good choice for an authoritative print source on a research project.

2) C: Option C is the only secondary source listed; options A, B, and D all contain firsthand information and would therefore be considered primary sources.

3) D: The example in option D includes a specific authoritative source, an active verb, and an integration of the quotation into the text.

4) D: This paraphrase is a rewording and syntactical alteration by the author of the paper; it is both accurate and academic.

5) C: Broadcast media is transmitted to the public in real time and includes film, TV, and radio.

6) C: The teacher is highlighting the framing theory by showing students how the media's chosen point of view affects how the story is perceived.

7) D: Information in various media can best be confirmed by comparing it to other sources.

8) C: Public domain and certain types of Creative Commons (CC) licenses allow use without permission.

Listening and Speaking

Listening and Speaking

Oral Language Development

Oral (spoken) language and the development of reading skills are entwined in children's lives from a young age. Students who understand the role of oral language in communication and how to produce and "consume" oral language will have a head start in learning how to read and write well.

Students who have a large spoken vocabulary will be far more likely to identify words in text. Those who have heard and participated in complex conversations and discussions will make connections and activate background knowledge as they read. Further, oral language and an understanding of its structures are critical components in phonics instruction (Chapter 2), which relies on the connections between written and spoken language.

Students should be expected to use oral language to think critically and communicate their thoughts. This process relies on both **receptive oral language** (the ability to understand what is being said) and **expressive oral language** (the ability to use language to communicate ideas appropriately). For older students, techniques for developing oral language skills for critical thinking and creative expression include the following:

- oral discussion or critiques of literature or expository texts
- reciprocal teaching (students become the teachers and guide a small-group reading activity)
- "book club" or book discussion activities in large or small groups
- oral discussions with peers on current events or issues that require critical reflection
- persuasive speeches or presentations
- plays or dramatic performances
- writing and reading a piece of creative writing aloud
- impromptu dialogues or role-plays

Nuances related to each student's home language (dialect, register, and so forth) should be respected in assessing and building oral language skills. While educators might have certain notions of the "right" or "wrong" way to speak, such distinctions do not exist organically. While some speech may not be well matched for a particular setting or audience, it is not "wrong." In assessing and building oral language proficiency, such a distinction should be kept in mind. An overemphasis on speaking English "correctly" without consideration for unique registers and dialects removes language from its pragmatic context and fails to account for the broad diversity within the spectrum of spoken English.

Practice Question

1) A ninth-grade English teacher asks a reading specialist how to incorporate oral language for critical thinking into his unit on Shakespeare's *Romeo and Juliet*. Which instructional strategy is the reading specialist MOST likely to recommend?
   A. filling out a graphic organizer before, during, and after reading the play
   B. reading the play aloud with dramatic inflection
   C. holding a class-wide debate on whose fault the tragedy really was
   D. encouraging students to use fix-up strategies as they orally read the tragedy

Oral Communication Activities

Oral communication exercises in the classroom come in a variety of forms:

- They may be formal or informal.
- They may occur one-on-one.
- They may occur in small groups.
- They may involve the whole class.

In planning an oral communication exercise, teachers make numerous considerations to ensure that the work is productive and purposeful. Effective teachers must

- know the objective of the lesson,
- choose an appropriate and relevant topic for discussion,
- decide on a format,
- define appropriate student behavior, and
- determine accountability measures.

The objectives of oral communication exercises are often twofold in an ELA classroom:

- They are usually conducted in the context of a broader unit and therefore may be centered on a particular reading objective (for example) and used in part to assess a student's grasp of a particular reading assignment, chapter, or unit.

> **Helpful Hint**:
> **Pragmatics** refers to the way we use language (oral or otherwise) for practical purposes.

- They address oral communication objectives such as fluency, coherence, and clarity.

First and foremost, the topic of an oral communication exercise must stem from the lesson objective. The exercise must also be age appropriate and have some relevance to students' lives or the world at large. In choosing a suitable topic, effective teachers consider the emotional and intellectual development of their students, the required background knowledge for discussion of the topic, and the objectives that they hope to see their students master. After choosing a topic, the teacher should decide what form the exercise will take:

- Will students give a speech, presentation, or participate in a debate or discussion?
- Will they interact with only one other student, a group of students, or the whole class?

Listening and Speaking

- Will communication flow in all directions or just in one?
- How directly will the teacher be involved?

Teachers may assign a **debate** in order to test students' abilities to both speak intelligently on topics they have researched as well defend their positions with evidence. Debates also assess the ability of students to handle stress and respond to academic arguments with composure. A debate can take many specific forms in the classroom; in general terms, it requires students to take a side on a particular issue and provide evidence for their reasoning. Depending on the teacher's objective, debates can take place one-on-one, in small groups, or with the whole class.

A teacher may assign a **speech** in order to evaluate students' formal public speaking abilities and observe their fluency and ability to communicate emotionally with an audience. A speech requires students—usually one at a time—to stand in front of a group and speak on a particular topic. The speech format is fairly versatile: speeches can range in length and formality depending on purpose, audience, and topic—all of which can vary widely. More information on the delivery of speeches is provided below.

Discussions may also be assigned in order to assess students' informal speaking and listening abilities as well as their verbal reasoning skills. In general, discussions allow participants to gain a deeper understanding of a specific topic or text but otherwise are varied in format. Effective teachers might consider the objective and the culture of their classrooms when choosing discussion formats.

For less complex topics, one-on-one discussions may be assigned in the form of **think-pair-shares**, in which students have the opportunity to first share briefly with a partner before sharing their responses with the whole class. Think-pair-shares are appropriate when everyone in the class can comment on a topic without much prompting or when every student is expected to have a response. This method is also helpful in new classes, where students are still getting to know each other and might feel more comfortable testing their responses out on just one classmate first.

Small-group discussions also allow for a level of safety since students are asked to share on a smaller, more intimate scale. They are therefore particularly helpful in classes where students may be unwilling to speak in front of a large group. In classes that are large or particularly vocal, small groups can also be helpful for getting every student engaged and giving everyone an opportunity to share. Teachers might discover, however, that small group discussions can be difficult to manage since many discussions must be monitored at once. For this reason, accountability measures are especially important in small groups.

Whole-class discussions, especially those conducted in classrooms that are safe and productive, can be especially useful for taking on broad, complex ideas that require many perspectives. Larger thematic questions related to the human condition, for example, can be explored in more dimensions when a larger number of perspectives and opinions comes together. The **Socratic seminar** format, in which a leader (the teacher or a student, depending on the classroom culture) prompts discussion by asking questions and allowing the class to share, respond to, and build upon one another's ideas, is especially effective and engaging.

Once the objective, topic, and format of the oral exercise have been determined, teachers should consider and define appropriate student behavior for the exercise and share this information with students. Some teachers may prefer to involve their students when defining these parameters by asking them what they consider to be appropriate discussion or debate behavior. When determining parameters, it is important to keep the following particulars in mind:

- Are students required to participate?

- If so, when and how much?
- Is there a maximum that students can contribute?
- Will they be required to use academic language during the exercise?
- What is appropriate behavior in response to a disagreement?
- Can students talk over each other? If not, how will that be managed?
- What is an effective or meaningful contribution?
- How will the group respond to comments that are inappropriate, irrelevant, or distracting?

In addition to defining appropriate behavior for students, teachers should also be prepared to share with students how they will be held accountable for their contributions to a discussion or debate. **Accountability** may take the form of a rubric-based grade, a follow-up written assignment, or a related project that requires tangible output.

Important Works

"The Gettysburg Address"

Speaker: Abraham Lincoln

Date: November 19, 1863

Summary: Lincoln delivered this brief address at the dedication of the national cemetery at Gettysburg, Pennsylvania—the site of the Civil War's bloodiest battle. He begins by reminding listeners of the Declaration of Independence and the ideals upon which the US was founded. He explains that a cemetery in this location is fitting but that the men who died there—not the people gathered on that day—are the ones consecrating the ground. He encourages listeners to persevere in the war effort so that these men will not have died in vain. He closes with another reference to the nation's founding and calls for the establishment of "a new birth of freedom" and a government that continues to be by, for, and of the people.

Themes and Rhetorical Strategies: appeal to patriotism and history, death and rebirth, struggle

Practice Questions

2) Which option would be the MOST appropriate assignment for assessing how well students can integrate evidence into an argument in order to prove a point?
    A. a speech
    B. a debate
    C. a think-pair-share
    D. a Socratic seminar

3) Mr. Green's class will soon be completing a discussion on F. Scott Fitzgerald's use of figurative language in *The Great Gatsby*. Which of the following is NOT an effective way for Mr. Green to hold his students accountable for this activity?
- A. He can require students to participate a minimum number of times during the discussion and then track the students' contributions.
- B. He can have students complete a series of multiple choice questions covering figurative language in *The Great Gatsby*.
- C. He can assign students to write an independent response after the debate to discuss any moments that stood out or changed their minds about something.
- D. He can ask students to complete a prediscussion list of questions to turn in on discussion day.

Effective Speeches and Presentations

In preparation for the professional world, today's students must know not only how to write a speech but also how to deliver a speech or presentation effectively. As with writing, purpose and audience are the two most important considerations in writing and giving a speech. Other elements of effective presentations include but are not limited to the following:

- tone
- bias
- conciseness
- clarity
- visuals

Audiences pick up on nuances of tone almost as quickly as they recognize a lack of eye contact or the use of unusual body language. Indeed, how the speaker delivers the message of a speech may be just as—if not far more—important than what is said. Before delivering a speech, speakers should rehearse extensively in order to ensure that they are employing the appropriate gradations of emotional tone:

- genuine or sarcastic
- casual or formal
- cold or warm
- sincere or insincere
- familiar or distant
- kind or harsh
- judgmental or nonjudgmental
- passionate or disinterested

Helpful Hint:

Semantics refers to the meaning of words. English dictionaries are the resources containing the semantics of the English language.

Conciseness in writing and speech delivery means much more than shortness; it involves the conscious ridding of superfluous wording, including clichés, fillers, and verbose sentence structures. A speech writer who is editing for conciseness cuts words not purely for the sake of shortening a speech but for the sake of choosing language that is clear and simple and that the audience will easily be able to understand.

Writers must sometimes continuously play with words until conciseness and clarity result. They may move, replace, cut, and add words until their sentence says exactly—no more than and no less than—

what they want it to say. While this practice can be tedious, the process of revising for clarity and conciseness allows writers to apply their knowledge of word nuances to achieve a satisfying end.

When it comes to speeches and presentations, **visual aids** can be extremely helpful and allow writers or speakers to emphasize elements throughout their presentations. If used incorrectly, however, visual aids can be a detriment to a good presentation. Some recommendations about the use of visual aids appear in Table 8.1.

Table 8.1. Visual Aids

Recommendation for Visual Aids	Explanation
Do not let the visual aid overpower the presenter.	The speaker—not the visual aid—should be the focus throughout most of a presentation. A PowerPoint presentation, for example, can be distracting if too much detail or animation is included on the slides.
Do not stand in front of a visual aid.	Most importantly, the speaker must avoid blocking the audience's view of the visual aid for any portion of the presentation. With a projection, standing in front of the visual aid creates a silhouette effect. Both are distracting and prevent the audience from experiencing the effect of the presentation as a whole.
Practicing with the visual is important.	Sometimes good intentions with a powerful visual aid go awry because the speaker has not sufficiently practiced with it or has not considered possible mishaps. Especially when using technology, speakers should be familiar with troubleshooting methods and have an alternative approach ready should their technology fail.
Look at the audience despite the visual aid.	Nervous speakers might depend on the visual aid for support and look more at the visual aid than at the audience. This signals a lack of confidence and prevents speakers from fully connecting with their audiences.
Make sure the room is appropriate for the visual aid.	Sometimes visual aids will be too large or too small for the location or audience, either of which can be distracting. Speakers should therefore be familiar with the presentation space and location of their audiences.
Make sure the visual aid has a clear purpose.	A visual aid—especially a chart, graph, or image—will only be effective if the audience understands its purpose. If a visual aid is never explained or referred to throughout the course of a presentation, it can probably be removed.
Keep it simple.	When it comes to visual aids, simpler is often better. Endless bullet points, too many sensory images, or too much information can overwhelm an audience and cause viewers to lose interest in the visual, the speaker, or both.

Developing students' skills with presentation software (e.g., Microsoft PowerPoint or Prezi) is also part of an effective ELA teacher's curriculum. Presentation software, slides, images, videos, movie clips, charts, graphs, songs, sound clips—or any combination of these and other technologies—can be integrated into presentations to support and emphasize the speaker's main points. Teachers must understand these technologies not only so that they can apply them in their classrooms but also so that they can instruct students on how to use these technologies most effectively—a skill that will continue to benefit them throughout their academic careers and into the workplace.

Helpful Hint:

When it comes to using visual aids, teachers should make the same considerations as speakers do by embracing such tools and learning how to apply and execute them appropriately in the context of a lesson. Like presentations, lessons can be derailed by faulty, unnecessary, or otherwise distracting visual aids.

Important Works

"On Women's Right to Vote"

(Title variations include: "Women's Right to the Suffrage" and "Is it a Crime to Vote?")

Speaker: Susan B. Anthony

Date: 1873

Summary: After being arrested, tried, and found guilty of voting in the 1872 presidential election, Anthony was required to pay a $100 fine. This speech explains why she refused to pay and why she believed she was innocent. She begins by quoting the preamble of the Constitution, explaining that "we the people" refers to all people—not just men. She argues that denying women voting rights denies the consent of the governed and creates a "hateful oligarchy of sex." Anthony concludes by explaining that women are citizens and thus have the right to consent to be governed. Therefore, any law that discriminates against women and African Americans is void because it denies their rights as American citizens.

Themes and Rhetorical Strategies: appeal to logic rooted in the Constitution, citizenship, equality, personhood, discrimination

Practice Question

4) What are some guidelines that a speaker should follow when using presentation software for a speech about city planning?
   A. to simply sit down by the computer with a clicker in hand, and let the slides speak for themselves
   B. to fill the slideshow with graphics, animation, word art, music, and surprise sounds to entertain the audience since the message will be most effective with a flashy and exciting design
   C. to use the slideshow as a visual tool with carefully chosen, dynamic images, incorporated at specifically chosen moments
   D. to create several slides with bullet points and then add transitions that cause the words to bounce in and out of each slide to keep the attention of the audience

Nonverbal Communication Skills

Developing students' nonverbal communication skills is equally as important as developing their oral language skills. **Nonverbal communication** refers to any way communication occurs outside of speech. Examples of nonverbal communication include the following:

- **paralinguistics** (tone, loudness, inflection, and pitch)
- facial expressions
- gestures
- body language/posture
- proximity
- eye contact

Each of the instructional activities discussed in this chapter can also focus on nonverbal communication skills as part of overall oral communication. Additionally, activities such as having students play charades or act out a "silent" movie can show them how even nonverbal communication has an impact.

Students can focus on paralinguistics by practicing speaking for an audience and then reviewing an audio or video recording of themselves. They can also analyze audio or video recordings of famous speeches for tone and inflection or other nonverbal communication, such as gestures or eye contact.

Eye contact and **body language** are integral in effective speech delivery. A speaker who makes eye contact with the audience, for example, will likely be perceived as more honest, genuine, and accessible than a speaker who looks above the audience or does not meet the eyes of the general audience at all.

Effective speakers also make emotional connections with their audiences by meeting the gaze of as many members as possible throughout the course of a speech. Additionally, effective speakers consider body language and seek to present themselves as calm and confident in their gestures and posture.

Educators should not judge culturally nuanced means of nonverbal communication as incorrect or correct but should instead focus on what is most appropriate for a given situation. Students should also be made aware that nonverbal communication varies based on locale, and different cultures have different norms or standards for gestures, eye contact, volume of voice, and so on.

Important Works

Martin Luther King Jr's "I Have a Dream" speech

Speaker: Martin Luther King Jr.

Date: August 28, 1963

Summary: King gave this famous speech at the March on Washington, a protest against racial discrimination. He begins by referencing the unfulfilled promises of the Emancipation Proclamation as African Americans still do not have the same freedoms as White Americans. He then calls for continued nonviolence in protests and to unite with White allies. He encourages listeners to continue to fight for justice when they return to their homes throughout the nation. King then explains his dream for the future of the country in which all people will be judged by their character and not their skin color. He ends with a call for people to work together so that America, founded on the principle of freedom for all, can truly be a nation of freedom for all.

Themes and Rhetorical Strategies: anaphora (i.e., repetition of "I have a dream"); nonviolent resistance; hope; freedom; the fight against racism

Practice Question

5) A high school English class watches and then discusses a video of an international technology expert's online presentation about artificial intelligence. The class agrees that they enjoyed the speaker's presentation but that his tone seemed too angry, which obscured the message. Which aspect of oral communication did the class critique?
- A. paralinguistics
- B. prosody
- C. morphology
- D. semantics

Listening Skills

Listening skills can be slower to develop than language skills, especially among younger children. A popular technique with younger students is **whole-body listening**. This strategy gives students explicit instruction on how to listen using their entire body:

- *Eyes* should be on the speaker.
- *Ears* should be listening.
- *Mouth* should be quiet.
- *Hands* should be in the lap or away from others.
- *Feet* should be still.
- *Body* should be pointed toward the speaker.
- *Brain* should be thinking about what it is hearing.
- *Heart* should be considerate of others.

Active listening is the process of fully concentrating on speakers and their messages; it is focused and empathetic. Students should be taught the following aspects of active listening:

- **Focusing:** Students practice keeping their attention on the person who is speaking.
- **Positive nonverbal cues:** Students demonstrate interest by looking at the speaker and using appropriate facial expressions and body language.
- **Allowing the speaker to finish uninterrupted:** Students wait for a speaker to finish, and then they concentrate on the message before formulating a response.
- **Nonjudgment:** Students listen and respond with respect for the speaker's views and feelings. They agree or disagree by using methods that maintain respect within the whole group.
- **Paraphrasing:** Students verify understanding by restating the speaker's main points concisely and in different words.

Practice Question

6) Which of the following quotes is a demonstration of active listening?
    A. "If I understand correctly, you think the class needs more time on this project."
    B. "I think you meant to say that you need more time to finish this project."
    C. "You didn't say how much more time you would need to finish."
    D. "There's no way I can let you have more time to finish this project."

Answer Key

1) C: In a class-wide debate, students have to think about the play critically, form an opinion, and then express that opinion orally. Of the options presented, option C offers the best way to incorporate oral language for critical thinking into the teacher's unit on Shakespeare's *Romeo and Juliet*.

2) B: A debate requires students to research a particular topic and gather evidence to support their positions on it.

3) B: This approach is not effective because it would not necessitate participation in the discussion; the students could likely answer these questions without engaging with the discussion.

4) C: Visuals should be used sparingly and purposefully.

5) A: Paralinguistics refers to the parts of speaking outside of the words themselves, such as tone, loudness, inflection, and pitch.

6) A: This quote demonstrates active listening because the listener is paraphrasing the message to clarify understanding.

Differentiation Strategies and Communication

Instructing Students with Reading Difficulties and Disabilities

Students with reading difficulties and disabilities that impact reading performance need explicit, systematic, direct instruction. Instruction must also be based on each student's needs as revealed through assessment and data collection. If instruction is not targeted in this way, it may be ineffective and/or increase student frustration.

Instructional strategies and intervention techniques for students with reading difficulties and disabilities are generally provided to either increase word identification or decoding on the word level or increase overall comprehension. Specific strategies and interventions are discussed below.

Scaffolding refers to the supports used by teachers (or sometimes peers) during classroom activities. Scaffolds should be built into all lessons per the **Universal Design for Learning (UDL)**, which states that all students should be able to learn from the same curriculum. (The UDL is discussed in more detail later on in this section.)

Shaping refers to providing incremental reinforcers and is helpful in instructing students with reading difficulties and disabilities. For example, as students progress by memorizing more grade-level high-frequency words, they should receive frequent, positive feedback from educators. This feedback is important for students who struggle with reading since they may not receive the consistent positive reinforcers, such as high grades or praise from peers, that other students who excel academically typically receive.

Students with reading difficulties on the comprehension level benefit most from instruction and interventions that help them develop metacognition to self-assess understanding and apply strategies to integrate information and synthesize it with existing knowledge. Such strategies include semantic mapping or other visual organizers, reciprocal teaching (Chapters 2 and 3), and the PQ4R method.

In the **PQ4R method**—an extension of the SQ3R method (Chapter 3)—students preview the reading material, generate questions, and read to answer the questions. They then reflect on what they have read, recite or retell from memory what they have read, and then review the material for any missed information.

In addition to the instructional strategies above, students with disabilities that impact reading (e.g., dyslexia) can benefit from certain accommodations. **Accommodations** are changes to materials or instructional methodologies that allow all students to learn the same material as their peers. Material and instructional accommodations include those listed in Table 9.1.

Table 9.1. Material and Instructional Accommodations

Material Accommodations	Instructional Accommodations
underlining or highlighting the key words in directions	<ul><li>clarifying directions through oral repetition</li><li>providing a written version of directions</li></ul>
chunking assignments or presenting them in smaller increments	<ul><li>implementing daily routines to clarify expectations</li></ul>
using a glossary or list of key vocabulary terms	<ul><li>providing visual aids whenever possible</li></ul>
using chapter-by-chapter, page-by-page, or even paragraph-by-paragraph reading guides	<ul><li>encouraging the use of mnemonic devices</li></ul>
using assistive technology	<ul><li>providing students a hard copy of notes</li></ul>
audio recordings or books on tape	<ul><li>implementing frequent review and reinforcement activities at the end of each lesson</li></ul>
e-readers or tablets	<ul><li>reviewing previously learned concepts at the beginning of a new lesson</li></ul>
text-to-speech software	<ul><li>creating opportunities for additional or extended practice using peer learning strategies</li></ul>

At times, students with reading disabilities will also need modifications to what they are expected to learn. **Modifications** are usually listed on the student's Individualized Education Program (IEP) and may include a reduced number of questions or items on assessments, different grading criteria, and so on. ELA teachers may collaborate with special education teachers to develop and monitor accommodations and modifications for students with learning disabilities that impact reading performance.

Practice Question

1) A tenth-grade English teacher wants to help one of her students who has dyslexia and is very frustrated and overwhelmed by the assigned novel the class is reading. Which of the following would be MOST appropriate?
   A. have the student read a study guide of the novel instead of the novel
   B. encourage the student to read at least fifty to one hundred pages each day
   C. give the student an audio recording of the book to aid in comprehension
   D. read the entire novel aloud in class, asking a different student to read orally each day

The Universal Design for Learning (UDL)

The **Universal Design for Learning (UDL)** is a framework to optimize teaching and learning. It is evidence-based with a focus on how humans learn. When developing fluencies, students may require scaffolds to support them in their practice. Opportunities to learn should take this into account and be appropriately flexible. Every learner has unique needs; some may require more scaffolding, while others can maintain a high degree of independence.

There should be numerous options to help build students up. One option is providing differentiated models to emulate, which helps demonstrate how the same outcome can be reached through various approaches. This can mean providing differentiated mentors who use different guidance techniques. The use of digital reading and writing software that scales to the independence and skills of the student is also a valuable tool. Giving students multiple solutions to the problems that they encounter is an important part of building fluency and independence.

Student participation is key for academic success. This is true for one-to-one, small-group, and large-group settings. Students' interests, experiences, and knowledge should be recognized and used to promote development and a positive attitude toward learning. From assessments and participation results, it should become clear which learners require adjustments and scaffolding.

Students with 504 plans or IEPs will require appropriate and effective accommodations based on their needs. The modifications will be outlined in the plan or program. Assessment and participation will help determine what additional needs the student has and how they should be met. It is appropriate and recommended to meet with other professionals to discuss the plan. Being educated on the categories of disabilities outlined in the Individuals with Disabilities Education Act and of Child Find obligations will be helpful when identifying unique learning differences.

The key to optimizing teaching and learning for all students, regardless of their individualized paths, is to maintain flexibility. It may take numerous methods to find a learning style that works for a particular student. Offering students choices may be an effective way to see how they engage with material, how they collaborate, and what makes them feel confident. It is also a good idea to get feedback and input from students regarding which methods they feel are most helpful. This also empowers students to feel confident and excited about their learning paths.

Practice Question

2) A teacher has noticed that the students in her class are at various levels of progress with the current lesson plan, and some students are far more advanced than others. Which scaffolding tool would be MOST effective for addressing this situation?
    A. to continue with standardized lessons until everyone is caught up to the same level
    B. to go back a few lessons so that everyone can catch up from that point onward
    C. to use reading and writing software that adapts to individual skill levels
    D. to pair up students and allow them to teach each other

Legal Issues Related to Reading Disabilities

Today's special education landscape has been shaped by federal legislation over the last fifty years. Before federal legislation mandating school access passed, many individuals with disabilities were institutionalized rather than given opportunities for education. In institutions, systemic neglect and abuse were common. In the 1960s, alongside other civil rights movements, the **disability rights movement** raised public awareness about the treatment of individuals with disabilities. The federal government responded with legislation, described in Table 9.2., that supports educational opportunities for people with disabilities.

Table 9.2. Federal Special Education Acts

Act	Description
Elementary and Secondary Education Act (ESEA) 1965	<ul><li>seeks to improve student academic achievement through supplementary educational services and increased educational research and training</li><li>provides financial assistance to schools servicing a high percentage of students from low-income families (Title I funding)</li></ul>
Rehabilitation Act of 1973	<ul><li>ensures all students with disabilities a right to public education</li></ul>
Section 504 of the Rehabilitation Act	<ul><li>prohibits programs that receive federal financial assistance from discriminating on the basis of disability</li><li>requires that public schools provide students with disabilities a comparable education to those without disabilities</li><li>allows for students with disabilities to receive related services, accommodations, and modifications to ensure equal access to education</li></ul>
Education for All Handicapped Children Act (EHA or P.L. 94-142) 1975	<ul><li>ensures that students with disabilities can access any accommodations, modifications, related services, and specially designed instruction needed to make adequate educational progress in a public school setting</li></ul>
Americans with Disabilities Act (ADA) 1990	<ul><li>prohibits discrimination on the basis of disability in the workplace and all public places</li><li>provides another layer of legal protection for the right of students with disabilities to have equal access to public education</li></ul>
Individuals with Disabilities Education Act (IDEA)	<ul><li>discussed in detail in Table 9.3.</li></ul>
No Child Left Behind (NCLB) 2001	<ul><li>sought to improve the academic performance of all students through increased accountability for results, emphasizing research-based instruction, and ensuring such instruction is delivered by highly qualified teachers (HQT)</li></ul>
Every Student Succeeds Act (ESSA)	<ul><li>replaced NCLB</li></ul>

Table 9.2. Federal Special Education Acts	
Act	Description
2015	<ul><li>rolls back many of the federal education requirements, giving power back to the states</li><li>requires states to create accountability plans, track state-set accountability goals, and incorporate accountability systems</li></ul>

Congress reauthorized EHA as the **Individuals with Disabilities Education Act (IDEA) in 1990** and again with amendments in 1997 and 2004. **Part B** of IDEA provides for services for students between the ages of three and twenty-one, while **Part C** provides for early intervention services for students from birth to three years old and their families. Since its original authorization, IDEA has operated under six foundational principles as described in Table 9.3.

Table 9.3. The Six Foundational Principles of the Individuals with Disabilities Education Act (IDEA)	
Principle	Description
Free Appropriate Public Education (FAPE)	<ul><li>FAPE maintains that students with disabilities have a right to an education at no additional cost to parents</li></ul>
Appropriate and nondiscriminatory evaluation	<ul><li>Evaluations must be completed by a team of trained professionals, such as teachers or school psychologists, and should include information from parents.</li><li>Evaluations should address all areas of concern, be nondiscriminatory, and be completed in a timely manner.</li><li>Reevaluations must occur a minimum of every three years.</li></ul>
Individualized Education Program (IEP)	<ul><li>An IEP is a legal document developed by the IEP team (parents, general educators, special educators, administrators, related service providers) that reports present levels of performance, annual goals and objectives, accommodations, modifications, related services, and specially designed instruction to help students make adequate educational progress.</li></ul>
Least Restrictive Environment (LRE)	<ul><li>Students with disabilities must be provided supports with nondisabled peers to the maximum extent appropriate for them to make educational progress.</li></ul>

Table 9.3. The Six Foundational Principles of the Individuals with Disabilities Education Act (IDEA)

Principle	Description
Parent and teacher participation	- Parents must have a shared role in all special education decisions, including IEP reviews, evaluation, and placement decisions.
Procedural safeguards	- Parents must receive written notice of procedural safeguards, parent and student rights, meetings, and all educational decisions. - Parents may take due process measures in the event of a disagreement between the parent and a school district.

The most recent authorization of IDEA is the **2004 Individuals with Disabilities Education Improvement Act**. IDEA 2004 expands procedures for identifying students with learning disabilities to include identification through response to intervention. IDEA 2004 also includes several changes to align with NCLB. If students with disabilities do not qualify for services under IDEA, they may still receive support through a 504 plan. The specifics of each plan are discussed in Table 9.4.

Table 9.4. IEP Versus Section 504 Plan

	IEP	Section 504 Plan
Law	Individuals with Disabilities Education Act (IDEA)	Section 504 of the Rehabilitation Act of 1973
Department	Department of Education	Office of Civil Rights
Eligibility	a disability as defined in IDEA that impacts educational performance	a disability that impacts a major life function
Included	specialized education services, accommodations, modifications, related services	- accommodations - modifications - related services
Age	0 – 21 years	no age limits
Location	schools through grade 12	- schools through grade 12 - college - work

Practice Question

3) Which of the following would NOT be a service provided to a student under a 504 plan?
   A. occupational therapy
   B. testing accommodations
   C. extra transition time between classes
   D. specially designed instruction

Culturally Responsive Practices and Considerations

In today's language classrooms, diversity extends both to language itself and to the learning process as a whole. Teachers must understand variations in language usage across time and place and be able to instruct students to not only use language in the context of their own cultures and communities but also to understand and adapt to the unique characteristics of language usage in other places and times as well.

Teachers must simultaneously be conscious of how language and culture are impacting their own classrooms and be able to employ varied, research-based instructional techniques to meet the diverse needs of their students. To do this, it is imperative that teachers make a number of considerations to ensure that the needs of each student are being met.

It is imperative that teachers create a **safe learning environment:** Students must be taught what is appropriate and inappropriate in an academic environment, especially with regard to academic risk-taking and personal identity. Students should never be shamed (by the teacher or by other students) for making mistakes or sharing their opinions; doing so can prevent them from making efforts altogether.

An **inclusive environment** should also be created by involving numerous, varied voices in classroom discussions, offering reading material by authors of different backgrounds, and having students write and speak about their own experiences. Together, these tactics can breed acceptance in the classroom. Ultimately, all students need to feel that they, their perspectives, and their opinions and ideas are valuable in the classroom environment.

Teachers must also understand the **identities** of their students—both as individuals and as a group—in order to practice instruction that is responsive to their needs and circumstances. For example, a class that consists of college-bound seniors may have a different set of needs from a class of seniors who plan to graduate and move immediately into the workforce. A classroom with a high immigrant population will have different needs from a classroom of students who speak English as their first language.

Practice Question

4) A ninth-grade English teacher uses class discussions on controversial issues as a prewriting technique to help students form opinions for persuasive essay topics. The teacher notices that the discussions sometimes get very heated, and several students appear to have hurt feelings. What changes to this method should the teacher make so that the discussions can be beneficial to all involved?
   A. avoid oral discussions of controversial issues since ninth graders lack the socio-emotional competence to understand diverse perspectives
   B. conduct prewriting activities individually and not cooperatively since diverse perspectives obscure the intended focus
   C. set class-wide ground rules about appropriate language and interactions with peers who express diverse or contradictory perspectives
   D. focus the discussion on topics that students have no fixed opinion about so that perspectives will be less diverse and discussions less heated

Code of Ethics and Standard Practices for Texas Educators

It is necessary to have a working knowledge of the *Code of Ethics and Standard Practices for Texas Educators*. This is a set of guidelines for Texas educators to follow in order to maintain professional conduct with students, colleagues, administrative employees, and families. These guidelines state that educators should also follow the policies and rules set out by their school districts and institutions. The *Code of Ethics and Standard Practices* includes standards for professional ethical conduct, ethical conduct toward professional colleagues, and ethical conduct toward students.

The following list includes just some examples of rules covered in the "Professional Ethical Conduct" section:

- no participating in deceptive practices
- no falsifying records
- maintaining good moral character
- not using illegal drugs
- not using alcohol on school property or during school activities

The "Ethical Conduct Toward Professional Colleagues" section includes the following types of rules:

- no false statements about colleagues
- no interference with a colleague's political or citizenship rights
- no attempts to influence the professional decisions of a colleague
- no discrimination against colleagues based on race, gender, age, etc.

Examples of rules included in the "Ethical Conduct Toward Students" section include the following:

- no disclosure of confidential information regarding students
- no conduct that harms the learning ability, health, or safety of the student

- no discrimination or advantages toward students on the basis of race, gender, religion, etc.
- no romantic or sexual conduct with students.

This above lists are not complete; it is the responsibility of educators to familiarize themselves with the *Code of Ethics and Standard Practices* in its entirety.

Practice Question

5) A teacher notices that a faculty member has been partaking in alcohol consumption during his lunch hour. What is the correct path forward for the teacher in this scenario?
   A. to tell the other teachers that the faculty member is partaking in illegal drug use
   B. to report the faculty member to the appropriate authorities, as he has violated the *Code of Ethics*
   C. to confront the faculty member and tell him that he has to move schools, or else you will report him
   D. to do nothing since reporting the faculty member would be a breach of the privacy rules within the *Code of Ethics*

Communication with Stakeholders

Communicating with the Campus Community

Effective communication with the campus community, administrators, and staff is key to creating a positive and productive workplace. This means that communication should be consistent, clear, and respectful at all times. In order to accomplish this, it is necessary to establish protocols and guidelines for how communication occurs.

Some guidelines for communicating include understanding the importance of clear and concise language. Language that has been carefully selected is less likely to cause misunderstandings. It is also helpful to have information structured in a way that is easy to read. This may mean using headings, bullet points, and well-formatted paragraphs when using written communication.

"Email etiquette" is also something that should be practiced when communicating professionally in a school environment. Some rules for email etiquette include the following:

- sending an appropriate number of emails per day
- not emailing outside of reasonable work hours
- waiting a fair amount of time before following up for a response

Being respectful in communication means being understanding and empathetic toward what others are sharing. It also means being inclusive of community members who may have different perspectives due to their cultures or personal experiences. When replying to correspondence, it is important to do so promptly; doing so shows respect and acknowledgement of the other party and the information they are sharing.

Communication should remain as open and transparent as possible. All parties should be able to speak freely and trust in the credibility of their colleagues; however, it is important to take note of information that may require privacy or confidentiality. Teachers should also take care to be diligent when sharing sensitive information and be sure to share such information with relevant parties only. This may include personal information about students, families, or other educators.

Practice Question

6) A teacher has frequently been emailing late at night and following up in the morning with passive-aggressive language when a reply has not yet been received. Another teacher has been emailing other staff to casually discuss the home lives of specific students. Which of the following responses would be MOST appropriate to align with communication standards for educators?
   A. to send an email to the entire faculty and staff outlining the importance of email etiquette and confidentiality
   B. to email the two teachers individually and reprimand them for their actions
   C. to revoke email privileges for the two teachers
   D. to do nothing, since responding would only create conflict

Communicating with Families

Communicating with parents/guardians, families, and stakeholders about a student's education is key to that student's academic success. When all parties in a student's life are involved in their education, it is easier for the student to find support and encouragement when pursuing their goals. All communication should be appropriate and professional. It is imperative to use a respectful tone as well as sensitivity toward the unique home life of each student.

Practicing effective communication means staying in regular contact. Intervals for contact, such as communicating once weekly or once monthly, should be established. Determining intervals for contact will depend on the student's needs and the needs of their parents or guardians. Communication may be done via school portals, email, and phone; however, it is also important to set up parent-teacher conferences to communicate in person and with greater detail.

Just as with the campus community, administrators, and other staff, it is important to maintain clear and concise language. Progress reports should be broken down into segments that are easy to understand for the parents/guardians. This may mean dividing such reports into sections for various academic subjects and the student's behavior throughout the day, for example. Doing so can help provide insight into what the student may need extra support with at home. For example, if a student is performing poorly on reading assignments, it would be beneficial for the parents/guardians to encourage the student to read more at home.

When communicating about a student's progress, it is important to make sure that all feedback is detailed and constructive in nature. An accurate representation of the student's strengths and weaknesses should also be provided. These strengths and weaknesses should be explained with facts, such as assignment grades or real examples of the student's behavior. Suggestions for parents/guardians to support the student's interests or make attempts to foster stronger connections in weak areas should also be provided. Keeping the tone of these conversations positive and hopeful will help both students and their families feel motivated about improvement.

Practice Question

7) A teacher has a student who suddenly experienced a significant drop in her grades and academic progress. Which of the following communication methods would be MOST appropriate to inform the student's parents of the change?
    A. to inform the student that she needs to tell her parents about her declining grades
    B. to organize a parent-teacher conference where the student's decline in progress is the main subject and a positive path forward will be suggested
    C. to send home a progress report that must be signed
    D. to hold off on establishing communication and see if the grades can be improved first

Answer Key

1) C: Access to an audio recording of the book will help the student feel less overwhelmed and also scaffold comprehension since the focus is on listening skills rather than on reading skills.

2) C: Option C is the most effective scaffolding tool because it is a differentiated method that will help students of all levels. Software programs will take into account the skill level of individual students and give them content that is challenging yet doable. This also means providing assistance to those students who may be struggling in certain areas. It can also be an effective tool for those with 504 plans or IEPs, since the software is adjustable. Option A is incorrect because students who require extra assistance are unlikely to catch up on their own. Option B is incorrect because going back a few lessons would be redundant for the students who are already proficient in those lessons. Option D is incorrect because students who require assistance should be given professional differentiated tools and mentors with whom to work.

3) D: Specially designed instruction is provided as part of an Individualized Education Program (IEP), but it is not part of a 504 plan.

4) C: Rules such as "always focus comments on the argument, not the person," and "use the most respectful language possible when expressing disagreement" can help students conduct these discussions more effectively and with fewer hurt feelings.

5) B: Option B is correct because the faculty member's alcohol consumption during school hours is a violation of the *Code of Ethics and Standard Practices for Texas Educators*, specifically under the "Professional Ethical Conduct" section. Reporting this behavior to the appropriate authorities not only ensures that the issue is handled properly, it is also the duty of any educator who witnesses such violations. Option A is incorrect because spreading false information about a colleague (such as claiming he is using illegal drugs when he is not) violates the "Ethical Conduct Toward Professional Colleagues" section. Option C is incorrect because confronting the faculty member with an ultimatum and threatening to report him if he does not move schools is inappropriate and may violate the code regarding influencing professional decisions. Option D is incorrect because the *Code of Ethics* requires educators to act in the best interests of students and the school community, which includes reporting unethical behavior.

6) A: Option A is correct because it addresses the issues of email etiquette and confidentiality. Sending an email to the entire faculty and staff will serve as a reminder of the communication standards without singling out any individuals. Option B is incorrect because it is overly antagonistic and may create a poor work environment; it also does not address the widespread communication issues involving other staff. Option C is incorrect because the teachers need their emails for their work; punishing them also does not address the widespread communication issues. Option D is incorrect because the inappropriate communication will continue if it is not addressed.

7) B: Option B is correct because it is the most thorough and effective option. It is worrying when a student experiences a sudden decline, since there may be outside factors at play. Setting up a face-to-face conference is the option most likely to bring answers as to why the student may be struggling. It is the most straightforward option, and a positive path forward can be established while everyone is present and engaged. Option A is incorrect because the student may or may not inform her parents. As an educator, it is the teacher's responsibility to establish contact. Option C is incorrect because a progress report does not address the root issue of why the student's performance is suddenly declining.

Option D is incorrect because communication should be as transparent and up-front as possible. Parents/guardians of students have a right to know how their students are performing at all points in their educational journeys.

Data-Driven Practices and Assessments

Assessment

Effective assessment is the cornerstone of good teaching. Teachers who cannot properly assess their students can neither meaningfully adjust instruction nor provide useful feedback to encourage student growth. Knowledge of different kinds of assessments and their applications is therefore necessary for educators in order to provide the best instruction possible for their students.

Different methods of assessment have different applications, and each method has unique strengths and flaws. Understanding these qualities will allow educators to choose effective assessment techniques that are truly aligned with the objectives they are hoping to evaluate.

Standardized Assessment

There are numerous published assessment instruments which have standardized questions or criteria and are administered in a consistent manner. These assessments fall into two categories: norm-referenced and criterion referenced:

- **Norm-referenced assessments** measure an individual student against a group of other test takers, typically those of the same age or grade level. Results are reported in a percentile ranking or as grade-equivalent scores.
    - A **percentile** is a score that shows where a student ranks in comparison to ninety-nine other students. For example, a percentile of 81 means that the student in question has performed equal to or outperformed eighty-one out of the other ninety-nine students who took the same test.
    - **Grade-equivalent scores** provide results as a grade level, meaning that the student's performance is equal to the median performance corresponding to other students of a certain grade level.
- **Achievement tests**, such as the Iowa Test of Basic Skills (ITBS) and the Peabody Individual Achievement Test, measure which skills a student has mastered. These assessments often fall under categories like reading and mathematics, typically use multiple-choice question formats, and require test takers to answer a standardized set of questions.
- Like achievement tests, **aptitude tests** measure learned abilities, such as mathematics and verbal reasoning. They also help predict the course of future learning.
    - The SAT and ACT are two very common aptitude tests used to predict the probability of a student's success in a college environment.

- **Criterion-referenced tests** measure an individual's performance as it relates to predetermined benchmarks or criteria. These tests are generally used to measure a student's progress toward meeting certain objectives; they do not compare test takers to one another but rather compare student knowledge against the set criteria.
    - Criterion-referenced tests include everything from annual state tests to those created by teachers or educational publishers to assess mastery of learning objectives.
    - One new incarnation of the criterion-referenced test used by many states is **standards-referenced testing** or **standards-based assessment**. These tests measure a student's performance against certain content standards as defined by each grade level and subject and are typically scored in categories such as basic, proficient, and advanced; unsatisfactory, satisfactory, and advanced.
    - Most annual state accountability tests, including the State of Texas Assessments of Academic Readiness (STAAR) and the Partnership for Assessment of Readiness for College and Careers (PARCC) are standards-based, criterion-referenced tests.

Practice Question

1) When planning lessons, a teacher wants to use test scores as a starting point in order to improve vocabulary knowledge among students. Which assessment results would be MOST appropriate for her to reference?
   A. Iowa Test of Basic Skills
   B. annual state accountability test
   C. SAT scores
   D. results from running records

Types of Assessments

Formal assessments refer to test results that are reported in either a percentile or percentage format; examples include the following:

- standardized tests
- chapter or unit tests
- end-of-course exams

Informal assessments evaluate students outside of the traditional, written test format and help give a more complete picture of ongoing progress. In certain situations, particularly when students experience stress in high-stakes testing scenarios, the following types of informal assessments can be used:

- observation
- portfolios
- projects
- presentations
- oral checks

Whether formal or informal, assessments can also be either formative or summative. **Formative assessment** refers to the ongoing monitoring of student progress toward learning objectives. These are often informal assessments in which teachers seek more information to streamline instruction; however, they can be more formal, such as a short quiz about the day's material. Formative assessments do not significantly impact a student's course grade or chances of promotion to the next grade.

> **Helpful Hint**:
>
> **Diagnostic assessments** are used to determine what students already know. They are given by many teachers at the beginning of the school year or before each unit of study to calibrate the level of instruction and track progress over time.

Summative assessment is designed to evaluate student learning after the end of a defined unit of study. It compares student knowledge to the initial learning objectives that were addressed throughout the unit of study. It may be formal or informal but often takes the form of a unit test, midterm, final exam, or final paper or project. Summative assessments are generally considered high stakes because they carry high point values. They are often critical to a student's overall grade, ability to pass a course, or promotion to the next grade.

A middle ground between a formative assessment and a summative assessment is the **benchmark assessment**, which is more formal than a formative assessment but not as high stakes as standardized summative assessments. Benchmark assessments are sometimes called **interim assessments** or **predictive assessments**. They track student progress and determine the degree to which students are on track to perform well on future summative assessments.

Authentic assessment measures the student's ability to use knowledge in direct, relevant, and real-world ways. In authentic literacy assessments, students apply reading and writing skills in pragmatic or practical ways. For example, an authentic assessment of the skills needed to write for a formal audience might include having high school students work on writing a resume or a profile on a professional networking platform.

> **Helpful Hint**:
>
> Formative assessments are used while students are *forming* their knowledge. Summative assessments are used to add up all of student learning into one lump *sum*.

Teachers may also ask other students to participate in the assessment process. This is known as **peer assessment**—the evaluation of student work by peers. If students receive appropriate guidance and practice, peer assessment can be used effectively in many secondary classrooms. In a peer assessment, students are given a rubric or list of criteria upon which to assess another student's work. They are then asked to offer specific feedback for improvement. This process can help students who are unsure of how to revise or edit their work since they are given clear and actionable suggestions.

> **Helpful Hint**:
>
> While most peer assessments do not result in formal grades, they can be invaluable in helping students revise their work before submitting it for grading.

Multi-perspective assessments are also used during cooperative learning activities. In these types of assessments, peers, the individual student, and teachers all collaborate to assess learning outcomes. This method can be helpful when parts of a group project occur both in and out of the classroom. In a multi-perspective assessment, the teacher may weigh input from various assessors differently when computing the total overall grade. For example:

- The teacher evaluation of the finished project may count for 75 percent of the grade.

- The peer assessment of group members might count for another 10 percent of the grade.
- Finally, the student's self-assessment could count for the remaining 15 percent of the grade.

Practice Questions

2) A teacher wants to assess student retainment of skills at the end of a small-group intervention aimed at vocabulary acquisition. Which method of assessment should be used?
   A. a norm-referenced assessment
   B. asking students to write down three new words they learned
   C. having students take a 25-question multiple-choice test
   D. a standardized achievement test

3) A tenth-grade English teacher wants to create an authentic assessment to evaluate students' skills with writing coherent paragraphs. Which assignment would be BEST?
   A. directing students to give a presentation to the class on something they know how to do well
   B. asking students to analyze the way paragraphs are used in a newspaper article
   C. assigning students to write the draft of an email they will eventually send to someone
   D. having students use a graphic organizer to formulate their thoughts into paragraphs before writing an essay

Assessing Reading and Writing Skills

Assessing Reading Skills

Assessing reading skills requires acknowledging how listening, speaking, reading, writing, and thinking are interconnected. Assessments should be designed to guide reading instruction and evaluate comprehension before moving on to new content. Reading assessments should be ongoing and created using evidence-based practices. A standard that students must meet through assessments should be implemented within the instruction.

Numerous factors may affect student success on reading proficiency assessments. The students' previous teachings and knowledge may influence how they grasp new concepts. Instruction should therefore take into account background knowledge and areas of potential struggle. The amount of reading practice that the students get per day will also affect their reading proficiencies. Rather than focusing on memorization and worksheets, students should be using whole, complex texts for learning. This instruction should be culturally responsive to improve student engagement and success. This means using a diverse range of texts that allow students to connect with their own backgrounds.

Another factor to consider when assessing reading skills is second-language acquisition. Some students may already read and write in a different language before learning English. These English learners may need extra support. Their proficiency levels may not match their grade levels due to limited English exposure and struggles to transfer reading and writing skills that they have already learned from their first language to English. For example, someone who has moved from another country may be at the tenth-grade level but only understand English at a seventh-grade level. English learners may benefit from slower paced instruction, increased vocabulary instruction, and a focus on linking background knowledge and culture to instruction. Visual aids during assessment may also prove helpful.

Practice Question

4) An English instructor in a dual language classroom is conducting an assessment on a recent news article the class read together. Although the ESL students contributed to the in-class discussion about the article, a multiple-choice quiz about the topic shows that many of the ESL students struggle to connect the content in the article with the answer options presented. Which assessment strategy would BEST help the ESL students?
- A. having the teacher read the test questions and answer options aloud
- B. assigning additional assessments to align with vocabulary instruction
- C. giving the assessment as a take-home assignment
- D. providing pictures or other visual clues alongside the answer options

Assessing Vocabulary Skills

Vocabulary development should be guided through assessments. How students perform on these assessments will guide the instruction and pacing of new content. The assessments should be consistently given while following standards and methods provided by research evidence. Students should be given frequent opportunities to use new vocabulary. Comprehension should be sufficient before moving on to new instruction. Students with unique needs should receive appropriate adjustments to ensure their success. Several factors can influence vocabulary development in students:

- Familial and cultural factors can impede progress made at home.
    - In homes where English is not the first language, students may lack support with their vocabulary progress.
    - Linguistically, students who speak a first language that is not English may struggle to adapt to new word structures, phonology, and code-switching.
- Students may come from different educational backgrounds that affect how they learn.
- Socioeconomic status may affect students' access to support, such as outside tutoring.
- The developmental status of students also plays a role in how quickly they learn new vocabulary.

Students will learn three different tiers of vocabulary:

- **Tier 1** is everyday vocabulary.
    - This is vocabulary that is used in everyday conversation.
- **Tier 2** vocabulary includes words that are often used in academic settings.
    - This vocabulary is relevant across multiple subjects.
    - These words may not come up in students' everyday conversations, but they are highly relevant to their education.
- **Tier 3** vocabulary words are specific to a field of study.
    - These are low-frequency words that are necessary when discussing specific subjects.

Instruction of vocabulary words should include the principles of word formation in English. These include the use of affixes and roots as well as a working knowledge of the origin of words. Students should be able to use both print and digital resources to learn about a word's meaning, syllabication, pronunciation, origin, and part of speech. They can then learn the denotative, connotative, and figurative meanings behind the word. This will provide a precise understanding of the word in its entirety. It is important to use research-based strategies to assess students' development; both formal and informal methods should be used. Quizzes, flashcards, summative exams, and writing assignments can all test for a student's progress. The results of these assessments should guide further instruction and potential intervention.

Practice Question

5) A student with a primary language other than English is struggling to grasp vocabulary words specific to history lessons. To get the student on track with her classmates, which intervention should take place?
    A. take the student aside to revisit Tier 2 vocabulary and the principles of word formation
    B. continue on with normal lessons, which will force the student to catch up
    C. give the student additional writing assignments to practice her skills
    D. allow the student to do vocabulary work in her primary language instead

Assessing Writing Skills

Assessing writing skills in a holistic, constructive way is a unique challenge for secondary ELA teachers, who must find ways to both assign scores to students' work and provide feedback to help them improve their writing skills. The goal for all of the assessment tools and response strategies discussed in this section is to provide students with useful feedback about their writing.

Teachers who plan to provide a traditional, numbered score (usually zero to one hundred) on a writing assignment may want to include a rubric. **Rubrics** are assessment tools that teachers use to objectively assign scores to projects or assignments whose merits are difficult to quantify, especially writing assignments.

> **Helpful Hint**:
> Useful feedback consists neither of falsified praise nor crushing criticism; it is an authentic celebration of strengths and a suggested pathway for improvement in the future.

Well-designed rubrics make grading guidelines clear for both the teacher and the students so that confusion and subjectivity are eliminated as much as possible. Two commonly used rubrics are the holistic rubric and the analytical rubric:

- **Holistic rubrics** provide a grade based on the overall effectiveness of the product. For example, holistic rubrics might assign a score based on the overall effectiveness of an argumentative essay.
- **Analytic rubrics** break the product down so that points are assigned based on the component parts. For example, an analytic rubric for an argumentative essay would separately score the thesis, evidence, organization, and grammar to produce an overall score.

In addition to rubrics, writing teachers employ a variety of other assessment techniques to provide students with useful, timely feedback. Providing feedback is a skill in itself and a responsibility that can be shared between the teacher and students. Effective teachers understand the value of constructive criticism and prioritize the need for regular writing feedback.

Sometimes, teachers may hold writing conferences—either as needed or at particular times throughout the year—to provide the feedback themselves. The purpose of a writing conference is to help students improve their writing skills by highlighting individual strengths and identifying areas that are most in need of improvement. Portfolios are also useful tools for assessment since they allow both the teacher and students to track and observe growth over time.

Practice Question

6) A ninth-grade English teacher is grading a nonfiction writing assignment using a holistic rubric. Which of the following should the teacher NOT do?
   A. mark the number of points deducted for each criteria not met by the student
   B. ensure that each student receives credit for effort
   C. consider how well the student addressed the writing prompt
   D. assign each student a grade based on the overall quality of the individual works

Answer Key

1) B: Most annual state accountability tests are standards-based assessments that are criterion-referenced based on state standards. These results would help the teacher align her lessons with both her students' needs and her state's standards.

2) B: Asking students to write down three new words they learned is a short, informal assessment that gives the teacher the needed data about what has been retained from the session.

3) C: Assigning students to write the draft of an email they will eventually send to someone is an authentic assessment because students will actually send the email to someone, so the assessment has a real-world application. It also allows the teacher to assess the students' use of paragraphs.

4) D: Providing visual aids on assessments can help English language learners tap into background knowledge and connect what they already know to what they are learning.

5) A: Option A is correct because, by revisiting Tier 2 vocabulary and the principles of word formation, the student will build upon the foundation necessary to tackle Tier 3 vocabulary (subject-specific). Option B is incorrect because a student who is falling behind in a specific area should not be forced to continue on. Without addressing the issue now, the student will struggle with highly specific vocabulary in other academic subjects, which will hurt her education overall. Option C is incorrect because, although writing assignments may help the student practice her vocabulary, the student needs additional support beyond independent work: her foundational skills need to be reinforced and taught by someone with expertise. Option D is incorrect because learning the vocabulary in the student's primary language will not help with her English development, which is a necessity for continuing her educational journey.

6) A: Holistic rubrics do not attach point values to specific criteria; instead, a single score is given based on the criteria laid out in the rubric for each score range.

Developing Data-Driven Instruction

Overview of the Constructed-Response Portion of the Exam

The TExES English Language Arts and Reading 7 – 12 (331) exam requires test takers to answer a question in a constructed-response format that demonstrates the candidate's comprehension of teaching principles and strategies that can be used to achieve a stated learning goal. The principles and strategies that the test taker discusses must be driven by data and based on standards. Stated learning goals in this portion of the exam may include the following:

- developing a specific learning goal that corresponds to a specific ELA academic standard and based on a literary (or informational) text or excerpt
- using strategies to assess students' command of a stated learning goal and being able to identify any learning challenges
- using teaching strategies to address learning challenges that have already been identified
- providing students with opportunities to build knowledge through texts, real-life experiences, and background knowledge
- using various strategies to differentiate instruction in order to meet the diverse needs of students
- using strategies to assess the growth of students as concerns meeting stated learning goals and using data to gauge student progress and inform instruction

Test takers will be provided with an "exhibit" that includes additional information related to the prompt as well as a grade-level literary or informational text excerpt. A constructed (i.e., written) response is then required. In this response, English language arts standards must be met as the educator develops a specific learning plan for the text. Note that the written response must adhere to the conventions of Standard English.

Educators should also be able to assess a student's mastery of specific learning goals. Doing so includes being able to identify learning challenges. Once challenges are identified, educators should be able to apply knowledge of instructional strategies to address the issue. If those strategies do not work, educators should be able to pivot toward other strategies or utilize other forms of professional assistance.

All students should be given the opportunity to use a variety of texts that allow them to make deeper connections between the texts they are reading and build knowledge by leveraging prior understanding, and using real-world experiences. It is the role of the educator to set students up for success with this and encourage progression. Educators should know how to effectively use strategies to provide students with the ability to use texts in this way.

Educators should be able to use knowledge of strategies for differentiating instruction to align with the diverse needs of all students. Students will have different learning capabilities, needs, and preferences. Educators should be able to identify these and then use a variety of instructional methods to create the most effective educational environment for students to succeed academically.

It is also vital that educators are able to assess student growth through a variety of strategies. This progress will be aligned with a specific learning goal, which means using standards-based assessments and analyzing the data they provide to measure progress and plan future instruction according to the results.

Sample Prompt

- An educator is teaching her students how to identify multiple themes within a text and explain how they connect to everyday life.

- The students are assigned an excerpt from *The Prince and the Pauper*. They are told to identify two themes within the text and then use textual evidence to explain how those themes are interconnected.

- **Your task:** Using evidence-based standards and data, describe a learning plan that will support students in identifying themes from the chosen text and explaining the interconnectedness of those themes based on textual evidence.

The Prince and the Pauper by Mark Twain

In the ancient city of London, on a certain autumn day in the second quarter of the sixteenth century, a boy was born to a poor family of the name of Canty, who did not want him. On the same day another English child was born to a rich family of the name of Tudor, who did want him. All England wanted him too. England had so longed for him, and hoped for him, and prayed God for him, that, now that he was really come, the people went nearly mad for joy. Mere acquaintances hugged and kissed each other and cried. Everybody took a holiday, and high and low, rich and poor, feasted and danced and sang, and got very mellow; and they kept this up for days and nights together. By day, London was a sight to see, with gay banners waving from every balcony and housetop, and splendid pageants marching along. By night, it was again a sight to see, with its great bonfires at every corner, and its troops of revellers making merry around them. There was no talk in all England but of the new baby, Edward Tudor, Prince of Wales, who lay lapped in silks and satins, unconscious of all this fuss, and not knowing that great lords and ladies were tending him and watching over him—and not caring, either. But there was no talk about the other baby, Tom Canty, lapped in his poor rags, except among the family of paupers whom he had just come to trouble with his presence.

Sample Constructed Response

In order to encourage students to find themes within the text and connect them with the real world and their experiences, I would first have them read *The Prince and the Pauper*, which has very clear themes of social class and inequality. After individual reading, I would then encourage a class discussion where students can share how they feel about the characters' circumstances in the excerpt. This could be accompanied by the students writing key words from the discussion on the whiteboard or digital board. For example, if students share words such as *unfair* or *wealth*, they would then be written for the class to take note of. This would lead the discussion in the direction of identifying the major themes.

After identifying the major themes during class-wide discussion, the students would be instructed to write journal entries in which they share experiences they have had in their lives that remind them of the story. This would allow them to connect the themes that they are learning about with the real world. Prompting students to talk about how the excerpt made them feel and what they would do if they were in the story would encourage an additional depth of understanding of the textual themes. In an individual journal entry assignment, students may feel more open to sharing personal experiences that they would otherwise not feel comfortable sharing in front of the class. Additionally, for the teacher reading these journal entries, it is easier to understand what levels students are at with their independent comprehension.

To then expand upon the assignment, students would be told to pick out words or phrases that indicate the themes of the work. These words or phrases could be written on flashcards and paired together in various ways. For example, for the theme of social inequality, students might point out the sentence in which the entirety of England was praying for Edward Tudor to be born versus the one that states nobody was talking about Tom Canty. Vocabulary comparisons could be *rich* versus *poor* and *silks* versus *rags*. These word pairings demonstrate the theme of inequality. This type of assignment would help students learn how to use textual evidence to support their claims regarding theme. It would also provide a visualization tool for students who learn best through such methods.

Sample Response Analysis

The response demonstrates a solid understanding of teaching strategies for theme identification and textual evidence use. It uses teaching methods such as class discussions, personal reflections, and vocabulary comparisons to aid in the students' understanding of the text's themes and how they reflect the world around them.

The first paragraph discusses an effective strategy to help the students identify themes within the excerpt that they were instructed to read. The strategy ensures engagement and participation by having the students physically write key words for the class to see. The class discussion of the text will lead to more creative brainstorming and allow for a variety of perspectives to be shared. It will also encourage critical thinking.

The second paragraph provides students with a personal assignment that allows them to reflect and connect themes with their own experiences. This increases their depth of understanding regarding the excerpt and its themes. It also explains how this assignment will aid in the teacher's assessment of the students' skills.

The third paragraph shares an assignment designed to aid in developing the students' skills in connecting themes with textual evidence. This is an especially important skill in writing and analysis. Including a physical component, such as flashcards, increases engagement levels. This assignment will once again deepen the students' connection to the text and thus help achieve the objective of identifying themes, understanding how they connect with real life, and showing how textual evidence supports those themes.

Although the response provides strong, relevant examples of teaching methods, there is room for improvement. The response could further explain what the teacher will take away from these assignments and how the findings will aid in the teacher's evaluation of the students. Monitoring progress is a vital part of reaching new objectives. The response could also provide methods of differentiation for students who may not benefit from these assignments.

Practice Test

1) A teacher is hoping to aid students in acquiring background knowledge through the reading of informational texts. What is the MOST effective strategy for doing this?
    A. instruct the class to read aloud and then discuss the text through guided questions
    B. have students read texts at home without in-class discussion or instruction
    C. encourage students to look up additional information at home to deepen their understanding
    D. follow an unstructured method where it is up to the students to find the method that works best for them

2) A middle school teacher is struggling to keep the attention of his students during his prepared lessons. According to the Universal Design of Learning principles, how should the educator approach diverse learning needs?
    A. have small-group instruction where more advanced learners can teach those who are behind in certain subjects
    B. use a one-size-fits-all approach so that the diverse learning needs are not a problem later on in the students' education
    C. give standardized tests at the beginning and end of the year to determine the current needs of the students
    D. prepare multiple options for diverse engagement, expression, and representation dependent on the students' needs

3) What is the main goal of providing students with an arsenal of word-attack strategies?
    A. to increase oral fluency and prosody
    B. to develop automaticity through sight word awareness
    C. to improve the decoding of unfamiliar words
    D. to decrease reliance on context clues

4) An ELA teacher is trying to create learning environments that respect cultural and linguistic diversity but still aim to meet challenging state standards for oral communication. Which of the following strategies should the teacher include in her lesson planning?
    A. strategies to eliminate an accent based on careful and scripted training
    B. strategies to promote code-switching once students enter the school
    C. opportunities to teach strategies for adjusting register based on audience
    D. opportunities to recognize and correct the use of slang and idioms in speech

5) Which of the following is the LEAST credible print source?
    A. *Journal of the American Medical Association*
    B. a PETA brochure
    C. *Across Five Aprils* by Irene Hunt
    D. *MLA Style Manual and Guide to Scholarly Publishing*

6) Which of the following sentences contains a comma usage error?
    A. On her way home she stopped to pick up groceries, pay her electric bill, and buy some flowers.
    B. I used to drink coffee every morning but my office took away the coffee machine.
    C. Elizabeth will order the cake for the party after she orders the hats.
    D. My cousin, who lives in Indiana, is coming to visit this weekend.

Questions 7 – 8 refer to the following excerpt from "The Whistle" by Benjamin Franklin:

When I was a child of seven years old, my friends on a holiday filled my pocket with coppers. I went directly to a shop where they sold toys for children; and, being charmed with the sound of a whistle that I met by the way in the hands of another boy, I voluntarily offered and gave all my money for one. I then came home, and went whistling all over the house, much pleased with my whistle, but disturbing all the family. My brothers and sisters and cousins, understanding the bargain I had made, told me I had given four times as much for it as it was worth; put me in mind what good things I might have bought with the rest of the money, and laughed at me so much for my folly, that I cried with vexation; and the reflection gave me more chagrin than the whistle gave me pleasure. . . . When I see a beautiful, sweet-tempered girl married to an ill-natured brute of a husband, What a pity, say I, that she should pay so much for a whistle! In short, I conceive that great part of the miseries of mankind are brought upon them by the false estimates they have made of the value of things, and by their giving too much for their whistles.

7) Which of the following does the author use to engage the reader's attention?
    A. sarcasm
    B. an implicit assertion
    C. an anecdote
    D. understatement

8) What can be inferred about the motives of the narrator's family?
    A. The family wants to teach the narrator caution in spending his money.
    B. The family is simply teasing the narrator, who seems to take things too seriously.
    C. The family wants to discourage the narrator from playing the whistle.
    D. The family wants to make sure the narrator will not grow up to be easily influenced by others.

9) Which type of phrase is underlined in the following sentence?

Mark, <u>a native of Massachusetts</u>, worked one summer at the *Boston Globe*.
    A. appositive
    B. absolute
    C. prepositional
    D. gerund

10) A new student joins the classroom halfway through the year after moving from another country. While the student grasps most material, he is struggling with reading complex texts at his assigned grade level. Which of the following approaches would BEST support the student's reading progress?
   A. Give the student culturally responsive texts and provide slower instruction with additional support from past lessons.
   B. Pair the student with an advanced reader and assign that student the task of determining if the new student has dyslexia.
   C. Assign memorization tasks for a variety of complex vocabulary words.
   D. Allow the student to read at his reading proficiency level and retest at the end of the year to see if there has been improvement.

11) Which of the following represents common knowledge that would NOT need documentation in a research paper?
   A. the fact that the US Civil War lasted from 1861 to 1865
   B. metadata from a study on the effects of sleep deprivation on driving
   C. the results of a survey on a major university campus regarding the subject of free speech
   D. a police report summarizing the murder rates from the top ten most populous cities in the United States

12) A middle school teacher has been assigned a new class of students. They have taken note that the students come from diverse cultures. What strategy should the teacher implement to create a positive, inclusive environment for all students?
   A. limit the use of bilingual resources in order to ensure English-only discussion
   B. assign homework that asks students to study their culture and discuss it with family
   C. standardize lessons so that there is uniformity within the classroom
   D. provide open-ended assignments that allow students to integrate their cultural backgrounds and experiences

13) To find the comparative and superlative forms of a word, which of the following sources should a writer consult?
   A. a table of contents
   B. a dictionary
   C. a thesaurus
   D. a glossary

14) An educator is preparing materials to give to high school students before a summer study abroad trip. Which of the following is the BEST topic on nonverbal communication to include?
   A. an explanation of how nonverbal and verbal communication work together
   B. definitions of important terms like paralinguistics
   C. research that explains the importance of nonverbal communication
   D. a list of nonverbal communication that might be different abroad from what students are used to at home

15) Which of the following is an example of an authentic assessment?
   A. After a unit on letter-writing, students are asked to write and send a letter to a person they know.
   B. After a unit on letter-writing, students are given an oral exam on key terms they have learned.
   C. After a unit on making inferences, students take a written multiple-choice test.
   D. After a unit on making inferences, students write an essay about what they have learned.

16) What is one main assertion of reader-response theory?
    A. There is one correct interpretation of a literary text.
    B. Readers do not interpret literary text; they simply experience it.
    C. There is a simple process for understanding text that involves paying careful attention to the repeated elements of the text and the emotions elicited by those elements.
    D. Readers participate in the creative process; the meaning of a literary text is found partially in the author's design and partially in the reader's experience of the text.

Questions 17 – 18 refer to the poem "Smoke" by Henry David Thoreau:

Light-winged Smoke, Icarian bird,

Melting thy pinions in thy upward flight,

Lark without song, and messenger of dawn

Circling above the hamlets as they nest;

Or else, departing dream, and shadowy form

Of midnight vision, gathering up thy skirts;

By night star-veiling, and by day

Darkening the light and blotting out the sun;

Go thou my incense upward from this hearth,

And ask the gods to pardon this clear flame.

17) Which term BEST describes this poem?
    A. a sonnet
    B. an extended metaphor
    C. a ballad
    D. an ironic statement

18) What does the word *pinions* mean?
    A. restraints that tie the arms to the body
    B. cuts to the end of a bird's wing that prevent it from flying
    C. the fall of Icarus
    D. the outer feathers on a bird's wing

Questions 19 – 20 refer to the first stanza of the poem "The Second Coming" by William Butler Yeats:

Turning and turning in the widening gyre

The falcon cannot hear the falconer;

Things fall apart; the centre cannot hold;

Mere anarchy is loosed upon the world,

The blood-dimmed tide is loosed, and everywhere

The ceremony of innocence is drowned;

The best lack all conviction, while the worst

Are full of passionate intensity.

19) "The blood-dimmed tide is loosed" is which of the following?
   A. a metaphor
   B. hyperbole
   C. an understatement
   D. a simile

20) The novel *Things Fall Apart* by Chinua Achebe takes its title from "The Second Coming" poem. What is the connection between the poem and the novel?
   A. The novel *Things Fall Apart* relates the decline of the British monarchy.
   B. In the novel *Things Fall Apart*, the account of disease and suffering in Africa has the same emotional effect as Yeats' poem.
   C. The novel *Things Fall Apart* shows the destructive impact of British imperialism on the culture of people in Africa.
   D. The Atlantic slave trade, which caused the destruction of many African villages, is described in the novel *Things Fall Apart*; Achebe used Yeats' poem to draw parallels to the suffering of its victims.

21) A seventh-grade teacher hopes to enhance his students' abilities to comprehend and use advanced vocabulary in their writing. The teacher wants the students to be able to decipher the meanings of unfamiliar words on their own and with ease. Which activity would MOST effectively help students determine the meaning of unknown vocabulary words?
   A. assign writing in the form of a research essay that requires Tier 3 vocabulary usage
   B. have students use flashcards with prefixes, roots, and suffixes to practice combining them
   C. have students read aloud and sound out words with which they are unfamiliar
   D. give students a dictionary to look up any unknown words during reading

22) An ELA teacher is co-planning with a special education teacher to meet the needs of a student with dysgraphia. Which of the following scaffolds is MOST appropriate to include in the plan?
   A. a text reader
   B. large-print text
   C. speech-to-text software
   D. texts at a lower Lexile level

23) Which introduction to a quotation within the body of a research paper would sound the MOST academic and lend credibility to the source?
   A. In their online article for the medical supply company, Dr. Smith and Dr. Jones indicate that . . .
   B. Several well-known authors agree with the following assertion:
   C. Medical professionals all across the United States have testified that . . .
   D. Dr. Frank Johnson, orthopedic surgeon from Medical University, asserts in his latest article that the . . .

24) James Russell Lowell is MOST closely associated with which group of poets?
   A. the Transcendentalist poets
   B. the Fireside poets
   C. the Imagists
   D. the Beat poets

25) A middle school teacher has noticed that her students are struggling to engage in independent, self-sustained reading while developing text comprehension. What is the MOST effective solution to this problem?
   A. assign more independent reading homework to increase practice time
   B. reduce independent reading time and have students read in small groups where they can discuss the text
   C. focus on teaching self-monitoring skills while allowing students to select texts of interest to them
   D. scale back on the text difficulty so that students are only working with simple vocabulary and comprehension

26) Which of the following would make the greatest impact on students' writing abilities?
   A. inviting professional writers to share their experiences with the class
   B. setting aside time each day for sentence diagramming and oral drills
   C. having students write only about topics they care about deeply
   D. allowing time for writing each day or during each class

Questions 27 – 29 refer to the initial lines from the poem "The Pyramids of Egypt," in *Introductory to Egypt, Nubia, and Abyssinia* by Philip Freneau:

'TIS darkness all, with hateful silence joined—

Here drowsy bats enjoy a dull repose,

And marble coffins, vacant of their bones,

Show where the royal dead in ruin lay!

27) Which statement BEST summarizes how imagery conveys the author's idea of the Egyptian pyramids?
   A. The image of royal people who are dead is frightening and disturbing.
   B. The imagery of coffins reveals the pointlessness of having power.
   C. The imagery of tombs suggests emptiness and ruin.
   D. The image of hateful silence suggests sadness and danger.

Practice Test   175

28) How would a semantic map of the poem help students understand the poet's use of concrete imagery to suggest an abstract idea?
   A. With "hateful silence" in the center circle, students could fill in the other circles with the concrete details related to hateful silence.
   B. Students could fill in the circles with the images of the poem.
   C. Students could pull out all of the adjectives and nouns in the poem and then draw lines that link the adjectives to the nouns they modify.
   D. Students could fill the circles with each word that is related to Egyptian pyramids.

29) If a teacher asks her students to use details of this poem to explain how the words *darkness*, *coffins*, and *silence* make them feel, which critical approach is she using?
   A. formalism
   B. reader-response
   C. semiotic analysis
   D. Marxist criticism

30) A teacher is using foundational elements of Multi-Tiered Systems of Supports (MTSS) to differentiate tiered instruction. Which type of data point should be used for this task?
   A. formative assessments, teacher observations, and standardized test scores
   B. standardized test scores from the beginning and end of the year
   C. homework grades and the number of books read per week
   D. teacher's notes about behavior during class

31) A high school teacher has noticed that some of her students who have IEPs are not meeting their specific learning goals. What is the BEST course of action that the teacher can take in this scenario?
   A. collaborate with the IEP team and parents/guardians to adjust strategies and provide support
   B. ask the students for input on what they believe would be helpful for them in reaching their goals
   C. continue on with the current IEP goals to see if any progress is made over the coming weeks
   D. give the students assignments that are a few levels easier than what they are currently working on

32) Which of the following topics is appropriate for a four- to six-page research paper?
   A. American poetry
   B. the causes of WWI
   C. the dangers of fad diets
   D. the development of grammar from the 1900s forward

Question 33 refers to the introductory sentences below from Louisa May Alcott's "Street Scenes in Washington":

The mules were my especial delight; and an hour's study of a constant succession of them introduced me to many of their characteristics; for six of these odd little beasts drew each army wagon and went hopping like frogs through the stream of mud that gently rolled along the street. The coquettish mule had small feet, a nicely trimmed tassel of a tail, perked-up ears, and seemed much given to little tosses of the head, affected skips and prances; and, if he wore the bells or were bedizened with a bit of finery, put on as many airs as any belle. The moral mule was a stout, hard-working creature, always tugging with all his might, often pulling away after the rest had stopped, laboring under the conscientious delusion that food for the entire army depended upon his private exertions. I respected this style of mule; and, had I possessed a juicy cabbage, would have pressed it upon him with thanks for his excellent example.

33) What is Louisa May Alcott's purpose in this section of text from "Street Scenes in Washington"?
   A. to inform readers about the activity on the streets of Washington
   B. to persuade readers that life in the city is fascinating
   C. to convince people to take the time to observe human activity
   D. to express her thoughts as she observes mules on a street in Washington

34) Which option suggests the BEST way to revise the underlined portion of the following sentence?

During the Civil War, a significant number of soldiers died during battle; <u>indeed,</u> large numbers of soldiers and civilians fell ill and died as a result of living conditions during the war.
   A. in addition,
   B. therefore,
   C. however,
   D. on the other hand,

35) A ninth-grade English teacher asks students to submit possible topics for their 2,000-word research papers. One student submits the topic of "television." What is the BEST feedback for the teacher to provide?
   A. "Think about how to narrow the focus."
   B. "Develop a pro-con list based on the topic."
   C. "Focus on gathering primary sources."
   D. "Begin with an outline to guide drafting."

36) A student has joined a classroom after being homeschooled. Her teacher has noticed that, due to the student's previous educational experiences, she lacks daily reading practice. As a result, her reading proficiency is slightly behind the expected level. Which strategy would BEST support this student's reading development?
   A. to continue on with reading lessons and allow the student to catch up on her own
   B. to assign autobiographical writing assignments to learn more about the student
   C. to provide vocabulary flashcards so that the student can study them at home
   D. to integrate complex texts into the student's daily reading and tailor instruction based on areas of struggle

37) In a connected text, a middle school student receiving supplemental reading instruction encounters the word *admiration*. Which strategy should the interventionist encourage the student to use to determine the meaning of this unknown word?
   A. syllabication
   B. identifying roots and affixes
   C. sematic cueing
   D. emphasizing onset and rime

38) Which of the following is a characteristic of Metaphysical poetry?
   A. using a serious, stern tone
   B. addressing the practical, everyday concerns of life
   C. addressing the value of scientific discoveries
   D. using paradoxes and puns as well as everyday language

39) Which activity BEST aligns with the goal of building confidence in students who are nervous about speaking in front of a group?
   A. whole-class discussion
   B. small-group presentation
   C. reader's theater
   D. Socratic seminar

40) While observing writing conferences in a high school classroom, a teacher hears a student suggest to a peer that he delete an irrelevant sentence from his essay. The teacher would MOST likely praise the student for her suggestion to improve which component of the essay?
   A. tone
   B. organization
   C. style
   D. focus

41) Consider the first lines (below) of "Autumn" from *The Belfry of Bruges and Other Poems* by Henry Wadsworth Longfellow. What sound device is used in the line "With banners, by great gales incessant fanned" from the following excerpt?

THOU comest, Autumn, heralded by the rain,

With banners, by great gales incessant fanned,

Brighter than brightest silks of Samarcand,

And stately oxen harnessed to thy wain!
   A. assonance
   B. mood
   C. symbolism
   D. tone

42) Which citation shows the correct way to cite a direct quote in APA style?
   A. (Harper)
   B. (Harper, p. 22)
   C. (Harper, 2006, p. 22)
   D. (Harper, page 22)

43) A sixth-grade student receiving literacy interventions writes the following introductory paragraph for his autobiographical essay:

My name is Joel my friends sometimes call me Joe. I have lived in Boston all my life I enjoy baseball fishing and marshal arts. After school. I live in a large house my two brothers live there to.

Which type of targeted mechanics instruction should the interventionist plan?
   A. basic orthography
   B. sentence structure
   C. basic capitalization
   D. preposition use

44) Which assessment would be MOST valid in measuring foundational reading skills?
   A. OLSAT
   B. DIBELS
   C. WrAP
   D. COGAT

Question 45 refers to the following stanzas from "The Haunted Oak" by Paul Laurence Dunbar:

PRAY why are you so bare, so bare,

Oh bough of the old oak-tree;

And why, when I go through the shade you throw,

Runs a shudder over me?

My leaves were green as the best, I trow,

And sap ran free in my veins,

But I saw in the moonlight dim and weird

A guiltless victim's pains.

I bent me down to hear his sigh;

I shook with his gurgling moan,

And I trembled sore when they rode away,

And left him here alone.

…

I feel the rope against my bark,

And the weight of him in my grain,

I feel the throe of his final woe

The touch of my own last pain.

And never more shall leaves come forth

On a bough that bears the ban;

I am burned with dread, I am dried and dead,

From the curse of a guiltless man.

45) The initial speaker of the poem asks an old oak tree "why are you so bare, so bare . . . ?" When a student explains she is convinced that the old oak tree is bare because an innocent man was hanged on one of the tree's branches, she is doing what?
   A. making an inference
   B. making a prediction
   C. stating a theme of the poem
   D. stating a pattern in the poem

46) A ninth-grade ELA teacher wants to help the class, which has limited experience with public speaking, prepare for a short speaking assignment. Which strategy is MOST likely to be helpful to students?
   A. writing the speech down and then reciting it from memory
   B. writing the speech down and reading it verbatim
   C. writing key points of the speech on note cards to refer to as necessary
   D. writing down anticipated questions from the audience to refer to as necessary

47) Which of the following strategies is MOST appropriate for helping students acquire and retain content-specific vocabulary words?
   A. providing students with a thesaurus to refer to as they encounter new vocabulary
   B. teaching students some of the most commonly used roots and affixes for content-area words
   C. encouraging students to read fiction texts on similar topics that feature content-area words
   D. giving students a brief refresher on the basics of the graphophonic cueing system

48) What is the BEST reason to include references to counterclaims in argumentative writing?
   A. to show mastery of the subject matter
   B. to promote the use of ethos appeals
   C. to praise alternate perspectives
   D. to offer reasonable refutations

49) Which of the following parts of speech describes how the word *travels* is used in the following sentence?

Abby's travels in Asia provided her the opportunity to try many foods that she would not have been able to try at home in the United States.
   A. verb
   B. noun
   C. adjective
   D. adverb

50) Which strategy would be MOST helpful for a student who has just arrived in the US and who is in the earliest stage of second-language acquisition?
   A. participating in peer tutoring
   B. receiving extra time for test completion
   C. completing a graphic organizer
   D. using a picture dictionary

Question 51 is based on the following excerpt from the short story "The Legend of Sleepy Hollow" by Washington Irving:

I recollect that, when a stripling, my first exploit in squirrel-shooting was in a grove of tall walnut-trees that shades one side of the valley. I had wandered into it at noontime, when all nature is peculiarly quiet, and was startled by the roar of my own gun, as it broke the Sabbath stillness around and was prolonged and reverberated by the angry echoes. If ever I should wish for a retreat whither I might steal from the world and its distractions, and dream quietly away the remnant of a troubled life, I know of none more promising than this little valley.

51) Which of the following BEST describes the organization of the passage?
  A. It is a description that includes sensory detail.
  B. The text is the sequence of events during a day of squirrel shooting.
  C. The text is organized as an explanation of the reasons people seek solitude.
  D. The echoing roar of the gun is contrasted to the stillness of the little valley.

52) Which activity BEST meets the goals of students using content-area vocabulary in an authentic context?
  A. writing a letter to a pen pal in another nation
  B. creating a website to teach others about parts of a cell
  C. drafting an essay about Spanish colonies in the Americas
  D. making a model of a proposed community irrigation plan

53) A seventh-grade teacher asks a reading specialist how to help English language learner (ELL) students navigate the writing process, particularly the revising and editing phases. Which of the following strategies should the reading specialist recommend?
  A. encourage ELL students to read their work aloud to check for grammatical errors
  B. during writing conferences, pair ELL students with peers whose first language is English
  C. allow ELL students to type their essays and use the spell-check feature
  D. provide heavy scaffolding that includes the teacher directly identifying errors for the student

54) A reading specialist is working with a high school English teacher to develop more rigorous assessment items. The goal is to write questions that fall within Benjamin Bloom's second level of understanding. Which of the following assessment items meets this cognitive-level goal?
  A. asking which type of writing tries to persuade others
  B. critiquing a persuasive essay for its use of rhetorical conventions
  C. writing a three-sentence summary of a persuasive essay.
  D. creating an outline for a persuasive essay

55) A high school teacher requires students to have research paper topics approved beforehand. In designing a form for students to fill out about their proposed topics, which of the following questions is the BEST to include?
  A. What sources are available regarding this topic?
  B. How did you become interested in this topic?
  C. What do you already know about this topic?
  D. Who else would be interested in this topic?

56) An eighth-grade teacher has noticed that many of his students are struggling to use context clues to understand unfamiliar vocabulary words. Which of the following activities would BEST assist the students in inferring meaning through context?
   A. pair up students and have them challenge each other with vocabulary flashcards
   B. Have students read through a text and highlight relevant context information for the difficult vocabulary words
   C. ask students to identify the prefix, suffix, and root of every unknown vocabulary word
   D. assign students a writing task where they use as many vocabulary words in one sentence as possible

57) Which type of clause is underlined in the following sentence?

Alice missed the most exciting part of the game; <u>consequently, she returned to the car disappointed</u>.
   A. noun clause
   B. adverb clause
   C. adjective clause
   D. independent clause

58) A ninth-grade student gives an oral presentation to her English class full of slang that mocks the subject matter. Under which rubric category would the teacher MOST likely leave feedback for improvement?
   A. tone
   B. clarity
   C. conciseness
   D. articulation

Questions 59 – 60 refer to the following sections from the essay "On Lying News-Writers," from *The Idler* by Samuel Johnson:

NO species of literary men has lately been so much multiplied as the writers of news. Not many years ago the nation was content with one gazette; but now we have not only in the metropolis papers for every morning and every evening, but almost every large town has its weekly historian, who regularly circulates his periodical intelligence, and fills the villages of his district with conjectures on the events of war, and with debates on the true interest of Europe.

To write news in its perfection requires such a combination of qualities, that a man completely fitted for the task is not always to be found. In Sir Henry Wotton's jocular definition, "An ambassador is said to be a man of virtue sent abroad to tell lies for the advantage of his country; a news writer is a man without virtue, who writes lies at home for his own profit."

To these compositions is required neither genius nor knowledge, neither industry nor sprightliness; but contempt of shame and indifference to truth are absolutely necessary. He who by a long familiarity with infamy has obtained these qualities, may confidently tell to-day what he intends to contradict to-morrow; he may affirm fearlessly what he knows that he shall be obliged to recant, and may write letters from Amsterdam or Dresden to himself.

In a time of war the nation is always of one mind, eager to hear something good of themselves and ill of the enemy. At this time, the task of news-writers is easy; they have nothing to do but to tell that a battle is expected, and afterward that a battle has been fought, in which we and our friends, whether conquering or conquered, did all, and our enemies did nothing.

Among the calamities of war may be justly numbered the diminution of the love of truth, by the falsehoods which interest dictates and credulity encourages. A peace will equally leave the warrior and relater of wars destitute of employment; and I know not whether more is to be dreaded from the streets filled with soldiers accustomed to plunder, or from garrets filled with scribblers accustomed to lie.

59) How is the author's view of news writers delivered?
- A. It is stated explicitly.
- B. It is stated implicitly.
- C. It is revealed by the point of view.
- D. It is indicated by the matter-of-fact tone.

60) What kind of appeal does Johnson use to support his perspective?
- A. ethical appeal
- B. logical appeal
- C. emotional appeal
- D. evidential appeal

61) Which type of sentence is the following?

The carpet's coloring was rich, and its pattern was complex.
- A. simple
- B. complex
- C. compound
- D. compound-complex

62) During which period of British literature were many epic poems about heroes and morality shared orally?
- A. Anglo-Saxon
- B. Victorian
- C. Romantic
- D. Renaissance

63) Which word from the following sentence is slang?

It's a drag to do homework on the weekend, but I won't pass the class if I spend all day watching TV.
- A. drag
- B. homework
- C. weekend
- D. pass

64) Which early literacy activity would be conducted FIRST in terms of developmental sequence?
- A. students reading high-frequency sight words from a chart
- B. students reciting the sound of each letter in sequence
- C. students manipulating words through phoneme substitution
- D. students clapping out onset and rime as a word is spoken

Questions 65 – 66 refer to the following excerpt from *Anecdotes of the Late Samuel Johnson* by Hester Thrale.

There is no private house in which people can enjoy themselves so well as at a capital tavern. Let there be ever so great plenty of good things, ever so much grandeur, ever so much elegance, ever so much desire that everybody should be easy, in the nature of things it cannot be: there must always be some degree of care and anxiety. The master of the house is anxious to entertain his guests—the guests are anxious to be agreeable to him; and no man, but a very impudent dog indeed, can as freely command what is in another man's house as if it was his own. Whereas, at a tavern, there is a general freedom from anxiety. You are sure you are welcome; and the more noise you make, the more trouble you give, the more good things you call for, the welcomer you are. No servants will attend you with the alacrity which waiters do, who are incited by the prospect of an immediate reward in proportion as they please. No, sir, there is nothing which has yet been contrived by man, by which so much happiness is produced as by a good tavern or inn.

65) What is the author implying about taverns in this passage?
   A. People enjoy themselves in taverns because they are relaxed and not worried about pleasing anyone.
   B. People want to behave rudely, like impudent dogs, at house parties but do not because they will be thrown out.
   C. People who give house parties make their guests uncomfortable by hovering over them.
   D. People are only happy in taverns because they can boss around the waiters, who will listen because they want tips.

66) Which of the following assessment methods would be MOST effective to gauge student writing progress over time?
   A. norm-referenced assessment
   B. criterion-referenced assessment
   C. dynamic assessment
   D. portfolio assessment

67) Which organizational pattern is Johnson using in this section of text?
   A. sequential
   B. compare and contrast
   C. cause and effect
   D. chronological

68) While giving oral presentations, students should be encouraged to look at which of the following?
   A. the visual aid they are showing
   B. the audience in front of them
   C. the farthest wall in the room
   D. the person sitting closest to them

69) The main goal of a K-W-L chart is to help students do which of the following?
   A. organize new vocabulary based on similar semantic and syntactic qualities
   B. use a set framework for activating background knowledge, setting a purpose, and summarizing
   C. refer to a set list of fix-up strategies and then choose the most appropriate one for the situation
   D. learn how to make inferences, identify purpose, and distinguish between fact and opinion

70) Harun is writing an essay about the migration patterns of birds. Which of the following facts would NOT be relevant to his research?
   A. Within a species, the tendency to migrate might vary by the location of each population, as populations in areas that are warm year-round may not need to migrate in pursuit of food.
   B. Of the species of bird that migrate, not all do so by flying: some bird species, such as the penguin, migrate in other ways, like by swimming.
   C. Prior to the late eighteenth century, many people believed that birds hibernated during the winter; only later did they accept migration as an explanation for the absence of birds during winter.
   D. Migration patterns may vary within a bird species based on age and gender.

71) A standardized assessment instrument that measures reading and language skills is widely used across the nation. Recently, educators have become critical of the assessment results and their ability to screen for possible reading disabilities, noting that many students are being falsely identified. What additional information would be MOST helpful for the educators to gather regarding the norm-referenced assessment to determine its current efficacy?
   A. when the test was last calibrated with a representative norming group
   B. which other schools and districts are using the assessment
   C. how many questions the assessment has at each cognitive level
   D. which other norm-referenced assessments are similar to the test

72) Which type of sentence is the following?

Although the politician denied that he intended to run for the presidency, he behaved as if he might.
   A. simple
   B. complex
   C. compound
   D. compound-complex

73) In the following sentence, the prefix *pre–* indicates that the evaluation will take place at which time?

The patient's preoperative evaluation is scheduled for next Wednesday.
   A. before the operation
   B. after the operation
   C. during the operation
   D. at the end of the operation

Questions 74 – 75 refer to the speech "The Man with the Muck-rake" by Theodore Roosevelt, delivered April 14, 1906:

Over a century ago Washington laid the corner stone of the Capitol in what was then little more than a tract of wooded wilderness here beside the Potomac. We now find it necessary to provide by great additional buildings for the business of the government. This growth in the need for the housing of the government is but a proof and example of the way in which the nation has grown and the sphere of action of the national government has grown. We now administer the affairs of a nation in which the extraordinary growth of population has been outstripped by the growth of wealth in complex interests. The material problems that face us today are not such as they were in Washington's time, but the underlying facts of human nature are the same now as they were then. Under altered external form we war with the same tendencies toward evil that were evident in Washington's time, and are helped by the same tendencies for good. It is about some of these that I wish to say a word today.

74) What is the central idea of Roosevelt's speech?
   A. The growth of the United States has resulted in a war between the conflicting interests of many groups in government.
   B. While the US government and population have grown, the United States continues to deal with the basic characteristics of human nature, both positive and negative.
   C. Many Americans have gained great wealth and are now attempting to control the government.
   D. The country has grown so fast and has acquired so much wealth that the government is struggling to deal with rising inequality between the wealthy and the poor.

75) Roosevelt mentions construction of "great additional buildings for the business of government" to emphasize which of the following?
   A. changes that have taken place in the type of government
   B. the complexity of democratic principles.
   C. the power of the United States as a world leader.
   D. the growth of the United States.

76) The following statement reflects the usage of which logical fallacy?

The corruption of the leadership is inevitable because a fish rots from the head down.
   A. hasty generalization
   B. false analogy
   C. irrelevant argument (non-sequitur)
   D. false cause (post hoc, ergo propter hoc)

77) The underlined phrase in the sentence below functions as which of the following parts of speech?

<u>To save lots of money</u>, the young family shopped for clothing at the local thrift store.
   A. noun
   B. pronoun
   C. adjective
   D. adverb

78) Which skill is BEST assessed via running records?
   A. comprehension
   B. mechanics
   C. oral fluency
   D. sentence structure

79) An ELA teacher is working with a small group of students and asks them to use each of the bold headings in their textbook to generate questions they will answer after reading the chapter. This is a strategy to help students do what?
   A. read with purpose
   B. activate background knowledge
   C. apply fix-up strategies
   D. use context clues

80) A teacher has completed an assessment of his students' reading comprehension levels. Some students are excelling, while others need additional support in specific areas. Which instructional planning method would be MOST beneficial based on the results of the assessment?
    A. use differentiated lesson plans and intervention scaffolding tailored to each student's needs
    B. assign collaborative reading activities so that students can read texts outside their levels
    C. give more at-home reading homework to combine with the reading done during class time
    D. increase the text complexity to see if students can successfully adapt independently

81) An eighth-grade teacher is preparing for a writing conference and notices that a student's essay contains several sentences unrelated to the thesis. What would MOST likely be the focus of the writing conference?
    A. support
    B. mechanics
    C. organization
    D. unity

82) Which of the following scaffolding techniques is LEAST effective in presenting new content to students learning English?
    A. using modified reading materials
    B. previewing vocabulary prior to a lesson
    C. providing students with an outline for notes
    D. performing regular checks for understanding

Questions 83 – 84 refer to the speech "On Women's Right to Vote" by Susan B. Anthony, 1873:

Friends and fellow citizens: I stand before you tonight under indictment for the alleged crime of having voted at the last presidential election, without having a lawful right to vote. It shall be my work this evening to prove to you that in thus voting, I not only committed no crime, but, instead, simply exercised my citizen's rights, guaranteed to me and all United States citizens by the National Constitution, beyond the power of any state to deny. The only question left to be settled now is: Are women persons? And I hardly believe any of our opponents will have the hardihood to say they are not. Being persons, then, women are citizens; and no state has a right to make any law, or to enforce any old law, that shall abridge their privileges or immunities. Hence, every discrimination against women in the constitutions and laws of the several states is today null and void, precisely as is every one against Negroes.

83) What is the purpose of Susan B. Anthony's speech?
    A. to express her anger about being arrested
    B. to inform people about the injustice women face
    C. to persuade women to continue to fight against all discrimination
    D. to convince others that she has the lawful right to vote

84) Which TWO rhetorical strategies does Susan B. Anthony use? Select ALL that apply.
    A. rhetorical question
    B. understatement
    C. parallelism
    D. amplification

85) Which of the following is a standardized assessment instrument?
   A. a curriculum-based assessment
   B. a teacher-created summative assessment
   C. the Iowa Test of Basic Skills
   D. an exit ticket given at the end of a lesson

86) A high school educator teaching a dual-credit US history course notices students are struggling to understand the college-level textbook. Which of the following strategies would be MOST appropriate to help the students?
   A. focusing the class's attention on multimedia texts instead of written information
   B. giving students explicit strategies, such as the SQ3R method
   C. reading most of the textbook aloud in class
   D. switching to another textbook for the rest of the year

87) Inflection in speaking refers to changes in which of the following?
   A. nonverbal cues
   B. tone or pitch
   C. dialect or vernacular
   D. syntax

88) Which of the following sentences indicates the end of a sequence?
   A. Our ultimate objective was to find a quality coat at an affordable price.
   B. We chose this particular restaurant because of its outdoor seating.
   C. Finally, we were able to settle in to enjoy the movie.
   D. Initially, it seemed unlikely that we'd be able to keep the puppy.

89) A tenth-grade English teacher is beginning a unit where students will be reading a novel that includes challenging content-specific vocabulary. What is the BEST strategy for the teacher to employ?
   A. instruct students in a text annotation system to help them link unknown words and context clues
   B. rely on incidental vocabulary learning as students read the text independently at their own pace
   C. preteach the most frequently used words prior to asking students to begin reading the text
   D. give frequent vocabulary quizzes covering important terms as students read the novel

Question 90 refers to the following text:

Communicating with any human being in crisis—whether that crisis is physical or emotional—is going to be more difficult than normal, everyday communication. Thus, emergency responders and medical practitioners, like many other social service providers, need to learn how to be sensitive in interpersonal communication. Here are some tips about how to hone your craft as a communicator while working with people in crisis. These tips can also be used for everyday communication.

First, it is essential that you are aware of cultural differences. In some cultures, direct eye contact can be unsettling or disrespectful. People from different cultures may have different comfort levels with personal space: some might find physical closeness comforting; others might find it threatening. Your body language speaks volumes. Be sure you are aware of the symbolic nature of your posture, hand motions, and gestures.

It is also important to enunciate your verbal statements and directions in a clear, relevant way. Use terminology and directions that a patient will understand, and avoid lofty medical jargon. Believe it or not, you also want to be honest with the person in crisis, even if the conditions are dire. Also explain, if possible, what you might do to help alleviate even the most drastic conditions so that the person feels supported. Lastly, and most importantly, be prepared to listen. Even if there is a language barrier, condition, or disability limiting your communication with the person in crisis, try to position yourself as an active listener. These tips will help you support people who need clarity and sensitivity.

90) What is the BEST summary of the passage?
- A. In some cultures, direct eye contact can be unsettling or disrespectful.
- B. Posture, hand motions, and gestures can symbolize respect or disrespect.
- C. Medical practitioners must learn to be sensitive with people who are in crisis.
- D. Medical practitioners should give clear directions and avoid using lofty medical jargon.

Answer Key

1) A: Option A is the correct answer because it actively engages students in acquiring background knowledge through the reading of informational texts and then discussing the texts through guided questions. Guided questions will help discussion stay productive, while group discussion will encourage a variety of perspectives. Option B is incorrect because having students read the texts at home may not provide them with the guidance they need to acquire background knowledge. Option C is incorrect because, although students may be successful when looking up additional information at home, it would be best for their primary growth to happen in the classroom with structure and guidance. Option D is incorrect because an unstructured method may leave some students struggling while others succeed.

2) D: Option D is correct because it aligns with the principles of the Universal Design for Learning (UDL). These principles include providing multiple options for engagement, expression, and representation to meet the diverse learning needs of students. Option A is incorrect because small-group instruction does not offer the flexibility that some students may require. Option B is incorrect because a one-size-fits-all approach goes against the UDL principles entirely. Option C is incorrect because the use of standardized tests as the sole mode of assessment is not flexible enough for the needs of a diverse group of students.

3) C: The main purpose of helping students develop a variety of word attack strategies is to improve their decoding of unfamiliar words.

4) C: Students should understand that oral communication in different dialects and registers is not right or wrong, good or bad. Students should instead adjust their communication styles based on audience and situation.

5) B: A brochure from PETA, a well-known advocacy group for animals, is not a credible print source because it is potentially biased.

6) B: This compound sentence requires a comma before the conjunction *but*.

7) C: The author tells the short story, or anecdote, of overpaying for an appealing toy, which illustrates his main point.

8) C: The narrator played the whistle less because he was upset about spending too much for it.

9) A: The phrase "a native of Massachusetts" renames the noun *Mark*.

10) A: Option A is correct; providing culturally responsive texts ensures that the student can connect with the material on a personal level, which can enhance engagement and comprehension. Slower instruction with support from past lessons helps to continue building a solid foundation and ensures the student is not left behind. Option B is incorrect because assigning a student the task of determining if a peer has dyslexia is inappropriate and not something for which a student is responsible. Option C is incorrect because memorization of complex vocabulary words does not necessarily improve overall reading comprehension. Option D is incorrect because allowing the student to continue reading at his current level without intervention will not help his progress.

11) A: The dates of the US Civil War are widely known and do not need documentation.

12) D: Option D is correct because it creates an inclusive environment where students can research and share information about their cultural backgrounds in a way that is educational and productive. Option

A is incorrect because bilingual resources are important tools for students who do not have English as a primary language; the denial of such resources may draw shame to their cultural differences. Option B is incorrect because, although it increases the students' awareness of their own cultures, it does not translate into the classroom environment itself. Option C is incorrect because standardizing lessons does not allow for the expression of diversity or unique backgrounds and is therefore not an inclusive method.

13) B: One of the features of the dictionary is the identification of comparatives and superlatives.

14) D: Certain types of nonverbal communication, such as shaking hands and appropriate social space, can differ from place to place

15) A: Writing and sending a letter after a unit on letter-writing is an authentic assessment because it evaluates student knowledge in a relevant and real-world way.

16) D: Some of the ways in which readers participate in the creative process are by imagining, remembering, and feeling what the text reminds them about in their own experiences. The artistic choices of the author inspire the reader's reflections

17) B: Thoreau is using the Icarian bird as a vehicle to describe smoke. The reader needs to ask how smoke is like a bird that circles, becomes a shadowy form at night, and darkens the morning sky.

18) D: Pinions are the outer feathers on a bird's wing. The poem references the story of Icarus, whose wings melted when he flew too close to the sun.

19) A: "The blood-dimmed tide is loosed" is a metaphor to describe what happens when "[t]hings fall apart" and "innocence is drowned"; no literal tide of blood is streaming.

20) C: The novel depicts the culture of the Igbo people being destroyed by the British missionaries and colonists who impose their ideas on the Igbo.

21) B: Option B is correct because it aids in the students' abilities to break down and understand the components of unfamiliar words. Students then learn to recognize common word parts and use this knowledge to infer the meanings of unfamiliar words. Option A is incorrect because, while writing research essays can help with vocabulary knowledge, such an assignment does not teach students strategies for deciphering unknown words. Option C is incorrect because reading aloud and sounding out words does not necessarily improve students' abilities to determine the meaning of unfamiliar words. Option D is incorrect because, while a dictionary can help students learn the meanings of unknown words, it does not promote the independent deciphering that the teacher is aiming for.

22) C: Speech-to-text software would allow the student with dysgraphia to dictate written assignments that can be converted to text.

23) D: This introduction, which states the doctor's name and field of medicine, provides enough information to legitimize Dr. Johnson as an authoritative source.

24) B: Fireside poets, like Longfellow, Lowell, and Bryant, wrote about the nineteenth-century United States, expressed views on political issues, and used conventional forms.

25) C: Option C is correct because it addresses the underlying issues by focusing on teaching self-monitoring skills and allowing students to choose texts that interest them personally. This will keep the students engaged and active in their own independent learning. Option A is incorrect because simply assigning more independent reading homework may not address the core issue of the students' difficulties. Option B is incorrect because the focus should be on independent learning, not group work.

Answer Key

Option D is incorrect because scaling back on the difficulty will not help the students learn how to work through challenging vocabulary or complex concepts within texts.

26) D: Writing as much as possible is one of the best ways to improve writing ability.

27) C: The imagery of the tombs effectively summarizes and connects to this broader idea of the Egyptian pyramids.

28) A: A semantic map helps students see the connections or relationships between words and concepts. By placing an abstract phrase in the center of the map, students can then build onto it by adding the concrete images that contribute to their understanding of the abstract elements of the poem.

29) B: Reader-response emphasizes the responses readers have to the details of a text.

30) A: Option A is correct because it incorporates a variety of data points, which provides a broader view of a student's progress. Option B is incorrect because standardized tests alone do not provide enough data regarding the type of differentiated instruction a student may need. Option C is incorrect because homework grades and the number of books being read do not show a student's true progress. Assessments and in-class work are also important factors to consider. Option D is incorrect because a teacher's notes about behavior do not reflect academic performance and are not enough to inform differentiated instruction.

31) A: Option A is correct because it involves all possible stakeholders to ensure that each student's plan is being assessed and adjusted as needed. This means that nobody is left in the dark as to how the plan is progressing. This is also the best outcome for the student. Option B is incorrect because there should be a more collaborative effort that includes the IEP team and parents/guardians. The students may not know what the best path for them is. Option C is incorrect because the students' current plans are not meeting their needs; therefore, they must be adjusted. Option D is incorrect because the difficulty level of assignments may not be the issue; there could be underlying issues that are affecting the students' performances.

32) C: The dangers of fad diets could probably be covered adequately in four to six pages. The other topics are too broad to be covered in such a short paper.

33) D: The author is expressing her thoughts, saying that she is delighted by the mules and sharing what she notices.

34) A: *In addition* is the appropriate introductory phrase as it signifies the additive relationship between the two clauses.

35) A: "Television" is too broad a topic for a 2,000-word research paper, so the best feedback is to ask the student to think about how to narrow the focus.

36) D: Option D is correct because integrating complex texts into the student's daily reading will help her increase her reading practice and subsequently develop a higher level of proficiency. This is especially true when areas of struggle are directly addressed. Option A is incorrect because the student is not succeeding to her fullest potential with the current plan; therefore, it should be changed. Option B is incorrect because, while autobiographical assignments may help the teacher learn more about the student's previous schooling and interests, they will not address the core issue. Option C is incorrect because vocabulary flashcards may help with the student's reading proficiency, but the student also needs to increase her reading practice.

37) B: The root word *admire* and the suffix *–ion* could be used to help this student derive meaning from this word.

38) D: Metaphysical poetry is noted for plays on words and complex ideas about the contradictions of life.

39) B: Small-group presentations will enable students to practice speaking in front of a small group before speaking in front of a larger group.

40) D: This student is helping her peer ensure that his writing remains true to its overall point or focus.

41) A: Assonance is the repetition of the /an/ sound in the words banners, incessant, and fanned.

42) C: In APA format, the author's last name, date, and page number are needed in the in-text citation.

43) B: The student's writing is mostly run-on sentences and fragments, indicating that he needs explicit instruction in sentence structure.

44) B: The Dynamic Indicators of Basic Early Literacy Skills (DIBELS) is an oral assessment that can be used for students in grades K – 8.

45) A: The poet does not state that a person was hung on a bough of the oak tree; the reader is using her knowledge of hangings as well as details revealed in subsequent stanzas to infer this.

46) C: Writing key points on note cards will allow students to have some support but still give an engaging speech.

47) B: Morphemes like *micro*, *macro* and many other common roots and affixes can help students as they encounter content-area words.

48) D: Refuting counterclaims is a useful rhetorical technique as it directly addresses the opposition.

49) B: *Travels* functions as a noun; it is the subject of the sentence.

50) D: A student in the earliest preproduction, or "silent period," of second language acquisition would benefit most from a picture dictionary, which will help the student understand basic directions and classroom routines.

51) D: The passage begins with the narrator entering the grove of trees. When the narrator fires his gun, he says the sound "broke the Sabbath stillness around and was prolonged and reverberated by the angry echoes." The last sentence says the place would be a perfect retreat.

52) B: Creating the website would enable students to use science content-area words to describe cells; the website is an authentic context.

53) B: Having English language learners (ELLs) review their work with a peer whose first language is English is an effective way to use homogenous grouping and actively involve ELLs in the revision process.

54) C: Summarizing falls within Bloom's second level of understanding.

55) A: This question is essential because students must be able to find adequate sources of information on a topic in order to compose a research paper.

56) B: Option B is correct because it directly engages students in using context clues to understand unfamiliar vocabulary words. By reading through a text and highlighting relevant context information, students learn to identify clues that help them infer the meanings of difficult words within the text. Option A is incorrect because vocabulary flashcards do not specifically teach students how to use context clues to infer meanings from surrounding text. Option C is incorrect because, while identifying the prefixes, suffixes, and roots of words is important for vocabulary analysis, it will not help with identifying context clues. Option D is incorrect because, although the students may come up with their own context clues while including vocabulary words in a sentence, this task will not help them with identifying context clues in complex texts.

57) D: The underlined clause is independent. Remember, a semicolon must be preceded AND followed by an independent clause.

58) A: Tone refers to the attitude presented in the speech toward the subject matter. This student's tone is largely inappropriate for the classroom context.

59) A: The author directly states, "Among the calamities of war may be justly numbered the diminution of the love of truth, by the falsehoods which interest dictates and credulity encourages. . . . I know not whether more is to be dreaded from the streets filled with soldiers accustomed to plunder, or from garrets filled with scribblers accustomed to lie."

60) A: Johnson quotes someone who was apparently a respected, credible figure in his time: "In Sir Henry Wotton's jocular definition, 'An ambassador is said to be a man of virtue sent abroad to tell lies for the advantage of his country; a news writer is a man without virtue, who writes lies at home for his own profit.'"

61) C: Two independent clauses are divided properly with the coordinating conjunction *and*.

62) A: Some of these Anglo-Saxon epics, like *Beowulf*, were eventually recorded in the written word.

63) A: In the sentence, *drag* is used as a slang term that means "an annoying or boring task."

64) D: Clapping out onset and rime is a very basic and simple activity to promote beginning phonemic awareness. Students can clap out /d/ /og/.

65) A: The text says that at house parties, "there must always be some degree of care and anxiety. . . . Whereas, at a tavern, there is a general freedom from anxiety. You are sure you are welcome. . . ."

66) D: A portfolio shows student progress over a span of time. Writing samples will hopefully demonstrate growth as well as increased proficiency and complexity.

67) B: Socializing at a tavern is contrasted with the practice of socializing at someone's house during a house party.

68) B: During oral presentations, speakers should maintain eye contact with the audience throughout the presentation.

69) B: Students use a framework to activate background knowledge ("what I already know"), set a purpose for reading ("what I want to know"), and summarize what they have learned ("what I learned").

70) C: Though it is interesting, the history of humanity's understanding of bird migration is not necessarily relevant to an essay about bird migration.

71) A: The norms established by the test makers may not be current if the test was last calibrated a long time ago.

72) B: This sentence has one independent clause and three dependent clauses, so it is a complex sentence.

73) A: The prefix *pre–* means "before."

74) B: Roosevelt states his purpose when he says, "we war with the same tendencies toward evil that were evident in Washington's time, and are helped by the same tendencies for good. It is about some of these that I wish to say a word today."

75) D: According to the text, additional government buildings have been necessary to accommodate the growth in government activity that has accompanied the corresponding growth of the country.

76) B: A rotting fish is not analogous to a position of leadership.

77) D: The phrase "to save lots of money" is modifying the verb shopped and explains why the young family shopped at the local thrift store. (Note that all introductory infinitive phrases are adverbial.)

78) C: Running records are oral reading checks that assess rate, accuracy, and prosody.

79) A: Having set questions will help students read with the purpose of answering these questions.

80) A: Option A is correct because using differentiated lesson plans and interventions means that students' individual needs will be met. This method targets all levels of proficiency and any manner of challenges. Option B is incorrect because assigning collaborative reading activities may help with reading proficiency but does not address the specific needs of each student who is struggling. Option C is incorrect because additional homework may leave the students lacking support that they require from the teacher or trained professional. Option D is incorrect because students should have their needs met and struggles supported before moving on to increased difficulty.

81) D: Writing that has unity contains only information directly related to the thesis and topic sentences.

82) D: While checking on students' understanding and progress is important, this strategy does not help students grasp content material; it only helps the teacher evaluate where her students are in the learning process.

83) D: Susan B. Anthony says that she wants to prove she has the right to vote, which is an attempt to convince others.

84) A, D: Susan B. Anthony rhetorically asks, "The only question left to be settled now is: Are women persons?" Amplification is the repetition of a word or expression for emphasis. The words *persons* and *citizens* are repeated throughout the speech to encourage audience members to consider the meanings of these important terms.

85) C: The Iowa Test of Basic Skills is a single assessment tool used in multiple schools throughout the nation.

86) B: Giving students strategies, such as the SQ3R method, to help them comprehend a difficult text can be helpful across the content areas.

87) B: Speakers use inflection by changing tone or pitch to show changes in meaning or attitude.

88) C: The transition word *finally* indicates the end of a sequence.

89) C: Preteaching new vocabulary is a best practice in this situation since it will give students more confidence and self-efficacy as they tackle this difficult text.

90) C: "Medical practitioners must learn to be sensitive with people who are in crisis" is an adequate summary of the passage overall. The other options only provide specific details from the passage.

Answer Key

Constructed-Response Prompt

- An educator is teaching his students how to interpret figurative language and literary devices.
- The teacher has assigned a sample poem (below) for students to read and identify the literary devices used as well as the meaning of the figurative language used.
- **Your task:** Using evidence-based standards and data, describe a learning plan that will support students in reading and identifying literary devices from the chosen text and understanding the meaning of the figurative language that is used.

"I Wandered Lonely as a Cloud" by William Wordsworth

I wandered lonely as a cloud

That floats on high o'er vales and hills,

When all at once I saw a crowd,

A host, of golden daffodils;

Beside the lake, beneath the trees,

Fluttering and dancing in the breeze.

Continuous as the stars that shine

And twinkle on the milky way,

They stretched in never-ending line

Along the margin of a bay:

Ten thousand saw I at a glance,

Tossing their heads in sprightly dance.

The waves beside them danced; but they

Out-did the sparkling waves in glee:

A poet could not but be gay,

In such a jocund company:

I gazed—and gazed—but little thought

What wealth the show to me had brought:

For oft, when on my couch I lie

In vacant or in pensive mood,

They flash upon that inward eye

Which is the bliss of solitude;

And then my heart with pleasure fills,

And dances with the daffodils.

Sample Response and Analysis

Sample Response

In order to effectively teach literary devices and the meaning of figurative language, I would first begin by laying down some foundational work. This would include the teaching of literary device terms with examples. This would be best done with visual aids, such as flashcards. Students would pair up and use the flashcards to memorize the definitions of various literary devices. Once it becomes clear that students have a strong foundational grasp of the terms, it would then be appropriate to move on to the Wordsworth poem.

The students would first do an individual reading of the poem while annotating and highlighting any figurative devices they see. This would allow a form of independent progress before moving on to the next part of the assignment. Students would be instructed to group up with their classmates and reread the poem together. They would then discuss the literary devices that they identified earlier, and they could begin to collaborate on deciphering the meaning of any figurative language used. After each group has identified and analyzed the figurative language in the poem, they would be asked to share one example that they found with the rest of the class. As the teacher, I would be writing key words and meanings on the board so that students can easily follow along.

To encourage a creative element, the students would then go back to individual work and write a short poem that uses three of the literary devices found in the Wordsworth poem. After they complete these poems, I would plan to read and grade them based on how appropriate their usage of literary devices is. This would serve as a form of assessment to measure each student's progress with the learning objective.

These strategies ensure that students are provided with both individual and group work opportunities. With no strict group limits, there is flexibility for students to choose the group size that works best for them. The discussion serves as an effective tool for inspiring creative brainstorming and developing skills of collaboration and teamwork. A solo assignment that is creative in nature will improve not only the students' writing skills but also their command of literary devices and figurative language. This will ultimately aid in their reading comprehension.

Sample Analysis

This response shows a solid understanding of which teaching strategies would be effective for teaching literary devices and figurative language. The use of numerous methods, including independent work, group collaboration, class-wide discussion, and a creative assignment, provides several options for students with varied learning needs.

The first paragraph discusses how the educator would teach students the foundational information needed to identify literary devices. This includes repetition and pairing up with another student to use a physical aid. This is an engaging method that ensures the participation of each student. It will help students understand the definitions of key terms and be prepared for the next assignment.

The second paragraph allows students to experience the poem on their own before discussing it as a class. This allows students to flex their new knowledge and put it into use. Just by walking around the class, the teacher can get an idea of how each student is progressing based on how they annotate the poem. Sharing their findings with the class once again allows an opportunity for collaboration. It also encourages creative thinking, as students may consider perspectives that they did not initially think about.

The third paragraph presents students with a creative assignment where they can use literary devices and figurative language on their own. This adds a deeper understanding to the objectives, as it allows students to not only identify and analyze literary devices but also use them in their own writing, which serves to improve both writing skills and reading comprehension. The teacher can then collect these poems and assess each student's progress before moving on to the next learning objective. Students who did not quite grasp the concepts are then identified and can receive scaffolding as needed.

Although this is a strong plan for teaching literary devices and figurative language, there is room for improvement. The teacher could use a formative assessment, such as a quiz, to better assess the students' command of the subject. A creative assignment may not present the full picture as to what the student does and does not understand. A quiz or homework assignment could be assigned in addition to the already established plan, strengthening what the teacher—and students—are able to take away from the lesson.

ONLINE RESOURCES

Trivium includes online resources with the purchase of this study guide to help you fully prepare for the exam.

Review Questions

Need more practice? Our review questions use a variety of formats to help you memorize key terms and concepts.

Flash Cards

Trivium's flash cards allow you to review important terms easily on your computer or smartphone.

Cheat Sheets

Review the core skills you need to master the exam with easy-to-read Cheat Sheets.

From Stress to Success

Watch "From Stress to Success," a brief but insightful YouTube video that offers the tips, tricks, and secrets experts use to score higher on the exam.

Feedback

Let us know what you think!

Access these materials at: cirrustestprep.com/texes-ela-online-resources

Dear TExES ELAR test taker,

Great job completing this study guide. The hard work and effort you put into your test preparation will help you succeed on your upcoming TExES ELAR exam. Thank you for letting us be a part of your education journey!

We have other study guides and products that you may find useful. Search for us on Amazon.com or let us know what you are looking for. We offer a wide variety of study guides that cover a multitude of subjects.

If you would like to share your success stories with us, or if you have a suggestion, comment, or concern, please send us an email at support@triviumtestprep.com.

Thanks again for choosing us!
Happy Testing
Cirrus Test Prep Team

www.ingramcontent.com/pod-product-compliance
Lightning Source LLC
Chambersburg PA
CBHW080733300426
44114CB00019B/2581